175 Best
Instant Pot®
Recipes

175 Best Instant Pot® Recipes

For Your Programmable Electric Pressure Cooker

Marilyn Haugen

Robert
ROSE

For complete cataloguing information, see page 224.

Disclaimers

175 Best Instant Pot® Recipes is an independent publication of Robert Rose Inc. and has
not been authorized, sponsored or otherwise approved by any other party, including
Double Insight Inc., and Robert Rose Inc. is not a licensee of or otherwise associated
with Double Insight Inc.

The recipes in this book have been carefully tested by our kitchen and our tasters. To the best
of our knowledge, they are safe and nutritious for ordinary use and users. For those people
with food or other allergies, or who have special food requirements or health issues, please
read the suggested contents of each recipe carefully and determine whether or not they may
create a problem for you. All recipes are used at the risk of the consumer. Consumers should
always consult their multicooker manufacturer's manual for recommended procedures and
cooking times.

We cannot be responsible for any hazards, loss or damage that may occur as a result of
any recipe use.

For those with special needs, allergies, requirements or health problems, in the event of
any doubt, please contact your medical adviser prior to the use of any recipe.

Design and production: Kevin Cockburn/PageWave Graphics Inc.
Layout: Alicia McCarthy/PageWave Graphics Inc.
Editor: Sue Sumeraj
Recipe editor: Jennifer MacKenzie
Proofreader: Kelly Jones
Indexer: Gillian Watts
Photographer: Tango Photographie
Food stylist: Éric Régimbald
Prop stylist: Véronique Gagnon Lalanne

Cover image: Chuck Wagon Beef Stew (page 68)

Published by Robert Rose Inc.
120 Eglinton Avenue East, Suite 800, Toronto, Ontario, Canada M4P 1E2
Tel: (416) 322-6552 Fax: (416) 322-6936
www.robertrose.ca

Printed and bound in Canada

4 5 6 7 8 9 MI 24 23 22 21 20 19 18 17

Contents

Preface

I love small kitchen appliances and gadgets, and virtually any new toy for the kitchen. But even more, I love to cook — and to eat. So any time I come across an appliance that promises to help me make healthier and more delicious foods that are easy and fast to prepare, it has my attention. The Instant Pot offers all that and uses less energy and requires less cleanup. Now that's a seriously appealing combination!

My first plunge into multicooker cooking was to purchase an Instant Pot for my favorite guinea pig: my daughter. We bought it in the summer so we could test how it operated and try new recipes before she headed back to college in the fall. For a college student, this appliance was a dream come true. She could prepare a recipe in the morning, put it in the slow cooker and have dinner ready when she returned from a full day of classes. She could also prepare breakfast — a very important meal — the evening before and enjoy it in the morning before flying out the door.

While she was excited about slow cooking, I was intrigued by the Instant Pot's pressure cooking function. I was curious about how it worked and wanted to make sure she knew how to handle it safely. She found a simple recipe online, and after 10 minutes — barely enough time for us to get our side dishes ready — we had succulent braised chicken leg quarters. We were hooked!

So when my publisher, Bob Dees, approached me about writing a cookbook for the Instant Pot, I was ecstatic. It is hard to pass up an opportunity to create recipes using a pressure cooker, slow cooker, rice cooker, porridge maker, yogurt maker and more in one pot that is only about 12 inches (30 cm) high by 12 inches (30 cm) in diameter.

After experimenting with many different options (some outstanding and some seriously questionable), I came up with numerous inviting, mouthwatering dishes that I could test on friends, neighbors and my daughter (a valuable and brutally honest critic). The result is this book, which offers creative recipes for every meal of the day using the Instant Pot features that work best for you. In a hurry? Done. Low and slow? Got it. The perfect rice or risotto? No problem. Entertaining? I have you covered. Desserts? Why not?

With your multicooker and this cookbook at hand, you will impress your family and friends with the wide variety of satisfying dishes you can quickly and easily create. Many of these recipes are sure to become new family favorites that will be requested again and again.

If you enjoy the recipes and tips in this book, stop by my blog, www.FoodThymes.com, to see what new recipes I have in store for you. While you are there, please feel free to share your own recipes and foodie experiences. I sincerely enjoy hearing from you.

Sound good? Let's get started.

— *Marilyn Haugen*

Acknowledgments

I cannot begin to thank the many people who made this book possible without first and foremost giving my heartfelt thanks to my mother. Her endless love and encouragement taught me that you can accomplish anything. Without the confidence she instilled in me, this book would not have been possible. I wish she was here now to see it come to life.

I am delighted and touched by my many friends who are so encouraging about my recipes. Special thanks to my taste-testers, especially my wonderful daughter, Natalie, for endlessly tasting recipes and giving me valuable feedback and support.

My sincere appreciation to Bob Dees, my publisher, who gave me the opportunity to create this cookbook to share with you. My editor, Sue Sumeraj, who is always outstanding to work with, has extraordinary insight into what will make a great experience for our readers. I continue to learn so much from both Sue and Jennifer MacKenzie, a recipe developer, editor and author, about what makes an exceptional recipe and cookbook.

My heartfelt thanks to Martine Quibell, an outstanding publicist who always has the kindest words of encouragement, and to Nina McCreath, whose exceptional marketing skills help connect my cookbooks and me to you.

Many thanks to Kevin Cockburn of PageWave Graphics for the wonderful design; to the team at Colin Erricson Photography for the stunning photographs; and to all of the outstanding professionals at Robert Rose who made this process a truly enjoyable and successful experience.

Instant Pot Basics

If you are looking for an easier way to get scrumptious meals on your table, then a multicooker such as the Instant Pot is for you. The beauty of this appliance, whether you choose its pressure cooking or slow cooking functions, is that you can prepare a meal with little hands-on time, and the Instant Pot will deliver consistently delicious results. It's perfect for busy people who want to get a nutritious meal on the table with little effort and minimal cleanup. Plus, you may save on energy consumption because multicookers are so energy-efficient.

About Multicookers

A multicooker enables you to pressure cook, slow cook, cook rice, make porridge and even make yogurt, all in one small, handy countertop appliance. There are several brands available today at kitchen stores, big-box retailers and online. The recipes in this book use the Instant Pot's terminology, but can easily be made in any other brand of multicooker.

> Fewer nutrients are lost when food is cooked under pressure.

The Instant Pot has several function keys that help you get the best results. You can refer to the user manual that came with your appliance for a more detailed explanation of the functions, but in general there are four core processing functions:

- Pressure (including Soup, Meat/Stew, Bean/Chili, Poultry, Rice, Multigrain, Porridge, Steam and Manual Pressure)
- Slow Cook
- Sauté
- Yogurt (including sub-programs for making yogurt, pasteurizing milk and making jiuniang)

In addition, there are operation keys that enable you to adjust the pressure, temperature and cooking time. Each recipe will tell you which functions to use and what adjustments you need to make for that recipe. Keep in mind that it is very important to follow the steps exactly as written to ensure that you get the best results, safely and mess-free.

On the following page, you'll find some additional tips for success with your multicooker, whether you are following one of the recipes in this book or venturing out on your own.

Pressure Cooking

- The lid must always be closed and locked and the steam release handle turned to Sealing when you are using a pressure cooking function.
- You must have a minimum of 1 cup (250 mL) water (or broth) in the pot.
- The cooker must be no more than two-thirds full for any recipe, and no more than half full for ingredients, such as beans and grains, that may foam or expand during cooking.

> The actual cooking time does not start until after working pressure is reached, which can take approximately 10 to 20 minutes, depending on the volume of ingredients in the pot.

Releasing Pressure

- **Quick Release:** When the timer beeps, press Cancel and turn the steam release handle to Venting. This immediately releases all of the pressure in the pot and stops the cooking process. When the float valve drops down, you will be able to open the lid. Keep your hands and face away from the hole on the top of the steam release handle so you don't get scalded by the escaping steam.
- **10-Minute Release:** When the timer beeps, press Cancel and let the pot stand, covered, for 10 minutes. After 10 minutes, turn the steam release handle to Venting and remove the lid. This release method is often used for dishes that benefit from an additional 10 minutes in the cooker's steam. (Occasionally, recipes may call for more or less standing time.)

Soaking Beans

Dried beans can be pressure cooked, but presoaking them removes some of the indigestible sugars that can cause gas. It also reduces cooking time and breakage.

- **8- to 12-hour standard soak:** Rinse and drain the dried beans. Place them in a medium bowl and cover with 4 cups (1 L) cold water for every 1 cup (250 mL) of beans. Let stand for 8 to 12 hours, changing the water halfway through. Drain and rinse.

- **10-minute quick soak:** Rinse and drain the dried beans. Place them in the inner pot and add 4 cups (1 L) cold water and 1 tsp (5 mL) salt for every 1 cup (250 mL) of beans. (Do not fill the pot more than half full.) Place the pot inside the cooker housing, close and lock the lid and turn the steam release handle to Sealing. Press Manual; the indicator will read "High Pressure." Use the ⊖ button to decrease the time on the display to 2 minutes. When the timer beeps, press Cancel. Let stand, covered, until the float valve drops down. Turn the steam release handle to Venting and remove the lid.

- **Natural Release:** When the timer beeps, press Cancel and let the pot stand, covered, until the float valve drops down. Turn the steam release handle to Venting, as a precaution, and remove the lid. This method can take about 15 to 25 minutes, depending on the volume of ingredients and the pressure level. It is used for dishes that foam and could cause clogging of the exhaust valve or spewing of ingredients out through the exhaust valve. It is also used for certain dishes that benefit from the additional standing time.

Slow Cooking

- Unless you are directed by a recipe to leave the lid off, the lid should be closed and locked and the steam release handle turned to Venting.
- Fill the cooker half to three-quarters full to avoid over- or undercooking.
- Avoid removing the lid during the cooking time. Doing so releases valuable heat, which can alter the amount of cooking time your dish gets at the correct temperature.
- Do not use frozen meats, as the temperature of your dish may never reach a safe temperature.

> If looking at your slow-cooking dish is something you feel you must do, purchase a clear glass cooking lid that is specifically made to fit your Instant Pot.

Sautéing

- The lid must always be kept off when using this function. Do not even partially cover the pot with the lid, as you might do on the stovetop when simmering sauces, as pressure can build in the pot and be very dangerous.
- The Sauté function is at full temperature and ready to go when the display says "Hot."
- There are three temperature levels, which you can change by pressing Adjust; most of the recipes in this book sauté on the "Normal" heat level.
- Always press Cancel when you are done using the Sauté function.

Making Yogurt

- Making yogurt takes time, so you will need to plan ahead for any recipe in which you want to use homemade yogurt.
- You can make yogurt directly in the inner pot or in individual glass jars.
- There are two steps to making yogurt: pasteurizing the milk, then adding a yogurt starter and pressing Yogurt to start the second stage.
- The steps you take to pasteurize the milk depend on whether you are using the jar method or the pot method. Follow the instructions in my recipe (page 212) or in your user manual for best results.

> Jiuniang, also known as fermented glutinous rice, is made using the Steam and Yogurt functions. Follow the instructions in your user manual for making jiuniang.

All Functions

- The recipes in this book are designed for multicookers with a 6-quart (6 L) capacity but will work in multicookers up to 1 quart (1 L) larger or smaller. Do not double or halve any recipe unless it specifically says you can do so.
- All ingredients must be added to the inner pot, never directly into the cooker housing.
- Keep the steam release valve free from any obstructions.
- Keep your multicooker clear of any cupboards, to prevent damage from the steam released.
- Whenever you are opening the lid after cooking, tilt the cover away from you so you don't get scalded by escaping steam. The cover can then be positioned upright in one of the handles on the cooker housing.

At altitudes above 3,000 feet (914 meters), recipes will require a change in cooking time or temperature, or both. Contact your multicooker's manufacturer to learn the adjustments needed for your altitude.

Recommended Accessories

Aside from your Instant Pot and some standard kitchen utensils, there are a few other kitchen gadgets that you will need (or will find handy) when preparing the recipes in this book.

- **Large chef's knife:** A sharp chef's knife is the best tool for cutting meats and vegetables to fit into your pot.
- **Steamer basket:** Although the Instant Pot comes with a steam rack, you will need a separate steamer basket to hold vegetables and other ingredients such as meatballs and chicken wings while steaming.
- **Ovenproof bakeware:** 6-oz (175 mL) ramekins, a 6-cup (1.5 L) round casserole dish, a 4-cup (1 L) round soufflé dish and a 6-inch (15 cm) springform pan are useful for making desserts and egg dishes in your multicooker, or when cooking smaller volumes.
- **Electric mixer:** Either a stand mixer or a handheld mixer can make it much easier to mix ingredients for cakes and puddings.
- **Food processor:** In some recipes, you will need to process ingredients for spreads or sauces.
- **Strainer:** A fine-mesh strainer is useful for rinsing rice or beans, and for straining liquids.
- **Garlic press:** You can certainly mince garlic by hand, but a press makes this frequent task a snap.

It's a good idea to keep a pair of kitchen gloves on hand. They are very useful when you're handling hot peppers, certain spices and fruits or vegetables that can stain your hands.

The Multicooker Pantry

A multicooker offers many benefits to the home cook, but when it comes to ingredients, two bonuses in particular stand out:

1. You can often use tougher, and therefore less expensive, cuts of meat, and they will become fork-tender in your multicooker.
2. You can prepare beans, rice and yogurt from scratch, without any processed ingredients.

The recipes in this book use a wide variety of ingredients, but there are certain staples used in a large number of recipes that you will want to be sure to keep on hand:

Oils

Olive oil is used in many of the recipes in this book. The high quality and superior taste of extra virgin olive oil make it the best choice for salads and other recipes that are not cooked; however, since extra virgin olive oil has a relatively low smoke point, regular olive oil is a better (and less expensive) choice for recipes that are cooked.

Virgin coconut oil, peanut oil, sunflower oil, sesame oil, grapeseed oil and hemp oil are also good options to have on hand.

Vinegars

Vinegar can impact the texture, color, flavor and thickness of dishes, adding acidity and sourness that can increase our enjoyment of our food. There are many types of vinegar, each of which has its own unique flavor. The vinegars used in this book include balsamic vinegar, cider vinegar, red wine vinegar, white wine vinegar and rice vinegar. If you are unsure which ones to have on hand, start with whichever one is used in a recipe you want to make, then expand your pantry provisions from there.

Broths

Vegetable, chicken and beef broths are used in many recipes to add flavor and as a substitute for water as the liquid in recipes. Most of the recipes call for ready-to-use broth, but by all means substitute homemade stock, if you have it on hand, or use broth prepared from bouillon cubes.

Certain recipes call for reduced-sodium broth, for the best flavor balance (typically when the recipe contains several other high-sodium ingredients). If you are watching your sodium intake, you may wish to use reduced-sodium or no-salt-added broths even when they are not specified in the recipe. If you do, just keep in mind that the flavor balance of the dish will be affected; you may want to add a bit of salt to compensate. (At least in that case you control the amount of added sodium.)

> If you are confident in your cooking skills and are familiar with a recipe, you may want to adjust the type or amount of an ingredient. Experimentation is fun, but can be a little more risky when you're cooking under pressure. Make sure to alter only one ingredient at a time, and change amounts only in small increments.

> Using the type of broth specified in the recipe will give you the best balance of flavors in the finished dish.

Condiments

Versatile condiments that will add zest and flavor to your dishes include Dijon mustard, Sriracha, tamari, soy sauce, Worcestershire sauce and honey. Stock your pantry with a variety of condiments that suit your taste, as they can be used to enhance many dishes.

Herbs, Seasonings and Flavorings

When adding fresh or dried herbs, seasonings and flavorings, remember that a little goes a long way. Always use the amount specified in the recipe for the best flavor and consistency.

If a recipe calls for fresh ingredients, do not substitute dried; if a recipe calls for dried ingredients, do not substitute fresh. Ingredients behave very differently under pressure or when slow cooking than you may be used to.

Other Staples

Cornstarch, brown sugar, tomato paste and vanilla extract are frequently used in these recipes, as thickeners or flavor enhancers.

Let's Get Cooking!

Once you have decided on a recipe you want to prepare, scan the ingredient and equipment lists to make sure you have everything you need on hand. For best results, purchase fresh meats, poultry, fish, vegetables and fruits just before you want to use them or, at the most, 2 to 3 days ahead.

You will have the most success with your dishes if you have all of the ingredients prepped and ready to go before you start following the recipe steps (unless otherwise directed in the method).

Quick Tips for Best Results

- Use the manual included with your multicooker for a complete description of the control panel and all of the functions, operation keys and indicators. The manufacturer is the expert on how to use its equipment for best results and safety.
- Measure ingredients carefully for optimal results.
- Follow the recipe steps exactly and in the order listed.
- Clean the inner pot, lid and housing according to the manufacturer's directions after each use.
- Clean the anti-block shield on the inside of the lid, the exhaust valve, the condensation collector and the sealing ring regularly to keep your cooker functioning properly.

> **Always add ingredients in the order listed and according to the recipe directions.**

> **Safety Note:** As with any cooking appliance, parts of the multicooker will become very hot. Be careful when handling the inner pot and any bakeware or steamer inserts used for cooking, and always be very cautious when releasing the steam from the vent and when opening the lid.

Breakfasts

Pressure Cooker

Slow Cooker

Quick and Easy Cook Functions

Power-Packed Creamy Oats

This warm and hearty breakfast is bursting with power foods that will leave you feeling satisfied and energized.

INSTANT POT FUNCTION

• Manual Pressure •

1 cup	steel-cut oats	250 mL
1½ tsp	ground ginger	7 mL
½ tsp	kosher salt	2 mL
4 cups	water	1 L
2 tsp	liquid honey	10 mL
1¾ cups	fresh red currants, divided	425 mL
¼ cup	slivered almonds, toasted (see tip, below)	60 mL
2 tbsp	chia seeds	30 mL
3 tbsp	heavy or whipping (35%) cream	45 mL

1. In the inner pot, combine oats, ginger, salt, water and honey, stirring well.

2. Place the pot inside the cooker housing, close and lock the lid and turn the steam release handle to Sealing. Press Manual; the indicator will read "High Pressure." Use the ➖ button to decrease the time on the display to 3 minutes.

3. When the timer beeps, press Cancel. Let stand, covered, until the float valve drops down. Turn the steam release handle to Venting and remove the lid.

4. Stir oats. Stir in 1 cup (250 mL) currants, almonds and chia seeds. Cover and let stand for 5 minutes or until oats are desired consistency.

5. Divide oats among serving bowls, top with the remaining currants and drizzle with cream.

Tips

When preparing oatmeal or any type of porridge using the Manual Pressure or Porridge functions, make sure to fill the pot no more than halfway full. Do not attempt to double or triple the recipe; otherwise, the exhaust valve may become clogged as the porridge froths up under pressure.

You can toast the almonds in your Instant Pot before beginning step 1. Press Sauté; when the display says "Hot," add the almonds and cook, stirring, for 3 minutes or until fragrant and lightly browned. Press Cancel and transfer the almonds to a plate to cool.

Variations

You can substitute an equal amount of ground flax seeds (flaxseed meal) for the chia seeds.

If you don't have fresh currants on hand, substitute an equal amount of fresh blueberries. You can also use 1 cup (250 mL) dried currants or raisins, adding ¾ cup (175 mL) in step 4 and the remainder on top. When using dried, you may want to increase the amount of honey to your liking.

Steel-Cut Oats with Strawberries and Cream

Start your day with creamy bowls of oats laced with sweet red strawberries, and you have a hearty and delicious breakfast that will fill you with warmth and goodness.

MAKES 4 SERVINGS

INSTANT POT FUNCTIONS

- Sauté -
- Manual Pressure -

1 tbsp	butter	15 mL
1 cup	steel-cut oats	250 mL
3 tbsp	packed brown sugar	45 mL
¼ tsp	salt	1 mL
3½ cups	water	875 mL
½ cup	heavy or whipping (35%) cream	125 mL
1½ cups	sliced strawberries	375 mL
3 tbsp	ground flax seeds (flaxseed meal) (optional)	45 mL

Tips

When preparing oatmeal or any type of porridge using the Manual Pressure or Porridge functions, make sure to fill the pot no more than halfway full. Do not attempt to double or triple the recipe; otherwise, the exhaust valve may become clogged as the porridge froths up under pressure.

Open the lid of the pressure cooker slowly, with the top of the lid facing you, to prevent burns from the hot steam.

1. Press Sauté; the indicator will read "Normal." When the display says "Hot," add butter to the pot and heat until melted. Add oats and cook, stirring, for 3 to 5 minutes or until fragrant. Press Cancel. Add sugar, salt, water and cream, stirring well.

2. Close and lock the lid and turn the steam release handle to Sealing. Press Manual; the indicator will read "High Pressure." Use the − button to decrease the time on the display to 3 minutes.

3. When the timer beeps, press Cancel. Let stand, covered, until the float valve drops down. Turn the steam release handle to Venting and remove the lid.

4. Stir oats. Fold in strawberries and flax seeds (if using). Cover and let stand for 5 minutes or until oats are desired consistency.

Apple Yogurt Chia Power Breakfast

The flavors of a warm apple pie meld together in this comforting, powered-up breakfast. But don't stop there — check out the variation for a surprisingly decadent dessert twist.

INSTANT POT FUNCTIONS

- Sauté -
- Manual Pressure -

1 tbsp	butter	15 mL
1 cup	steel-cut oats	250 mL
1	large firm sweet apple (such as Gala or Rome), peeled and diced	1
2 tbsp	packed light brown sugar	30 mL
1½ tsp	ground cinnamon	7 mL
¼ tsp	kosher salt	1 mL
3½ cups	water	875 mL
¼ cup	chia seeds	60 mL
¼ cup	plain Greek yogurt	60 mL
¼ cup	chopped walnuts	60 mL

Tip

When preparing oatmeal or any type of porridge using the Manual Pressure or Porridge functions, make sure to fill the pot no more than halfway full. Do not attempt to double or triple the recipe; otherwise, the exhaust valve may become clogged as the porridge froths up under pressure.

1. Press Sauté; the indicator will read "Normal." When the display says "Hot," add butter to the pot and heat until melted. Add oats and cook, stirring, for 3 to 5 minutes or until fragrant. Press Cancel. Add apple, brown sugar, cinnamon, salt and water, stirring well.

2. Close and lock the lid and turn the steam release handle to Sealing. Press Manual; the indicator will read "High Pressure." Use the ⊖ button to decrease the time on the display to 3 minutes.

3. When the timer beeps, press Cancel. Let stand, covered, until the float valve drops down. Turn the steam release handle to Venting and remove the lid.

4. Stir oats. Stir in chia seeds. Cover and let stand for 5 minutes or until oats are desired consistency.

5. Divide oats among serving bowls, top each with a dollop of yogurt and sprinkle with walnuts.

Variation

Apple Oatmeal Brûlée: Preheat broiler. After step 4, divide oatmeal among four 6-oz (175 mL) ramekins. In a small bowl, combine ¼ cup (60 mL) packed brown sugar and 2 tbsp (30 mL) granulated sugar. Sprinkle mixture evenly over oatmeal. Place ramekins on a baking sheet and broil for 3 to 5 minutes or until sugars are brown and crystallized. Let cool slightly. Serve sprinkled with berries and walnuts, if desired. (Do not top with yogurt.)

Maple Cinnamon Breakfast Quinoa

This dish is a morning star with the slightly nutty flavor of quinoa — a darling of gluten-free grains — and swirling with sweet cinnamon notes.

MAKES 6 SERVINGS

INSTANT POT FUNCTIONS

• Sauté •

• Manual Pressure •

2 tsp	grapeseed oil	10 mL
1 cup	quinoa, rinsed	250 mL
¼ tsp	ground cinnamon	1 mL
Pinch	kosher salt	Pinch
2 cups	water	500 mL
2 tbsp	pure maple syrup	30 mL
1 tsp	vanilla extract	5 mL

Tips

When preparing foods that expand as they cook, such as quinoa, make sure to fill the pot no more than halfway full. Do not attempt to double or triple the recipe; otherwise, the exhaust valve may become clogged, resulting in excess pressure.

I used grapeseed oil in this recipe because it does not impart any additional flavors to the quinoa. However, you can use any other good-quality oil you have on hand.

Quinoa has a bitter coating that protects the grain. You may find pre-rinsed quinoa, but I still prefer to rinse it one more time to remove any bitter residue.

1. Press Sauté; the indicator will read "Normal." When the display says "Hot," add oil to the pot and heat until shimmering. Add quinoa and cook, stirring, for 4 to 6 minutes or until golden brown. Press Cancel. Add cinnamon, salt, water, maple syrup and vanilla, stirring well.

2. Close and lock the lid and turn the steam release handle to Sealing. Press Manual; the indicator will read "High Pressure." Use the ⊖ button to decrease the time on the display to 1 minute.

3. When the timer beeps, press Cancel and let the pot stand, covered, for 10 minutes. After 10 minutes, turn the steam release handle to Venting and remove the lid.

4. Using a fork, fluff quinoa and transfer to serving bowls.

Forbidden Black Rice with Coconut

Black rice was once regarded as so superior in quality and nutritional value that it was reserved for Chinese royalty. Give yourself the royal treatment with this highly prized rice, crowned with toasted coconut and bananas.

MAKES 2 SERVINGS

INSTANT POT FUNCTION

• Manual Pressure •

1 cup	forbidden black rice, rinsed (see tips, below)	250 mL
Pinch	kosher salt	Pinch
¾ cup	water	175 mL
⅔ cup	coconut milk, divided	150 mL
½ tsp	almond extract	2 mL
½ cup	unsweetened flaked coconut	125 mL
1	banana, sliced	1

Tips

When preparing foods that expand as they cook, such as rice, make sure to fill the pot no more than halfway full. Do not attempt to double or triple the recipe; otherwise, the vent pipe may become clogged, resulting in excess pressure.

Wash and rinse black rice two or three times. When washing, rub the rice grains together with your fingers to remove any excess starch and reduce clumping when cooked. Completely rinse the rice in a fine-mesh strainer under cold water.

Black rice is naturally chewier than white rice. If you want it to have a texture more like risotto, cover it with cold water and soak in the refrigerator for 4 hours or overnight. Rinse and drain thoroughly before adding to the pot.

1. In the inner pot, combine rice, salt, water, ½ cup (125 mL) coconut milk and almond extract, stirring well.

2. Place the pot inside the cooker housing, close and lock the lid and turn the steam release handle to Sealing. Press Manual; the indicator will read "High Pressure." Use the ⊖ button to decrease the time on the display to 20 minutes.

3. Meanwhile, in a small skillet over high heat, toast coconut, stirring occasionally, for 3 minutes or until golden brown. Remove from heat and set aside.

4. When the timer beeps, press Cancel. Let stand, covered, until the float valve drops down. Turn the steam release handle to Venting and remove the lid.

5. Stir rice thoroughly. Divide rice among serving bowls and top with banana and toasted coconut. Drizzle with the remaining coconut milk.

Ham, Egg and Spinach Pot

Called *oeufs en cocotte* in French, this deliciously creamy brunch dish is simple to make, yet a full-bodied breakfast that will leave you satisfied and ready to start your day.

MAKES 1 SERVING

INSTANT POT FUNCTION

• Manual Pressure •

- **6-oz (175 mL) ramekin, bottom and sides buttered**
- **Instant Pot steam rack**

2 tbsp	diced ham	30 mL
4	baby spinach leaves, stems removed	4
1½ tbsp	shredded Cheddar cheese, divided	22 mL
2	large eggs	2
	Torn fresh basil	
	Freshly ground black pepper	

Tips

A bowl of fresh berries makes the perfect accompaniment to these delightful pots.

When using the Quick Release method to release pressure, keep your hands and face away from the hole on the top of the steam release handle so you don't get scalded by the escaping steam.

1. Layer ham, spinach and 1 tbsp (15 mL) cheese in the prepared ramekin. Crack eggs side by side on top of the cheese. Sprinkle eggs with the remaining cheese.

2. Add 1 cup (250 mL) water to the inner pot and place the steam rack in the pot. Place the ramekin on the rack. Close and lock the lid and turn the steam release handle to Sealing. Press Manual; the indicator will read "High Pressure." Use the ⊖ button to decrease the time on the display to 10 minutes.

3. When the timer beeps, press Cancel and turn the steam release handle to Venting. When the float valve drops down, remove the lid. Carefully remove the ramekin from the pot.

4. Sprinkle with basil and season with pepper.

Huevos Rancheros

Many years ago, I was traveling for my job to a small Texas town where the only restaurant for miles served only Mexican food. It was there that I quickly became a lifelong fan of these simple, quick and incredibly tasty ranchers-style eggs.

MAKES 1 SERVING

INSTANT POT FUNCTION
• Manual Pressure •

- **6-oz (175 mL) ramekin, sprayed with nonstick cooking spray**
- **4-oz (125 mL) ramekin**
- **18- by 12-inch (45 by 30 cm) sheet heavy-duty foil**
- **Instant Pot steam rack**

½ cup	salsa	125 mL
½ tsp	soy sauce	2 mL
2	large eggs	2
½ cup	refried beans	125 mL
2	taco-size (6-inch/15 cm) flour tortillas	2
2 tbsp	shredded Mexican cheese blend	30 mL
	Coarsely chopped fresh cilantro	

Tips

You can get two servings of refried beans from an 8-oz (227 mL) can.

Try the Mexican Refried Beans (page 132) in this recipe. It can be made ahead of time so you can still make breakfast quickly.

1. In the prepared 6-oz (175 mL) ramekin, combine salsa and soy sauce. Crack eggs side by side on top.

2. Place beans in the 4-oz (125 mL) ramekin. Wrap tortillas in foil.

3. Add 1 cup (250 mL) water to the inner pot and place the steam rack in the pot. Place both ramekins on the rack. Place foil-wrapped tortillas on top of the ramekins. Close and lock the lid and turn the steam release handle to Sealing. Press Manual; the indicator will read "High Pressure." Use the ⊖ button to decrease the time on the display to 10 minutes.

4. When the timer beeps, press Cancel and turn the steam release handle to Venting. When the float valve drops down, remove the lid. Using silicon-coated tongs, remove tortillas from pot, open foil carefully and transfer tortillas to a serving plate.

5. Carefully remove the ramekins from the pot and, using a large spoon, divide eggs evenly between tortillas. Pour salsa over top, leaving the yolks exposed. Sprinkle with cheese and cilantro. Serve with beans on the side.

Crustless Bacon Broccoli Quiche

Simple, elegant, colorful and sure to be a family favorite, this quiche is quickly ready for breakfast or lunch. Serve it with a side of fruit for breakfast or a side salad for lunch and feel like you have been transported to a Parisian bistro.

MAKES 4 SERVINGS

INSTANT POT FUNCTION

• Manual Pressure •

- **4-cup (1 L) round soufflé dish, bottom and sides buttered**
- **Instant Pot steam rack**

6	large eggs	6
2 tsp	dry mustard	10 mL
$\frac{1}{4}$ tsp	kosher salt	1 mL
Pinch	freshly ground black pepper	Pinch
$\frac{1}{2}$ cup	milk	125 mL
8	slices bacon, cooked crisp and crumbled	8
1	package (10 oz/300 g) frozen chopped broccoli, thawed and drained	1
1 cup	shredded Cheddar cheese	250 mL
2 tbsp	sliced green onions	30 mL

Tip

You can use virgin olive oil instead of butter to prepare your soufflé dish. Make sure the sides of the dish are coated all the way to the top, to allow the soufflé to rise and expand without sticking.

1. In a large bowl, whisk eggs. Whisk in mustard, salt, pepper and milk. Stir in bacon, broccoli, cheese and green onions. Pour mixture into prepared soufflé dish and cover loosely with foil.

2. Add $1\frac{1}{2}$ cups (375 mL) water to the inner pot and place the steam rack in the pot. Place the soufflé dish on the rack. Close and lock the lid and turn the steam release handle to Sealing. Press Manual; the indicator will read "High Pressure." Use the ⊖ button to decrease the time on the display to 10 minutes.

3. When the timer beeps, press Cancel and let the pot stand, covered, for 10 minutes. After 10 minutes, turn the steam release handle to Venting and remove the lid. Check to make sure a knife inserted in the center comes out clean. (If more cooking is needed, reset the manual pressure to "High Pressure" for 2 minutes.) Let the pot stand, uncovered, for 5 minutes, then remove the soufflé dish. Cut into 4 wedges and serve.

Cherry and Coconut Granola

If you have never made granola at home, it's time to give it a try. Making your own gives you the opportunity to choose the best-quality and best-priced ingredients and tweak the granola just to your liking. This slow-cook version makes it easy to get evenly browned, sensational-tasting granola.

MAKES ABOUT 6 CUPS (1.5 L)

INSTANT POT FUNCTION

• Slow Cook •

• **Baking sheet, lined with parchment paper**

4 cups	large-flake (old-fashioned) rolled oats	1 L
⅔ cup	slivered almonds	150 mL
½ tsp	ground ginger	2 mL
½ tsp	kosher salt	2 mL
⅓ cup	liquid honey	75 mL
¼ cup	butter	60 mL
½ tsp	vanilla extract	2 mL
½ cup	unsweetened shredded coconut	125 mL
½ cup	dried cherries	125 mL
½ cup	chopped dried apricots	125 mL
⅓ cup	sunflower seeds	75 mL

Tip

Sprinkle granola over plain yogurt, or alternate layers of yogurt and granola, for a fun morning treat or midday snack.

---

1. In the inner pot, combine oats, almonds, ginger, salt, honey, butter and vanilla, stirring well.

2. Place the pot inside the cooker housing, leaving the lid off. Press Slow Cook; the indicator will read "Normal." Press Adjust once to change the heat level to "More." Use the ⊖ button to decrease the time on the display to 1:00. Stir twice during the cooking time.

3. When the timer beeps, stir in coconut, cherries, apricots and sunflower seeds. Press Slow Cook; the indicator will read "Normal." Press Adjust twice to change the heat level to "Less." Leave the time at 4:00 and cook, stirring occasionally, until granola is completely dry.

4. Transfer granola to prepared baking sheet, spread out in a single layer and let cool. Transfer granola to an airtight container and store at room temperature for up to 2 weeks.

Almond Cinnamon Apples and Oats

Wake up to a warm bowl of creamy steel-cut oats with sweetened apples and a touch of almond and cinnamon to get your day started off with a wonderful breakfast.

INSTANT POT FUNCTION

• Slow Cook •

3	apples, divided	3
	Nonstick cooking spray	
1 cup	steel-cut oats	250 mL
¼ cup	packed brown sugar	60 mL
1 tbsp	ground cinnamon	15 mL
3 cups	water	750 mL
1 cup	unsweetened almond milk	250 mL
	Dried cranberries (optional)	
	Chopped walnuts (optional)	
	Pure maple syrup (optional)	

Tip

Crisp apples, such as Gala, Fuji, Cameo or Honeycrisp, will work best in this recipe.

1. Peel and core 2 apples and cut into ½-inch (1 cm) chunks.

2. Spray the inner pot with cooking spray. Add apple chunks, oats, brown sugar, cinnamon, water and almond milk to the pot, stirring gently to combine.

3. Place the pot inside the cooker housing, close and lock the lid and turn the steam release handle to Venting. Press Slow Cook; the indicator will read "Normal." Press Adjust twice to change the heat level to "Less." Use the ✚ button to increase the time on the display to 8:00.

4. When the timer beeps, remove the lid and stir well, scraping down the sides of the pot as necessary.

5. Core the remaining apple and cut into ½-inch (1 cm) chunks.

6. Transfer oatmeal to serving bowls and top with apple chunks. If desired, sprinkle with cranberries and walnuts and drizzle with maple syrup.

Variation

Fast Almond Cinnamon Apples and Oats: In step 3, after locking the lid, turn the steam release handle to Sealing. Press Porridge; the indicators will read "High Pressure" and "Normal." Press Pressure once to adjust the pressure to "Low Pressure." Press Adjust twice to change the cooking duration to "Less" (the time on the display will read "15"). When the timer beeps, press Cancel. Let stand, covered, until the float valve drops down. Turn the steam release handle to Venting and remove the lid. Stir well, scraping down the sides of the pot as necessary. Continue with step 5.

Applewood Smoked Bacon and Potatoes

This hearty breakfast or brunch dish will make even your hungriest eaters happy. Covered with melted Cheddar, it is perfect as a stand-alone breakfast, but you can also serve it with your choice of eggs.

INSTANT POT FUNCTION

• Slow Cook •

	Nonstick cooking spray	
3	russet potatoes (about 2 lbs/1 kg), peeled and cut into 1-inch (2.5 cm) cubes	3
1 cup	chopped onion	250 mL
	Kosher salt and freshly ground black pepper	
12	slices applewood-smoked bacon, cooked crisp and crumbled	12
1 cup	shredded sharp (old) Cheddar cheese	250 mL
½ tsp	dry mustard	2 mL
1 tbsp	ready-to-use chicken broth	15 mL

1. Spray the inner pot with cooking spray. Add half each of the potatoes and onion. Season with salt and pepper. Sprinkle with half each of the bacon and cheese. Repeat layers. Sprinkle with mustard and drizzle with broth.

2. Place the pot inside the cooker housing, close and lock the lid and turn the steam release handle to Venting. Press Slow Cook; the indicator will read "Normal." Press Adjust twice to change the heat level to "Less." Use the ✚ button to increase the time on the display to 6:00.

3. When the timer beeps, remove the lid and check to make sure the potatoes are fork-tender. (If more cooking is needed, reset the slow cooker to "Less" for 30 minutes.) Stir gently and serve.

Roasted Pepper, Kale, Feta and Eggs

This Mediterranean-inspired brunch bake is one of my favorite dishes to make when I have family and guests spending time during the holidays. It is colorful and satisfying, and offers a nice change from those large holiday feasts.

MAKES 6 SERVINGS

INSTANT POT FUNCTION

• Slow Cook •

	Nonstick cooking spray	
3½ cups	diced French bread	875 mL
8	slices bacon	8
1	large shallot, diced	1
2 cups	loosely packed torn trimmed kale	500 mL
8	large eggs	8
½ cup	milk	125 mL
1 cup	crumbled feta cheese	250 mL
¾ cup	roasted red bell peppers (about 3), drained and chopped	175 mL
	Kosher salt and freshly ground black pepper	

Tip

This dish can also be made in 2 hours. In step 6, press Adjust once to change the heat level to "More." Use the ⊖ button to decrease the time on the display to 2:00. Continue with step 7.

1. Spray the inner pot with cooking spray and place bread in the bottom of the pot.

2. In a large skillet, cook bacon over medium heat, turning once, for 5 to 6 minutes or until crispy. Using tongs, transfer bacon to a plate lined with paper towels and let cool.

3. Discard all but 1 tbsp (15 mL) bacon grease from the skillet. Add shallot and kale to the skillet and cook, stirring, for 1 to 2 minutes or until shallot is softened and kale is wilted. Add to the bread in the pot.

4. Dice cooled bacon and add to the pot, tossing to combine.

5. In a large bowl, whisk together eggs and milk. Stir in cheese and roasted peppers. Season with salt and pepper. Pour into the pot.

6. Place the pot inside the cooker housing, close and lock the lid and turn the steam release handle to Venting. Press Slow Cook; the indicator will read "Normal." Press Adjust twice to change the heat level to "Less." Use the ⊖ button to decrease the time on the display to 3:00.

7. When the timer beeps, remove the lid and check to make sure a knife inserted in the center comes out clean. (If more cooking is needed, reset the slow cooker to "Less" for 30 minutes.)

Ham, Swiss and Artichoke Frittata

This show-stopping strata takes the traditional layered casserole and gives it headlining ingredients of ham, Swiss cheese, green onions and my personal favorite, artichoke hearts.

MAKES 6 SERVINGS

INSTANT POT FUNCTION

• Slow Cook •

	Nonstick cooking spray	
6	slices sourdough bread, trimmed and torn into small pieces (about 4 cups/1 L)	6
2 cups	shredded Swiss cheese, divided	500 mL
1½ cups	diced ham	375 mL
⅔ cup	thinly sliced green onions, divided	150 mL
1	can (14 oz/398 mL) artichoke hearts, drained and finely chopped	1
4	large eggs	4
¾ cup	half-and-half (10%) cream	175 mL
1 tbsp	Worcestershire sauce	15 mL
½ tsp	dry mustard	2 mL

> **Tip**
> When you trim the crust from the bread, you don't need to cut all of it off. A little bit of crust will give this dish a firmer density.

1. Spray the inner pot with cooking spray and place bread in the bottom of the pot. Add layers of 1½ cups (375 mL) cheese, ham, ½ cup (125 mL) green onions and artichokes.

2. In a medium bowl, whisk together eggs, cream, Worcestershire sauce and mustard. Pour into the pot.

3. Place the pot inside the cooker housing, close and lock the lid and turn the steam release handle to Venting. Press Slow Cook; the indicator will read "Normal." Press Adjust twice to change the heat level to "Less." Use the ⊖ button to decrease the time on the display to 3:30.

4. When the timer beeps, remove the lid and check to make sure a knife inserted in the center comes out clean. (If more cooking is needed, reset the slow cooker to "Less" for 30 minutes.)

5. Sprinkle frittata with the remaining cheese and green onions. Cover and let stand for 10 minutes or until cheese is melted. Cut frittata into wedges and, using a thin, flexible spatula, transfer to plates.

Ham, Cheese and Bell Pepper Quiche

One of my favorite uses for leftover ham is to dice up those salty, savory chunks and add some creamy cheese, mushrooms and peppers for this custardy creation you can serve for breakfast or lunch.

INSTANT POT FUNCTION

• Slow Cook •

● **6-cup (1.5 L) round casserole dish, bottom and sides buttered**

1 tbsp	olive oil	15 mL
2 cups	chopped mushrooms (about 8 oz/250 g)	500 mL
½ cup	chopped red bell pepper	125 mL
1	package (10 oz/300 g) frozen spinach, thawed, drained and chopped	1
1½ cups	shredded Swiss cheese	375 mL
¾ cup	diced ham	175 mL
8	large eggs	8
2 cups	half-and-half (10%) cream	500 mL
½ tsp	kosher salt	2 mL
¼ tsp	freshly ground black pepper	1 mL
½ cup	all-purpose baking mix (such as Bisquick)	125 mL

Tip

This dish can also be made in 2½ hours. In step 3, press Adjust once to change the heat level to "More." Use the ● button to decrease the time on the display to 2:30. Continue with step 4.

1. In a large skillet, heat oil over medium heat. Add mushrooms and red pepper; cook, stirring, for 5 to 6 minutes or until softened. Remove from heat and stir in spinach, cheese and ham.

2. In a medium bowl, whisk eggs. Stir in cream, salt and pepper. Stir into mixture in skillet. Fold in baking mix. Pour egg mixture into prepared casserole dish.

3. Place the casserole dish in the inner pot. Close and lock the lid and turn the steam release handle to Venting. Press Slow Cook; the indicator will read "Normal." Press Adjust twice to change the heat level to "Less." Use the ● button to increase the time on the display to 5:00.

4. When the timer beeps, remove the lid and check to make sure a knife inserted in the center comes out clean. (If more cooking is needed, reset the slow cooker to "Less" for 30 minutes.) Carefully remove the casserole from the pot and let stand for 15 minutes before cutting and serving.

Variation

Broccoli Cheese Quiche: Substitute a 10-oz (300 g) package of frozen chopped broccoli, thawed and drained, for the spinach, and omit the ham.

Country Sausage, Egg and Hash Brown Casserole

This dish reminds me of morning breakfasts at my grandmother's house, where the crackling sound of frying sausages and hash browns was soon followed by the nose-tingling aroma of onions and peppers and subsequently the roar in my tummy.

MAKES 6 SERVINGS

INSTANT POT FUNCTION

• Slow Cook •

	Nonstick cooking spray	
1 lb	pork sausage (bulk or casings removed), browned and drained	500 g
½	package (28 oz/793 g) frozen O'Brien hash brown potatoes, thawed	½
3 cups	shredded sharp (old) Cheddar cheese	750 mL
12	large eggs	12
¼ cup	milk	60 mL
½ tsp	kosher salt	2 mL
¼ tsp	freshly ground black pepper	1 mL

Tips

Depending on your cravings, you can spice up your dish with breakfast sausage blends featuring Italian, chorizo or hot seasonings.

Traditional hash brown potatoes can be used in place of the O'Brien potatoes If you prefer to omit the peppers and onions.

1. Spray the inner pot with cooking spray. Add one-third of the sausage, followed by one-third each of the potatoes and cheese. Repeat layers twice more.

2. In a large bowl, whisk eggs. Stir in milk, salt and pepper. Pour into the pot.

3. Place the pot inside the cooker housing, close and lock the lid and turn the steam release handle to Venting. Press Slow Cook; the indicator will read "Normal." Press Adjust twice to change the heat level to "Less." Use the ✚ button to increase the time on the display to 6:00.

4. When the timer beeps, remove the lid and check to make sure a knife inserted in the center comes out clean. (If more cooking is needed, reset the slow cooker to "Less" for 30 minutes.)

Banana French Toast

If you are looking for a dreamy breakfast for a sleepy weekend morning, prepare this banana and peanut butter French toast the evening before and wake up to a warm and decadent breakfast.

- **6-cup (1.5 L) round casserole dish, bottom and sides buttered**
- **12-inch (30 cm) square sheet foil, sprayed with nonstick cooking spray**

¼ cup	peanut butter	60 mL
6	slices day-old brioche bread (¾ inch/2 cm thick)	6
3	bananas, sliced	3
¼ cup	dark chocolate chips (optional)	60 mL
6	large eggs	6
⅔ cup	granulated sugar	150 mL
½ tsp	ground cinnamon	2 mL
3 cups	half-and-half (10%) cream	750 mL
1 tsp	vanilla extract	5 mL
	Confectioners' (icing) sugar	
	Pure maple syrup	

Tips

You can use either chunky or smooth peanut butter.

Any type of rich egg bread, such as challah, can be used in this recipe.

1. Spread peanut butter on one side of each bread slice. Place 2 slices, spread side up, in prepared casserole dish, arranging them so the bread lies flat. Arrange half the bananas on top. Sprinkle with half the chocolate chips (if using). Top with 2 more bread slices, spread side up, then the remaining bananas and chocolate chips (if using). Place the remaining bread slices, spread side down, on top.

2. In a large bowl, whisk eggs. Stir in sugar, cinnamon, cream and vanilla. Pour over bread layers, pressing the liquid into the bread. Let stand for 10 minutes or until liquid is absorbed. Cover dish with prepared foil.

3. Place the casserole dish in the inner pot. Close and lock the lid and turn the steam release handle to Venting. Press Slow Cook; the indicator will read "Normal." Press Adjust once to change the heat level to "More." Use the ⊖ button to decrease the time on the display to 3:00.

4. When the timer beeps, remove the lid and check to make sure a knife inserted in the center comes out clean. (If more cooking is needed, reset the slow cooker to "More" for 15 minutes.) Carefully remove casserole from pot and let stand for 10 minutes before cutting. Dust with confectioners' sugar and serve with maple syrup.

Monkey Bread

Sweet, gooey and crunchy all come together in this rich breakfast or snack treat that everyone loves to pull apart and eat.

MAKES 6 SERVINGS

INSTANT POT FUNCTION

• Slow Cook •

⅔ cup	butter, melted, divided	150 mL
¾ cup	packed brown sugar, divided	175 mL
½ cup	chopped walnuts	125 mL
⅓ cup	water	75 mL
1 tsp	ground cinnamon	5 mL
¼ tsp	kosher salt	1 mL
1	can (16.3 oz/462 g) large refrigerated biscuits	1

Tip

The monkey bread can remain in the pot on the Keep Warm setting for up to 5 hours. If you plan to use the Keep Warm setting, increase the water to ⅔ cup (150 mL).

1. Butter the bottom and the lower third of the sides of the inner pot with 1 tbsp (15 mL) butter. Sprinkle ¼ cup (60 mL) sugar over the butter. Add walnuts, ¼ cup (60 mL) butter and water.

2. In a medium bowl, combine the remaining sugar, cinnamon and salt.

3. Cut each biscuit into 4 pieces. Roll each piece into a ball. Brush each ball with butter, roll in sugar mixture and place in the pot, arranging as needed to fit in one layer.

4. Place the pot inside the cooker housing, close and lock the lid and turn the steam release handle to Venting. Press Slow Cook; the indicator will read "Normal." Press Adjust twice to change the heat level to "Less." Use the ⊖ button to decrease the time on the display to 2:00.

5. When the timer beeps, remove the lid and check to make sure a tester inserted in the center of the biscuits comes out clean. (If more cooking is needed, reset the slow cooker to "Less" for 15 minutes.) Press Cancel and lift the pot out of the cooker. Place a plate upside down over the pot and carefully flip pot and plate over to release the monkey bread onto the plate. Serve by tearing off individual servings.

Apple Pie Coffee Cake

Can I be so bold as to say that this coffee cake will soon become a family favorite? The delicate crumb cake is infused with all the flavors of classic apple pie, then topped with a crunchy brown sugar streusel.

MAKES 8 SERVINGS

INSTANT POT FUNCTION

• Slow Cook •

- 7-inch (18 cm) nonstick springform pan, sprayed with nonstick cooking spray

Coffee Cake

1	large egg	1
2	crisp apples (such as Gala, Fuji, Cameo or Honeycrisp), peeled and diced	2
2 cups	all-purpose baking mix (such as Bisquick)	500 mL
2 tbsp	packed dark brown sugar	30 mL
1 tsp	ground cinnamon	5 mL
¼ tsp	ground nutmeg	1 mL
Pinch	ground cardamom	Pinch
Pinch	ground allspice	Pinch
⅔ cup	unsweetened applesauce	150 mL
¼ cup	milk	60 mL
2 tbsp	butter, melted	30 mL
1 tsp	vanilla extract	5 mL
½ tsp	apple cider vinegar	2 mL

Streusel

¼ cup	large-flake (old-fashioned) rolled oats	60 mL
¼ cup	all-purpose flour	60 mL
¼ cup	packed dark brown sugar	60 mL
¼ cup	butter, melted	60 mL

1. *Cake:* In a large bowl, using a fork, lightly beat egg. Stir in apples, baking mix, brown sugar, cinnamon, nutmeg, cardamom, allspice, applesauce, milk, butter, vanilla and vinegar until combined; batter will be lumpy. Pour batter into prepared pan.

2. *Streusel:* In a small bowl, combine oats, flour, brown sugar and butter. Sprinkle evenly over batter and lightly press it in.

3. Place the pan in the inner pot. Close and lock the lid and turn the steam release handle to Venting. Press Slow Cook; the indicator will read "Normal." Press Adjust twice to change the heat level to "Less." Use the ➕ button to increase the time on the display to 4:30.

4. When the timer beeps, remove the lid and check to make sure a tester inserted in the center of the cake comes out clean. (If more cooking is needed, reset the slow cooker to "Less" for 30 minutes.) Carefully remove pan from cooker and let stand for 15 minutes. Transfer cake to a serving platter, slice and serve.

Tips

The coffee cake can remain in the cooker on the Keep Warm setting for up to 2 hours.

Substitute chopped walnuts or pecans for the rolled oats in the streusel, if you like.

Maple Caramel–Glazed Cinnamon Coffee Cake

When the air outside gets crisp, it's time to fire up your slow cooker for some warm and inviting coffee cake. The smell of cinnamon wafting through the air like a warming breeze will have your household scrambling to the kitchen.

MAKES 6 SERVINGS

INSTANT POT FUNCTION

• Slow Cook •

- **15-inch (38 cm) square sheet parchment paper**
- **Stand mixer, fitted with flat beater**

Nonstick cooking spray

Streusel

¼ cup	all-purpose baking mix (such as Bisquick)	60 mL
¼ cup	packed brown sugar	60 mL
1 tsp	ground cinnamon	5 mL

Coffee Cake

1 cup	granulated sugar	250 mL
½ cup	butter, softened	125 mL
2	large eggs	2
1 cup	sour cream	250 mL
1 tsp	vanilla extract	5 mL
2 cups	all-purpose flour	500 mL
1 tsp	baking powder	5 mL
½ tsp	baking soda	2 mL

Maple Caramel Glaze

½ cup	granulated sugar	125 mL
3 tbsp	water	45 mL
¼ cup	pure maple syrup	60 mL
2 tbsp	butter, cut into pieces	30 mL

1. Place parchment paper in the inner pot, pressing as needed to cover the bottom and sides. Spray parchment with cooking spray.

2. *Streusel:* In a small bowl, combine baking mix, brown sugar and cinnamon. Set aside.

3. *Cake:* In the stand mixer bowl, beat sugar and butter until smooth. Mix in eggs, sour cream and vanilla until combined. On low speed, mix in flour, baking powder and baking soda, scraping down the sides of the bowl as needed, until batter is smooth; do not overmix.

4. Pour half the batter into prepared pot. Sprinkle streusel evenly on top. Pour in the remaining batter.

5. Place the pot inside the cooker housing, close and lock the lid and turn the steam release handle to Venting. Press Slow Cook; the indicator will read "Normal." Press Adjust once to change the heat level to "More." Use the ⊖ button to decrease the time on the display to 1:45.

6. When the timer beeps, remove the lid and check to make sure a tester inserted in the center of the cake comes out clean. (If more cooking is needed, reset the slow cooker to "More" for 10 minutes.) Press Cancel and let stand for 15 minutes. Use the parchment to carefully lift out the cake. Using a cake spatula, transfer cake to a serving plate.

7. *Glaze:* Meanwhile, in a medium saucepan, heat sugar and water over medium-high heat, stirring constantly, for 3 minutes or until sugar is dissolved. Boil without stirring for 3 to 5 minutes or until mixture is an amber color. Remove from heat and carefully stir in maple syrup and butter until butter is melted.

8. Drizzle glaze over top of cake. Cut cake into wedges to serve.

Variation

Maple Caramel Bacon Glaze: In a medium skillet, cook 4 slices of bacon over medium heat, turning once, for 7 minutes or until crispy. Transfer to a plate lined with paper towels and let cool, then chop bacon into tiny pieces. Stir into glaze in step 7, after adding the maple syrup and butter.

Tip

When removing the lid, turn it quickly to the side to prevent any accumulated moisture from dropping onto your cake.

Russian Kasha with Cranberries

Having been a mainstay of Russian cuisine for centuries, this classic millet porridge is truly something special. You'll understand why is has been such a long-standing favorite when you try this version, made with dried cranberries.

MAKES 2 SERVINGS

INSTANT POT FUNCTION
• Porridge •

1	large egg	1
½ cup	millet, rinsed	125 mL
¼ cup	dried cranberries	60 mL
1 cup	ready-to-use chicken broth	250 mL
2 tsp	butter	10 mL

Tips

When preparing porridge using the Manual Pressure or Porridge functions, make sure to fill the pot no more than halfway full. Do not attempt to double or triple the recipe; otherwise, the exhaust valve may become clogged as the porridge froths up under pressure.

Golden raisins or chopped dried cherries, or a combination, can be used in place of the cranberries.

If you don't have chicken broth on hand, replace it with an equal amount of water and add 1 tsp (5 mL) kosher salt.

1. In a small bowl, whisk the egg, then whisk in millet.

2. In the inner pot, combine millet mixture, cranberries and broth, stirring well.

3. Place the pot inside the cooker housing, close and lock the lid and turn the steam release handle to Sealing. Press Porridge; the indicators will read "High Pressure" and "Normal." Press Adjust twice to change the cooking duration to "Less" (the time on the display will read "15").

4. When the timer beeps, press Cancel. Let stand, covered, until the float valve drops down. Turn the steam release handle to Venting and remove the lid.

5. Stir millet, divide between serving bowls and top each with 1 tsp (5 mL) butter.

Creamy Millet with Strawberry Compote

What I love about millet is that it has a slight bit of crunch on the outside after cooking. So if you'd love a creamy, nutritious breakfast with a hint of crunch, this one is for you. Serve with additional coconut milk or sugar to your liking.

MAKES 3 TO 4 SERVINGS

INSTANT POT FUNCTION

• Porridge •

Porridge

	Nonstick cooking spray	
½ cup	millet, rinsed	125 mL
¼ tsp	ground cardamom	1 mL
Pinch	kosher salt	Pinch
½ cup	coconut milk	125 mL
½ cup	water	125 mL

Strawberry Compote

1 cup	frozen strawberries	250 mL
1 tbsp	orange juice	15 mL
½ tsp	granulated sugar	2 mL
Pinch	ground cinnamon	Pinch
Pinch	ground ginger	Pinch

Tips

When preparing porridge using the Manual Pressure or Porridge functions, make sure to fill the pot no more than halfway full. Do not attempt to double or triple the recipe; otherwise, the exhaust valve may become clogged as the porridge froths up under pressure.

Any combination of berries, or a combination of berries and cherries, will work equally well for the compote.

1. *Porridge:* Spray the inner pot with cooking spray. Add millet, cardamom, salt, coconut milk and water, stirring well.

2. Place the pot inside the cooker housing, close and lock the lid and turn the steam release handle to Sealing. Press Porridge; the indicators will read "High Pressure" and "Normal." Press Pressure once to adjust the pressure to "Low Pressure." Press Adjust twice to change the cooking duration to "Less" (the time on the display will read "15").

3. When the timer beeps, press Cancel. Let stand, covered, until the float valve drops down. Turn the steam release handle to Venting and remove the lid. Stir porridge.

4. *Compote:* Meanwhile, in a small saucepan, heat strawberries and orange juice over medium heat, mashing berries with a potato masher, for 3 minutes or until bubbling. Reduce heat to medium-low and stir in sugar, cinnamon and ginger. Cook, mashing and stirring occasionally, for 10 to 12 minutes or until mixture is a soft gel-like consistency.

5. Divide porridge among serving bowls and top with compote.

Cranberry Almond Quinoa and Millet Porridge

When I need a light, yet filling breakfast, I break out my Instant Pot and make this sweet, tart and savory porridge that perfectly satisfies all of my cravings.

MAKES 3 TO 4 SERVINGS

INSTANT POT FUNCTION

• Porridge •

⅓ cup	quinoa, rinsed	75 mL
¼ cup	millet, rinsed	60 mL
2 tbsp	dried cranberries	30 mL
Pinch	kosher salt	Pinch
2½ cups	unsweetened almond milk	625 mL
2 tbsp	pure maple syrup	30 mL
1 tsp	vanilla extract	5 mL

Tips

When preparing porridge using the Manual Pressure or Porridge functions, make sure to fill the pot no more than halfway full. Do not attempt to double or triple the recipe; otherwise, the exhaust valve may become clogged as the porridge froths up under pressure.

For a slightly nuttier flavor, toast the quinoa before adding the other ingredients. Press Sauté; the indicator will read "Normal." Press Adjust twice to adjust the heat level to "Less." When the display says "Hot," add quinoa and cook, stirring, for 5 to 7 minutes or until fragrant. Press Cancel. Continue with step 1.

1. In the inner pot, combine quinoa, millet, cranberries, salt, almond milk, maple syrup and vanilla, stirring well.

2. Place the pot inside the cooker housing, close and lock the lid and turn the steam release handle to Sealing. Press Porridge; the indicators will read "High Pressure" and "Normal." Press Adjust twice to change the cooking duration to "Less" (the time on the display will read "15").

3. When the timer beeps, press Cancel. Let stand, covered, until the float valve drops down. Turn the steam release handle to Venting and remove the lid. Stir well, scraping down the sides of the pot as necessary, before serving.

Harvest Basket Porridge

This porridge takes me to my festive farmers' market in autumn, where bright reds, oranges and purples explode from the tables, making my mouth water with the promise of sweet, tangy and chewy delights.

INSTANT POT FUNCTION

• Porridge •

2 cups	steel-cut oats	500 mL
½ cup	dried cranberries	125 mL
½ cup	chopped dried apricots	125 mL
½ cup	chopped dates	125 mL
½ cup	green pumpkin seeds (pepitas)	125 mL
¼ cup	packed brown sugar	60 mL
1 tsp	ground cardamom	5 mL
½ tsp	ground ginger	2 mL
½ tsp	kosher salt	2 mL
4 cups	water	1 L
4 cups	coconut water	1 L
2 tbsp	tahini	30 mL
1 tsp	vanilla extract	5 mL
	Grated zest of 1 orange	

1. In the inner pot, combine oats, cranberries, apricots, dates, pumpkin seeds, brown sugar, cardamom, ginger, salt, water, coconut water, tahini and vanilla, stirring well.

2. Place the pot inside the cooker housing, close and lock the lid and turn the steam release handle to Sealing. Press Porridge; the indicators will read "High Pressure" and "Normal." Press Adjust twice to change the cooking duration to "Less" (the time on the display will read "15").

3. When the timer beeps, press Cancel. Let stand, covered, until the float valve drops down. Turn the steam release handle to Venting and remove the lid. Stir well, scraping down the sides of the pot as necessary. Stir in orange zest.

Tips

When preparing porridge using the Manual Pressure or Porridge functions, make sure to fill the pot no more than halfway full. Do not attempt to double or triple the recipe; otherwise, the exhaust valve may become clogged as the porridge froths up under pressure.

Leftover porridge can be stored in an airtight container in the refrigerator for up to 5 days. Reheat the porridge in the microwave or on the stovetop over medium-low heat, gradually stirring in water or milk to bring it to your desired consistency.

Steel-Cut Oats and Amaranth Porridge with Dates

If you have tried amaranth, you already know the nutty, slight earthy taste and crunch of this healthy ancient grain. If not, get ready for an enjoyable breakfast porridge infused with sweet, chewy dates, maple syrup and a hint of nutmeg.

MAKES 4 SERVINGS

INSTANT POT FUNCTION
• Porridge •

½ cup	steel-cut oats	125 mL
½ cup	amaranth	125 mL
¼ cup	chopped dates	60 mL
½ tsp	salt	2 mL
½ tsp	ground nutmeg	2 mL
2 cups	coconut milk	500 mL
1 cup	water	250 mL
1 tbsp	pure maple syrup	15 mL
1 tsp	vanilla extract	5 mL
¼ cup	chopped walnuts	60 mL

Tip
When preparing porridge using the Manual Pressure or Porridge functions, make sure to fill the pot no more than halfway full. Do not attempt to double or triple the recipe; otherwise, the exhaust valve may become clogged as the porridge froths up under pressure.

1. In the inner pot, combine oats, amaranth, dates, salt, nutmeg, coconut milk, water, maple syrup and vanilla, stirring well.

2. Place the pot inside the cooker housing, close and lock the lid and turn the steam release handle to Sealing. Press Porridge; the indicators will read "High Pressure" and "Normal." Press Adjust twice to change the cooking duration to "Less" (the time on the display will read "15").

3. When the timer beeps, press Cancel. Let stand, covered, until the float valve drops down. Turn the steam release handle to Venting and remove the lid. Stir well, scraping down the sides of the pot as necessary.

4. Divide porridge among serving bowls and top with walnuts.

Caribbean Spice Porridge

While I never imagined that a warm oatmeal porridge would be a welcoming breakfast in Jamaica, this creamy oatmeal porridge immersed in a bounty of spices and topped with dried tropical fruits is one of my all-time favorites.

MAKES 4 SERVINGS

INSTANT POT FUNCTIONS

• Sauté •

• Porridge •

10	whole allspice berries	10
5	whole cloves	5
1	cinnamon stick	1
1	bay leaf	1
1 tsp	ground nutmeg	5 mL
2½ cups	water	625 mL
1 cup	large-flake (old-fashioned) rolled oats	250 mL
Pinch	kosher salt	Pinch
1 cup	coconut milk	250 mL
	Milk (optional)	
½ cup	dried tropical fruit mix, chopped	125 mL
¼ cup	chopped pecans	60 mL
	Shredded coconut (optional)	
	Cacao nibs (optional)	

Tips

When preparing porridge using the Manual Pressure or Porridge functions, make sure to fill the pot no more than halfway full. Do not attempt to double or triple the recipe; otherwise, the exhaust valve may become clogged as the porridge froths up under pressure.

Dried tropical fruit mix is typically a mix of mango, pineapple and banana. It often includes shredded coconut, too. If you don't have it on hand, 2 sliced bananas are a nice alternative.

1. In the inner pot, combine allspice berries, cloves, cinnamon stick, bay leaf, nutmeg and water. Place the pot inside the cooker housing and press Sauté; the indicator will read "Normal." Press Adjust once to increase the temperature to "More." Bring to a boil and boil for 5 minutes. Press Cancel. Using a slotted spoon, remove the allspice, cloves, cinnamon and bay leaf. Stir in oats, salt and coconut milk.

2. Close and lock the lid and turn the steam release handle to Sealing. Press Porridge; the indicators will read "High Pressure" and "Normal." Press Adjust twice to change the cooking duration to "Less" (the time on the display will read "15").

3. When the timer beeps, press Cancel. Let stand, covered, until the float valve drops down. Turn the steam release handle to Venting and remove the lid. Stir well, scraping down the sides of the pot as necessary. If desired, stir in milk until the porridge is your desired consistency.

4. Divide porridge among serving bowls and top with dried fruit and pecans. If desired, sprinkle with coconut and cacao nibs.

Portuguese Sausage and Rice

The sausage in this recipe contains a secret blend of spices that has been its signature flavor for centuries. Add in a slight Asian influence and you might feel like you are dining in the Hawaiian islands, where this dish is one of the local favorites.

MAKES 4 SERVINGS

INSTANT POT FUNCTIONS

- Sauté •
- Rice •

2 tbsp	virgin olive oil	30 mL
14 oz	cooked linguiça sausage, cut into ¼-inch (0.5 cm) slices	400 g
1 cup	chopped onion	250 mL
2 cups	short-grain white rice	500 mL
1 cup	frozen baby peas	250 mL
3 cups	ready-to-use chicken broth	750 mL
2 tsp	soy sauce	10 mL
1½ tbsp	butter	22 mL
4	large eggs	4
3	green onions, sliced	3
	Freshly ground black pepper (optional)	

Tips

Linguiça sausage is sometimes called Portuguese sausage. It is mild, lean and full of a secret blend of spices. It is really worth trying. You can also use it in chili or on pizza, or eat it grilled.

If you cannot find linguiça, a mild pork sausage such as kielbasa will also work well.

1. Press Sauté; the indicator will read "Normal." When the display says "Hot," add oil and heat until shimmering. Add sausage and onion; cook, stirring, for 7 to 9 minutes or until sausage is seared and onions are lightly browned. Press Cancel. Stir in rice, peas, broth and soy sauce.

2. Close and lock the lid and turn the steam release handle to Sealing. Press Rice; the indicator will read "Low Pressure."

3. When the timer beeps, press Cancel and let the pot stand, covered, for 10 minutes. After 10 minutes, turn the steam release handle to Venting and remove the lid.

4. Meanwhile, in a large skillet, heat butter over medium heat until bubbling. Crack eggs into the skillet and cook, turning once, for 5 minutes or until done to your liking.

5. Divide rice mixture among serving plates and top each with a fried egg. Garnish with green onions and season with pepper (if using).

Soups, Stews and Chilis

Pressure Cooker

Slow Cooker

Broccoli and Beer Cheese Soup

When you grow up in a state known for its dairy products and beer, you get pretty creative when coming up with dishes that include both. My take on creamy broccoli soup will leave you feeling warm and content.

MAKES 8 SERVINGS

INSTANT POT FUNCTIONS

- Sauté -
- Manual Pressure -

2 tbsp	butter	30 mL
1	small onion, finely chopped	1
3	stalks celery, finely chopped	3
2	carrots, shredded	2
3 cups	chopped broccoli florets	750 mL
2 tsp	dry mustard	10 mL
1 tsp	kosher salt	5 mL
½ tsp	freshly ground black pepper	2 mL
2½ cups	ready-to-use chicken broth	625 mL
1½ tsp	Worcestershire sauce	7 mL
2 cups	shredded Cheddar cheese	500 mL
1	can (12 oz/341 mL) lager-style beer, at room temperature	1
½ cup	heavy or whipping (35%) cream	125 mL
4	slices bacon, cooked crisp and crumbled (optional)	4
	Green onions, sliced (optional)	

1. Press Sauté; the indicator will read "Normal." When the display says "Hot," add butter to the pot and heat until melted. Add onions and cook, stirring, for 3 to 5 minutes or until translucent. Press Cancel. Add celery, carrots, broccoli, mustard, salt, pepper, broth and Worcestershire sauce, stirring well.

2. Close and lock the lid and turn the steam release handle to Sealing. Press Manual; the indicator will read "High Pressure." Use the ⊖ button to decrease the time on the display to 4 minutes.

3. When the timer beeps, press Cancel and turn the steam release handle to Venting. When the float valve drops down, remove the lid.

4. Stir in cheese, beer and cream until cheese is melted and well combined. If desired, serve garnished with bacon and/or green onions.

Tips

This soup can be stored in an airtight container in the freezer for up to 3 months. Thaw in the refrigerator overnight before reheating. You may want to freeze it in individual serving sizes for a quick single meal.

Additional toppings that work well on this soup include croutons, popcorn and shredded Cheddar cheese.

Homestyle Corn Chowder

Creamy, buttery and with just a little kick, this corn chowder is the thumbs-up favorite for a soothing, hearty soup. Top it with crumbled bacon, and you'll be coming back for more.

MAKES 6 SERVINGS

INSTANT POT FUNCTIONS
• Sauté •
• Manual Pressure •

6	ears sweet corn (preferably bicolor)	6
⅓ cup	butter, divided	75 mL
2	onions, finely chopped	2
2 tsp	dried parsley	10 mL
1 tsp	dried thyme	5 mL
½ tsp	garlic powder	2 mL
Pinch	granulated sugar	Pinch
3 cups	ready-to-use chicken broth	750 mL
2 tbsp	cornstarch	30 mL
1½ cups	half-and-half (10%) cream	375 mL
4	slices bacon, cooked crisp and crumbled	4
2 tsp	hot pepper flakes	10 mL
	Kosher salt and freshly ground black pepper	

Tips

I like to use early-season bicolor corn, as I find it to be much more tender and sweet. If you cannot find bicolor corn, use 3 ears each of yellow and white corn or 6 ears of any sweet corn variety of your choice.

When using the Quick Release method to release pressure, keep your hands and face away from the hole on the top of the steam release handle so you don't get scalded by the escaping steam.

1. Cut the kernels off of the corn. Press Sauté; the indicator will read "Normal." When the display says "Hot," add 2 tbsp (30 mL) butter to the pot and heat until melted. Add onions and cook, stirring, for 3 to 5 minutes or until translucent. Press Cancel. Add corn, parsley, thyme, garlic powder, sugar, broth and the remaining butter, stirring well.

2. Close and lock the lid and turn the steam release handle to Sealing. Press Manual; the indicator will read "High Pressure." Use the ⊖ button to decrease the time on the display to 2 minutes.

3. When the timer beeps, press Cancel and turn the steam release handle to Venting. When the float valve drops down, remove the lid.

4. In a small bowl, whisk together cornstarch and cream. Press Sauté. Add the cornstarch mixture to the pot, along with bacon and hot pepper flakes, and cook, stirring, for 3 minutes or until thickened. Season to taste with salt and pepper.

Golden Potato Soup with Crème Fraîche

This soup has all the comforting full flavors you expect from a down-home soup, but the new potatoes and crème fraîche give it a lighter, slightly tangy twist.

MAKES 6 SERVINGS

INSTANT POT FUNCTIONS

• Sauté •

• Manual Pressure •

3 tbsp	butter	45 mL
1	large shallot, finely chopped	1
1	clove garlic, minced	1
3 cups	chopped new potatoes (about 1 lb/500 g)	750 mL
3 cups	ready-to-use chicken broth	750 mL
½ cup	crème fraîche, divided	125 mL
	Kosher salt and freshly ground black pepper	
	Snipped fresh chives	

Tips

After step 3, you can blend the soup to make it smoother. Either use an immersion blender right in the pot or transfer the soup in batches to a blender or food processor.

You may want to try serving this soup cold as a starter. As a starter, it will serve 10 to 12 people. After step 3, let soup cool to room temperature. Cover and refrigerate for at least 3 hours or up to 3 days. When ready to serve, use an immersion blender to purée the soup until smooth. Continue with step 4.

1. Press Sauté; the indicator will read "Normal." When the display says "Hot," add butter to the pot and heat until melted. Add shallots and cook, stirring, for 2 to 3 minutes or until translucent. Add garlic and cook, stirring, for 30 seconds or until fragrant. Press Cancel. Add potatoes and broth, stirring well.

2. Close and lock the lid and turn the steam release handle to Sealing. Press Manual; the indicator will read "High Pressure." Use the ⊖ button to decrease the time on the display to 7 minutes.

3. When the timer beeps, press Cancel and turn the steam release handle to Venting. When the float valve drops down, remove the lid.

4. Stir in ¼ cup (60 mL) crème fraîche. Season to taste with salt and pepper. Ladle into serving bowls and serve dolloped with the remaining crème fraîche and garnished with chives.

Ginger Pumpkin Soup

This colorful soup has so many things going for it, you just must give it a try. It boasts a combination of sweet, spicy, zesty and creamy flavors and is perfect as a main dish or as a starter for an Indian-inspired meal.

MAKES 6 SERVINGS

INSTANT POT FUNCTIONS

• Sauté •

• Manual Pressure •

3 tbsp	butter	45 mL
3	cloves garlic, minced	3
1	large onion, minced	1
2 tbsp	minced gingerroot	30 mL
1 tsp	ground cumin	5 mL
½ tsp	curry powder	2 mL
4 cups	cubed seeded peeled pie pumpkin	1 L
2 tbsp	packed brown sugar	30 mL
1 tbsp	kosher salt	15 mL
3½ cups	water	875 mL
1⅔ cups	coconut milk	400 mL
2 tsp	sweet Thai chile sauce (optional)	10 mL
	Juice of 1 orange	
1 cup	plain Greek yogurt	250 mL
	Grated zest of 1 lime	
¼ cup	fresh basil chiffonade (see tip, at right)	60 mL

1. Press Sauté; the indicator will read "Normal." When the display says "Hot," add butter to the pot and heat until melted. Add garlic, onion, ginger, cumin and curry powder; cook, stirring, for 4 to 5 minutes or until onion is soft and spices are fragrant. Press Cancel. Add pumpkin, brown sugar, salt, water, coconut milk, chile sauce (if using) and orange juice, stirring well.

2. Close and lock the lid and turn the steam release handle to Sealing. Press Manual; the indicator will read "High Pressure." Press Pressure once to adjust the pressure to "Low Pressure." Use the ⊖ button to decrease the time on the display to 3 minutes.

3. When the timer beeps, press Cancel and turn the steam release handle to Venting. When the float valve drops down, remove the lid. The pumpkin should be very tender when tested with a fork. (If more cooking is needed, reset the manual pressure to "Low Pressure" for 1 minute.) Stir soup well and adjust seasoning, if desired.

4. In a small bowl, combine yogurt and lime zest. Ladle soup into serving bowls and serve dolloped with lime yogurt and garnished with basil.

Tips

Use pie pumpkins (also known as sugar pumpkins or sweet pumpkins), as they are much more flavorful than the larger ones typically used for decorating or carving.

This soup can be completed through step 3 and then refrigerated in airtight containers for up to 1 week.

To chiffonade basil, remove the stems and stack 10 or more leaves. Roll the leaves up lengthwise into a fairly tight spiral, then cut crosswise into thin strips. Fluff the strips.

Colombian Vegetable Soup

Soup is very popular in Colombia, and this is one of the most famous soups from the mountainous regions of the country. Think of it as a vegetable soup with a kick.

INSTANT POT FUNCTION		
• Manual Pressure •		

2	large russet potatoes, peeled and cut into ½-inch (1 cm) cubes	2
1	carrot, diced	1
1	ear sweet corn, cut into 6 crosswise slices	1
1½ cups	rinsed drained canned fava beans	375 mL
1 cup	frozen peas	250 mL
1 tsp	ground cumin	5 mL
6 cups	ready-to-use vegetable broth	1.5 L
	Kosher salt and freshly ground black pepper	
¼ cup	chopped fresh cilantro	60 mL
1	avocado, peeled and cut into 6 wedges	1

1. In the inner pot, combine potatoes, carrot, corn, fava beans, peas, cumin and broth.

2. Place the pot inside the cooker housing, close and lock the lid and turn the steam release handle to Sealing. Press Manual; the indicator will read "High Pressure." Use the ⊖ button to decrease the time on the display to 15 minutes.

3. When the timer beeps, press Cancel and turn the steam release handle to Venting. When the float valve drops down, remove the lid.

4. Stir well and season to taste with salt and pepper. Ladle into serving bowls, including 1 corn slice in each bowl. Garnish with cilantro and top each with 1 avocado wedge.

Tips

Substitute a package of frozen mixed vegetables that includes the carrots, peas and corn. You will need 3 cups (750 mL) frozen vegetables. You may also be able to use mini frozen ears of corn instead of cutting a whole ear of corn.

When using the Quick Release method to release pressure, keep your hands and face away from the hole on the top of the steam release handle so you don't get scalded by the escaping steam.

Chicken and Wild Rice Soup

When I lived in a region where we had many cold and snowy days, I soon realized why the locals were so enamored of wild rice soup. Not only does it taste fantastic, it seems to have the magical power to warm you to your bones.

MAKES 6 SERVINGS

INSTANT POT FUNCTIONS
- Sauté •
- Manual Pressure •

2 tbsp	butter	30 mL
1 cup	chopped onion	250 mL
1 cup	diced carrots	250 mL
1 cup	diced celery	250 mL
2	boneless skinless chicken breasts, cut into cubes	2
1	package (6 oz/175 g) long-grain and wild rice mix	1
1 tbsp	dried parsley	15 mL
1 tsp	kosher salt	5 mL
½ tsp	freshly ground black pepper	2 mL
1¾ cups	ready-to-use chicken broth	425 mL
1 tbsp	cornstarch	15 mL
2 tbsp	cold water	30 mL
4 oz	brick-style cream cheese, cubed	125 g
1 cup	milk	250 mL
1 cup	half-and-half (10%) cream	250 mL

1. Press Sauté; the indicator will read "Normal." When the display says "Hot," add butter to the pot and heat until melted. Add onion, carrots and celery; cook, stirring, for 4 to 5 minutes or until tender. Press Cancel. Add chicken, rice mix (without any seasoning packet), parsley, salt, pepper and broth, stirring well.

2. Close and lock the lid and turn the steam release handle to Sealing. Press Manual; the indicator will read "High Pressure." Use the ⊖ button to decrease the time on the display to 7 minutes.

3. When the timer beeps, press Cancel and let the pot stand, covered, for 5 minutes. After 5 minutes, turn the steam release handle to Venting and remove the lid. Check to make sure the chicken is no longer pink inside. (If more cooking is needed, reset the manual pressure to "High Pressure" for 1 minute.)

4. In a small bowl, whisk together cornstarch and cold water. Press Sauté. Stir the cornstarch mixture into the pot. Add cream cheese and stir until melted. Add milk and cream; cook, stirring, until heated through (do not let boil).

Variation

For a vegetarian version, use vegetable broth and omit the chicken.

Bouillabaisse with Rouille

With its fresh-catch ingredients imbued with fresh herbs, this full-flavored Provençal fish stew will encourage your mind to drift away to the warm breezes of the Mediterranean. The spicy, garlicky rouille is the perfect spread for crusty bread slices to serve with your bouillabaisse.

MAKES 6 SERVINGS

INSTANT POT FUNCTIONS

- Sauté -
- Manual Pressure -

• **Food processor**

Bouillabaisse

2 tbsp	virgin olive oil	30 mL
1	onion, chopped	1
1	leek (white and light green parts only), sliced	1
2	cloves garlic, chopped	2
10	sprigs fresh parsley (about ¼ bunch)	10
10	sprigs fresh thyme (about ¼ bunch)	10
2	bay leaves	2
	Fronds of 1 fennel bulb, divided	
Pinch	saffron threads	Pinch
1½ cups	chopped tomatoes	375 mL
8 cups	water	2 L
1½ lbs	mussels, scrubbed and debearded	750 g
1½ lbs	jumbo shrimp (21/25 count), peeled and deveined	750 g
1½ lbs	skinless halibut, cut into 2-inch (5 cm) chunks	750 g
1½ lbs	skinless cod, cut into 2-inch (5 cm) chunks	750 g

Rouille

1	roasted red bell pepper, drained	1
1	clove garlic	1
⅓ cup	almonds	75 mL
¼ cup	fresh parsley leaves	60 mL
½ tsp	kosher salt	2 mL
Pinch	cayenne pepper	Pinch
1 tbsp	freshly squeezed lemon juice	15 mL
⅓ cup	extra virgin olive oil	75 mL
	French bread, sliced	

1. *Bouillabaisse:* Press Sauté; the indicator will read "Normal." When the display says "Hot," add oil to the pot and heat until shimmering. Add onion and leek; cook, stirring, for 3 to 5 minutes or until softened. Add garlic and cook, stirring, for 1 minute or until fragrant. Press Cancel. Add parsley, thyme, bay leaves, half the fennel fronds, saffron, tomatoes and water, stirring well.

2. Close and lock the lid and turn the steam release handle to Sealing. Press Manual; the indicator will read "High Pressure." Use the ⊖ button to decrease the time on the display to 5 minutes.

3. When the timer beeps, press Cancel and turn the steam release handle to Venting. When the float valve drops down, remove the lid.

4. Strain liquid from pot into a bowl and discard solids. Return liquid to the pot and add mussels and shrimp. Press Sauté, cover pot and cook for 2 minutes. Add halibut and cod, cover and cook for 2 to 3 minutes or until mussels are opened, shrimp are pink, firm and opaque and fish flakes easily when tested with a fork. Discard any mussels that did not open.

5. *Rouille:* In food processor, combine roasted pepper, garlic, almonds, parsley, salt, cayenne and lemon juice; process until smooth. With the motor running, through the feed tube, gradually add oil, processing until a paste forms.

6. Ladle bouillabaisse into serving bowls and garnish with the remaining fennel fronds. Spread rouille on French bread and serve with bouillabaisse.

Tips

The rouille is wonderful as a condiment with other fish dishes. Refrigerate it in an airtight container for up to 3 days.

This dish originated with cooks buying the fresh catch of the day, offered by fishmongers. You can use any combination of fresh shellfish and fish that suits you. The fish should be a firm white fish, such as haddock, cod, sole, grouper or tilapia.

The fennel bulb is wonderful when thinly sliced and added to slaws or salads. For a tasty salad combination, toss the fennel with sliced green onions, a tangy vinaigrette and some shaved Parmesan or Romano cheese.

Spicy Navy Bean and Chicken Soup

A variety of peppers abound in this spicy, sensational soup that is loaded with tender chicken and beans.

INSTANT POT FUNCTIONS

• Sauté •
• Manual Pressure •

2½ lbs	bone-in skinless chicken thighs	1.25 kg
1 tbsp	ground cumin, divided	15 mL
2 tsp	chili powder, divided	10 mL
1½ tsp	kosher salt	7 mL
3 tbsp	virgin olive oil, divided	45 mL
6	cloves garlic, minced	6
2	onions, finely chopped	2
2	medium-heat chile peppers (such as serrano), seeded and chopped (optional)	2
1	chipotle pepper in adobo sauce, chopped	1
1½ cups	mild chile peppers (such as poblano), seeded and chopped	375 mL
2 tsp	dried oregano	10 mL
2	cans (each 14 to 19 oz/398 to 540 mL) navy beans, drained and rinsed	2
2	cans (each 4 oz/114 mL) chopped green chiles	2
5 cups	ready-to-use chicken broth	1.25 L
1 tbsp	cornmeal	15 mL
½ cup	finely chopped fresh cilantro	125 mL
	Sour cream (optional)	
	Minced red onion (optional)	
	Thinly sliced jalapeño peppers (optional)	

1. Season chicken with 1 tsp (5 mL) cumin, 1 tsp (5 mL) chili powder and salt. Press Sauté; the indicator will read "Normal." When the display says "Hot," add 2 tbsp (30 mL) oil to the pot and heat until shimmering. Working in batches, add chicken and cook, turning once, for 5 to 6 minutes or until golden brown on all sides. Transfer chicken to a plate.

2. Add garlic, onions, medium peppers (if using), chipotle peppers with sauce, mild peppers, oregano and the remaining cumin and chili powder to the pot; cook, stirring, for 4 to 6 minutes or until onions and peppers are softened. Press Cancel. Add beans, green chiles, broth and the remaining oil, stirring well.

3. Close and lock the lid and turn the steam release handle to Sealing. Press Manual; the indicator will read "High Pressure." Use the ⊖ button to decrease the time on the display to 25 minutes.

4. Meanwhile, remove the bone from the chicken thighs (see tip, opposite) and cut the meat into ½-inch (1 cm) pieces. Set aside.

5. When the timer beeps, press Cancel. Let stand, covered, until the float valve drops down. Turn the steam release handle to Venting and remove the lid.

6. Sprinkle cornmeal into the pot, then stir in chicken. Close and lock the lid and reset the manual pressure to "High Pressure" for 8 minutes.

7. When the timer beeps, press Cancel. Let stand, covered, until the float valve drops down. Turn the steam release handle to Venting and remove the lid. Check to make sure the juices run clear when the chicken is pierced with a fork and the beans are tender. (If more cooking is needed, reset the manual pressure to "High Pressure" for 2 minutes.)

8. Ladle soup into serving bowls and garnish with cilantro. If desired, garnish with sour cream, red onions and jalapeños.

Tips

When preparing beans of any type using the Manual Pressure function, make sure to fill the pot no more than halfway full. Do not attempt to double or triple the recipe; otherwise, the exhaust valve may become clogged as the beans froth up under pressure. Adding oil or butter with the beans will help to reduce the amount of froth.

To remove the bone from the browned chicken thighs, use a fork to hold a thigh firmly on a cutting board. Using a paring or boning knife, cut a line through the meat along either side of the bone. Expose the bone, scraping away any small pieces of meat. When the meat has been mostly scraped off the bone, separate the end of the bone from the meat. Trim off any leftover bone or gristle still on the thigh. Chicken can be very slippery, so curl your fingers when cutting to avoid exposing them to the knife.

Thai Coconut Chicken Soup

This mouthwatering soup features moist chicken thighs and creamy coconut tinged with curry, with added color and depth of flavor provided by the sweet potatoes. It's perfect for lunch!

MAKES 4 SERVINGS

INSTANT POT FUNCTIONS

• Manual Pressure •
• Sauté •

4 cups	ready-to-use chicken broth	1 L
1½ cups	coconut milk	375 mL
1 to 2 tbsp	Thai red curry paste	15 to 30 mL
4	bone-in skinless chicken thighs	4
3	green onions, diagonally sliced, divided	3
1½ cups	cubed peeled sweet potatoes (about 2 small)	375 mL
2 tbsp	chopped fresh thyme	30 mL
	Juice of 1 lime	
	Kosher salt	

Tips

You can substitute 3 boneless skinless chicken breasts for the thighs. Reduce the cooking time in step 2 to 7 minutes.

Use 1 tbsp (15 mL) curry paste for a mild soup; for a bolder, spicier soup, use up to 2 tbsp (30 mL).

1. In the inner pot, combine broth, coconut milk and 1 tbsp (15 mL) curry paste, stirring well. Add more curry paste as desired (see tip, at left). Add chicken, half the green onions and the sweet potatoes.

2. Place the pot inside the cooker housing, close and lock the lid and turn the steam release handle to Sealing. Press Manual; the indicator will read "High Pressure." Use the ● button to decrease the time on the display to 8 minutes.

3. When the timer beeps, press Cancel and let the pot stand, covered, for 4 minutes. After 4 minutes, turn the steam release handle to Venting and remove the lid. Check to make sure an instant-read thermometer inserted in the center of a thigh registers 165°F (74°C). (If more cooking is needed, reset the manual pressure to "High Pressure" for 2 minutes.) Transfer chicken to a cutting board and, using a fork, shred meat from bones, discarding bones.

4. Using a potato masher or immersion blender, mash sweet potatoes until mostly smooth. Press Sauté. Add shredded chicken, the remaining green onions and thyme; cook, stirring, for 2 minutes or until heated through. Stir in lime juice and season to taste with salt.

Swiss Market Soup with Split Peas and Root Vegetables

This creamy soup is very similar to a traditional split pea and ham soup, but is brought to a whole new level when you add more root vegetables and cook under pressure.

INSTANT POT FUNCTION

• Manual Pressure •

4	carrots, chopped	4
1	celery root, peeled and chopped	1
1	parsnip, chopped	1
2 cups	dried yellow split peas	500 mL
1½ cups	chopped onions	375 mL
¾ cup	chopped celery	175 mL
2	bay leaves	2
1 tsp	garlic powder	5 mL
8 cups	ready-to-use chicken broth	2 L
2 tbsp	butter	30 mL
1	ham bone or smoked pork hock	1

1. In the inner pot, combine carrots, celery root, parsnip, peas, onions, celery, bay leaves, garlic powder, broth and butter, stirring well. Add ham bone.

2. Place the pot inside the cooker housing, close and lock the lid and turn the steam release handle to Sealing. Press Manual; the indicator will read "High Pressure." Use the ⊖ button to decrease the time on the display to 10 minutes.

3. When the timer beeps, press Cancel. Let stand, covered, until the float valve drops down. Turn the steam release handle to Venting and remove the lid. Discard bay leaves.

4. Remove ham bone and shred meat from bone, discarding bone. Return meat to the pot, stirring well.

Tips

When preparing legumes of any type using the Manual Pressure function, make sure to fill the pot no more than halfway full. Do not attempt to double or triple the recipe; otherwise, the exhaust valve may become clogged as the beans froth up under pressure. Adding butter or oil with the legumes will help to reduce the amount of froth.

Save the bone from a baked ham you made, such as Slow-Braised Ham with Maple Mustard Glaze (page 167), for use in this soup. The ham bone can be refrigerated for up to 3 days or frozen for up to 3 months before use; thaw in the refrigerator before using.

Steakhouse Beef and Vegetable Soup

My grandmother made a melt-in-your-mouth beef and vegetable soup that always made us run to the table for dinner. Using a bounty of fresh vegetables and tender beef, this updated version continues to get me excited for dinner.

MAKES 8 SERVINGS

INSTANT POT FUNCTIONS

• Sauté •

• Manual Pressure •

2 tbsp	virgin olive oil	30 mL
1½ lbs	boneless beef chuck steak, cut into ½-inch (1 cm) cubes	750 g
2	carrots, sliced	2
2	stalk celery, sliced	2
1	onion, finely chopped	1
1	russet potato, cut into ½-inch (1 cm) cubes	1
7 cups	ready-to-use beef broth	1.75 L
3 tbsp	tomato paste	45 mL
1	can (14 oz/398 mL) diced tomatoes, with juice	1
	Kosher salt and freshly ground black pepper	

Tip

Cook the beef cubes in batches for more even browning. Transfer the browned cubes to a plate after each batch. Add them back to the pot when all are browned.

1. Press Sauté; the indicator will read "Normal." When the display says "Hot," add oil to the pot and heat until shimmering. Add beef (see tip, at left) and cook, stirring, for 4 to 5 minutes or until browned on all sides. Press Cancel. Add carrots, celery, onion, potato, broth and tomato paste, stirring well.

2. Close and lock the lid and turn the steam release handle to Sealing. Press Manual; the indicator will read "High Pressure." Use the ⊖ button to decrease the time on the display to 11 minutes.

3. When the timer beeps, press Cancel. Let stand, covered, until the float valve drops down. Turn the steam release handle to Venting and remove the lid. The beef should be melt-in-your-mouth tender. (If more cooking is needed, reset the manual pressure to "High Pressure" for 2 minutes.)

4. Press Sauté. Add tomatoes and cook, stirring often, for 7 to 9 minutes or until soup is your desired consistency. Season to taste with salt and pepper.

Pork Posole

This traditional Mexican holiday stew has an inviting blend of spices and a bit of a chewy texture from the hominy and melt-in-your-mouth pork. It's typically a long- and slow-cooking dish, but the multicooker speeds up your cooking and waiting time.

MAKES 6 SERVINGS

INSTANT POT FUNCTIONS

• Manual Pressure •
• Sauté •

2	cans (each 29 oz/822 mL) Mexican-style white hominy, drained and rinsed	2
4 cups	ready-to-use chicken broth	1 L
2 cups	water	500 mL
1½ lb	boneless pork shoulder blade roast, trimmed and cut into 2-inch (5 cm) cubes	750 kg
	Kosher salt and freshly ground black pepper	
4	cloves garlic, minced	4
1	small onion, chopped	1
2	bay leaves	2
2 tbsp	ancho chile powder	30 mL
1 tbsp	dried Mexican oregano	15 mL
1 tsp	ground cumin	5 mL
1	can (4 oz/114 mL) chopped green chiles	1
1	avocado, cut into chunks	1
⅓ cup	chopped fresh cilantro	75 mL
1	lime, cut into wedges	1

1. Drain hominy and add to the inner pot. Add broth and water, stirring well. Place the pot inside the cooker housing, close and lock the lid and turn the steam release handle to Sealing. Press Manual; the indicator will read "High Pressure." Use the ⊖ button to decrease the time on the display to 15 minutes.

2. When the timer beeps, press Cancel. Let stand, covered, until the float valve drops down. Turn the steam release handle to Venting and remove the lid.

3. Season pork with salt and pepper; add to the pot. Add garlic, onion, bay leaves, chile powder, oregano and cumin, stirring well. Close and lock the lid and reset the manual pressure to "High Pressure" for 10 minutes.

4. When the timer beeps, press Cancel. Let stand, covered, until the float valve drops down. Turn the steam release handle to Venting and remove the lid. Check to make sure the pork is no longer pink inside. (If more cooking is needed, reset the manual pressure to "High Pressure" for 2 minutes.) Discard bay leaves.

5. Press Sauté. Add green chiles and cook, stirring occasionally, for 7 to 11 minutes or until the stew is your desired consistency.

6. Ladle stew into bowls and garnish with avocado and cilantro. Serve with lime wedges.

Tips

If you cannot find Mexican-style hominy, two 15-oz (425 mL) cans of white hominy will also work in this recipe.

Mexican oregano has more citrus notes than its Mediterranean counterpart and goes especially well with chile peppers and cumin. In my opinion, these differences make it well worthwhile to have it on hand.

Chicken Chili Verde

This chili has an abundance of peppers that give it depth and a rich, well-honed sauce that balances out the chicken beautifully. Even if you are a die-hard red chili fan, you'll want to try this delectable green chili.

INSTANT POT FUNCTIONS

• Sauté •

• Manual Pressure •

• **Immersion blender (see tip, below)**

2 tbsp	virgin olive oil	30 mL
3 lbs	bone-in skin-on chicken thighs	1.5 kg
6	cloves garlic, peeled	6
4	tomatillos, husked and quartered	4
3	poblano peppers, seeded and coarsely chopped	3
2	Anaheim peppers, seeded and coarsely chopped	2
1	jalapeño pepper, seeded and coarsely chopped	1
1	onion, chopped	1
1 tbsp	cumin seeds, toasted and ground (see tip, below)	15 mL
	Kosher salt	
1 cup	loosely packed fresh cilantro leaves, divided	250 mL
1 tbsp	Worcestershire sauce	15 mL
	Cornbread wedges (optional)	
	Lime wedges (optional)	

1. Press Sauté; the indicator will read "Normal." When the display says "Hot," add oil to the pot and heat until shimmering. Add chicken, garlic, tomatillos, poblano peppers, Anaheim peppers, jalapeño, onion, cumin and 1 tsp (5 mL) salt to the pot; cook, stirring, until just sizzling. Press Cancel.

2. Close and lock the lid and turn the steam release handle to Sealing. Press Manual; the indicator will read "High Pressure." Use the ⊖ button to decrease the time on the display to 15 minutes.

3. When the timer beeps, press Cancel and turn the steam release handle to Venting. When the float valve drops down, remove the lid. Check to make sure an instant-read thermometer inserted in the center of a thigh registers 165°F (74°C). (If more cooking is needed, reset the manual pressure to "High Pressure" for 4 minutes.) Transfer chicken to a plate and set aside.

4. Add $\frac{1}{2}$ cup (125 mL) cilantro and Worcestershire sauce to the pot. Using the immersion blender, blend to your desired consistency. Season to taste with salt.

5. Shred chicken and return to sauce, stirring well.

6. Ladle chili into serving bowls and garnish with the remaining cilantro. If desired, serve with cornbread and lime wedges.

Tips

To toast cumin seeds, heat a small skillet over medium-high heat. Add cumin seeds and cook, stirring, for 3 minutes or until lightly toasted and fragrant. Transfer to a plate and let cool, then use a mortar and pestle or a clean grinder to grind the seeds.

If you don't have an immersion blender, you can use a regular blender to blend the chili. In step 4, after stirring in the cilantro and Worcestershire sauce, transfer the chili to the blender in batches and blend to the desired consistency. Return chili to the pot and season to taste with salt. Continue with step 5.

Tex-Mex Chili

One of the best things about chili is that there are almost as many variations as there are people who love it. But one thing is for certain: when you head down to Texas and the Southwest, get ready for a bit of a kick — and you better not mention beans in chili! This chili hits on all notes.

MAKES 4 SERVINGS

INSTANT POT FUNCTIONS
• Sauté •
• Manual Pressure •

2 lbs	beef stew meat, cut into 1-inch (2.5 cm) pieces	1 kg
1 tbsp	kosher salt	15 mL
2 tsp	virgin olive oil	10 mL
1	bottle (12 oz/341 mL) ale or lager	1
1 tbsp	chili powder	15 mL
2 tsp	ground cumin	10 mL
2	chipotle peppers in adobo sauce, chopped	2
2 cups	salsa	500 mL
1 tbsp	adobo sauce	15 mL
1 tbsp	tomato paste	15 mL
3 cups	tortilla chips	750 mL

Tips

Cut your beef into pieces of a similar size, so they cook evenly.

If you prefer not to use beer, you can use 1¹/₂ cups (375 mL) ready-to-use beef broth in its place. Either use reduced-sodium broth or reduce the salt in the recipe to ¹/₂ tsp (2 mL).

1. Season beef with salt. Press Sauté; the indicator will read "Normal." When the display says "Hot," add oil to the pot and heat until shimmering. Working in batches, add beef and cook, stirring, for 2 to 3 minutes or until browned on all sides. Transfer beef to a plate.

2. Add beer to the pot and heat for 2 minutes, scraping up any brown bits from the bottom of the pot. Press Cancel. Return beef and any accumulated juices to the pot and add chili powder, cumin, chipotle peppers with sauce, salsa, adobo sauce and tomato paste, stirring to combine.

3. Close and lock the lid and turn the steam release handle to Sealing. Press Manual; the indicator will read "High Pressure." Use the ⊖ button to decrease the time on the display to 15 minutes.

4. When the timer beeps, press Cancel and turn the steam release handle to Venting. When the float valve drops down, remove the lid. The beef should be very tender when pricked with a fork. (If more cooking is needed, reset the manual pressure to "High Pressure" for 5 minutes.)

5. Ladle chili into serving bowls. Serve tortilla chips on the side or crumble them over top.

Creamy Tomato Basil Soup

This soup will bring you back to the days when your mother made you a bowl of warm, creamy tomato soup with a grilled cheese sandwich. Still just as heartwarming, this soup is fresh and easy to make.

MAKES 6 SERVINGS

INSTANT POT FUNCTIONS

• Sauté •
• Slow Cook •

2 tbsp	virgin olive oil	30 mL
2	onions, thinly sliced	2
1 tsp	kosher salt	5 mL
¼ tsp	hot pepper flakes	1 mL
6	cloves garlic, thinly sliced	6
8	sprigs fresh thyme	8
2	sprigs fresh basil	2
3	cans (each 28 oz/796 mL) crushed tomatoes, drained	3
8 cups	ready-to-use chicken or vegetable broth	2 L
¼ cup	freshly grated Parmesan cheese	60 mL

Tips

Oyster crackers or herbed croutons make a great garnish for this soup.

Serve with grilled cheese sandwiches to bring back childhood memories.

1. Press Sauté; the indicator will read "Normal." When the display says "Hot," add oil to the pot and heat until shimmering. Add onions, salt and hot pepper flakes; cook, stirring, for 3 to 4 minutes or until onions are softened. Add garlic and cook, stirring, for 1 to 2 minutes or until fragrant and softened. Press Cancel. Add thyme, basil, tomatoes and broth, stirring well.

2. Close and lock the lid and turn the steam release handle to Venting. Press Slow Cook; the indicator will read "Normal." Press Adjust once to change the heat level to "More." Use the ✚ button to increase the time on the display to 6:00.

3. When the timer beeps, press Cancel, remove the lid and check to see if the soup is your desired consistency. (If more cooking is needed, press Sauté and cook, stirring occasionally, for 5 to 10 minutes or until soup is done to your liking.) Discard the thyme and basil sprigs.

4. Ladle soup into serving bowls and sprinkle with Parmesan.

Loaded Baked Potato Soup

If you are a fan of loaded baked potatoes, this soup will make you swoon. It mirrors the flavors of loaded potatoes, but in a creamy, head-to-toe-warming soup.

MAKES 6 SERVINGS		

INSTANT POT FUNCTIONS		
• Slow Cook •		
• Sauté •		

6	russet potatoes (about 2 lbs/1 kg), cut into ½-inch (1 cm) cubes	6
3	cloves garlic, minced	3
1	large onion, finely chopped	1
1 tbsp	kosher salt	15 mL
1 tsp	freshly ground black pepper	5 mL
4 cups	ready-to-use chicken broth	1 L
¼ cup	butter	60 mL
3 tbsp	chopped fresh chives	45 mL
1 cup	heavy or whipping (35%) cream	250 mL
1 cup	shredded sharp (old) Cheddar cheese, divided	250 mL
1 cup	sour cream	250 mL
8	slices bacon, cooked crisp and crumbled	8

Tip

This soup can also be made in 4 hours. In step 2, press Adjust once to change the heat level to "More" and leave the time at 4:00. Continue with step 3.

1. In the inner pot, combine potatoes, garlic, onion, salt, pepper, broth and butter, stirring well.

2. Place the pot inside the cooker housing, close and lock the lid and turn the steam release handle to Venting. Press Slow Cook; the indicator will read "Normal." Press Adjust twice to change the heat level to "Less." Use the ✚ button to increase the time on the display to 8:00.

3. When the timer beeps, remove the lid. Using a fork, check to make sure the potatoes are tender. (If more cooking is needed, reset the slow cooker to "Less" for 30 minutes.) Press Cancel.

4. Using a potato masher, coarsely mash the potatoes so that some chunks remain. Stir in chives and cream. Press Sauté; the indicator will read "Normal." Press Adjust twice to change the heat level to "Less." Cook, stirring occasionally, for 5 to 7 minutes or until soup is thickened to your liking. Press Cancel. Stir in ½ cup (125 mL) cheese.

5. Spoon soup into serving bowls and serve dolloped with sour cream and sprinkled with bacon and the remaining cheese.

Harvest Minestrone Soup

This Italian-inspired soup is exploding with vegetables and beans that swirl together with tubular pasta and an inspired broth.

INSTANT POT FUNCTIONS

• Slow Cook •
• Sauté •

4	cloves garlic, minced	4
1	onion, chopped	1
2 cups	chopped carrots	500 mL
2 cups	chopped potatoes	500 mL
1 cup	diced tomatoes	250 mL
2	bay leaves	2
1 tbsp	dried Italian seasoning	15 mL
1 tsp	kosher salt	5 mL
½ tsp	freshly ground black pepper	2 mL
4 cups	ready-to-use vegetable broth	1 L
2 cups	water	500 mL
3 cups	tomato juice	750 mL
1	zucchini, diced	1
2	cans (each 14 to 19 oz/398 to 540 mL) cannellini (white kidney) beans, drained	2
1	can (19 oz/540 mL) green beans, drained	1
1 cup	tube-shaped pasta	250 mL

1. In the inner pot, combine garlic, onion, carrots, potatoes, tomatoes, bay leaves, Italian seasoning, salt, pepper, broth, water and tomato juice, stirring well.

2. Place the pot inside the cooker housing, close and lock the lid and turn the steam release handle to Venting. Press Slow Cook; the indicator will read "Normal." Press Adjust twice to change the heat level to "Less." Use the ➕ button to increase the time on the display to 7:00.

3. When the timer beeps, press Cancel, remove the lid and stir in zucchini, cannellini beans, green beans and pasta. Press Sauté and cook, stirring occasionally, for 10 to 15 minutes or until pasta is tender. Discard bay leaves.

Tips

You can leave the skin on the carrots and the potatoes (make sure to scrub them well), or you can peel them, if you prefer.

You can substitute great northern beans or navy beans for the cannellini beans if they are more readily available.

For the tube-shaped pasta, choose bucatini, elbow macaroni, penne or ziti. The cooking times of different pastas may vary, so test the pasta for tenderness and adjust the cooking time as needed.

Chinese Hot-and-Sour Soup

This Chinese takeout staple boasts loads of mushrooms, bamboo shoots and water chestnuts swirling in a spicy chicken broth. My version is even better than takeout, because you can adjust the ingredients and spice to your taste.

MAKES 4 SERVINGS

INSTANT POT FUNCTIONS
- Sauté -
- Slow Cook -

1½ tbsp	sesame oil, divided	22 mL
4 oz	firm tofu, patted dry and cut into ½-inch (1 cm) cubes	125 g
1 cup	shredded rotisserie chicken	250 mL
6 oz	shiitake mushrooms, stems removed, caps sliced	175 g
1	can (8 oz/227 mL) sliced bamboo shoots, drained	1
1	can (8 oz/227 mL) sliced water chestnuts, drained	1
4 cups	ready-to-use chicken broth	1 L
3 tbsp	rice wine vinegar	45 mL
2 tbsp	soy sauce	30 mL
1 tsp	hot chili oil	5 mL
2 tbsp	cornstarch	30 mL
3 tbsp	cold water	45 mL
2	green onions, sliced	2

1. Press Sauté; the indicator will read "Normal." When the display says "Hot," add ½ tbsp (7 mL) sesame oil to the pot and heat until shimmering. Add tofu and cook, turning, for 2 to 3 minutes or until at least two sides of each cube are browned. Press Cancel. Transfer tofu to a plate and let cool, then cover and refrigerate.

2. Add chicken, mushrooms, bamboo shoots, water chestnuts, broth, vinegar, soy sauce and chili oil to the pot, stirring well.

3. Close and lock the lid and turn the steam release handle to Venting. Press Slow Cook; the indicator will read "Normal." Press Adjust twice to change the heat level to "Less." Use the ⊖ button to decrease the time on the display to 3:00.

4. When the timer beeps, remove the lid and check to make sure the chicken is warmed through and the flavors have melded. (If more cooking is needed, reset the slow cooker to "Less" for 30 minutes.) Press Cancel.

5. In a small bowl, whisk together cornstarch and cold water. Add cornstarch mixture, tofu and the remaining sesame oil to the pot, stirring well.

6. Close and lock the lid and press Slow Cook; the indicator will read "Normal." Press Adjust once to change the heat level to "More." Cook for 10 minutes or until soup is slightly thickened.

7. Ladle soup into serving bowls and serve sprinkled with green onions.

Variations

For a vegetarian version, use twice as much tofu, omit the chicken and use vegetable broth instead of chicken broth.

Mix and match the amounts of bamboo shoots and water chestnuts to your liking, but maintain about 16 oz (454 mL) of ingredients before draining.

Fisherman's Seafood Chowder

This seafood chowder is inspired by the hugely popular San Francisco cioppino. Cooked low and slow, the dish becomes gradually infused with the flavors of sensational seafood and tender vegetables.

MAKES 6 SERVINGS

INSTANT POT FUNCTION
• Slow Cook •

2	carrots, sliced	2
1	onion, chopped	1
1	green bell pepper, chopped	1
1	clove garlic, minced	1
1 cup	sliced mushrooms	250 mL
1 tsp	dried oregano	5 mL
1 tsp	paprika	5 mL
2 cups	ready-to-use chicken broth	500 mL
1¾ cups	tomato sauce	425 mL
½ cup	clam juice	125 mL
1 lb	skinless halibut, cubed	500 g
8 oz	cooked deveined peeled shrimp	250 g
1	can (7 oz/198 g) clams, with liquid	1
1	can (6 oz/170 g) backfin (lump) crabmeat, with liquid	1
2 tbsp	chopped fresh basil	30 mL

Tips

Any firm white fish, such as cod, will work well in place of the halibut.

As with any traditional fisherman's stew, you can mix and match the shellfish according to what is readily available.

1. In the inner pot, combine carrots, onion, green pepper, garlic, mushrooms, oregano, paprika, broth, tomato sauce and clam juice, stirring well.

2. Place the pot inside the cooker housing, close and lock the lid and turn the steam release handle to Venting. Press Slow Cook; the indicator will read "Normal." Press Adjust twice to change the heat level to "Less." Use the ➕ button to increase the time on the display to 7:00.

3. When the timer beeps, remove the lid and test to see if the halibut flakes easily with a fork. (If more cooking is needed, reset the slow cooker to "Less" for 1 hour.) Press Cancel.

4. Add halibut, shrimp, clams and crabmeat to the pot, stirring well. Close and lock the lid and press Slow Cook; the indicator will read "Normal." Press Adjust once to change the heat level to "More." Use the ➖ button to decrease the time on the display to 0:30.

5. After 25 minutes, remove the lid and test to see if the shrimp is pink, firm and opaque and the clams and crab are heated through. (If more cooking is needed, close the lid and continue cooking for 5 minutes.)

6. Ladle soup into serving bowls and serve garnished with basil.

Hearty Ham and Split Pea Soup

This is one of my all-time favorite comfort foods. My aunt's outstanding recipe used to be my favorite, but it requires more hands-on time. This slow cooker version achieves the same deep taste, but you just set it and forget it until dinnertime.

MAKES 8 SERVINGS		
INSTANT POT FUNCTION		
• Slow Cook •		
1 lb	dried green split peas	500 g
1	small meaty ham bone	1
2	cloves garlic, minced	2
1	large onion, finely chopped	1
1½ cups	thinly sliced carrots	375 mL
1 cup	chopped celery	250 mL
1	bay leaf	1
1 tsp	dried oregano	5 mL
¼ tsp	freshly ground black pepper	1 mL
5 cups	ready-to-use chicken broth	1.25 L
3 cups	water	750 mL

1. Add peas, ham bone, garlic, onion, carrots, celery, bay leaf, oregano, pepper, broth and water into the inner pot; do not stir.

2. Place the pot inside the cooker housing, close and lock the lid and turn the steam release handle to Venting. Press Slow Cook; the indicator will read "Normal." Press Adjust twice to change the heat level to "Less." Use the ➕ button to increase the time on the display to 9:00.

3. When the timer beeps, remove the lid and transfer ham bone and ham to a cutting board. Discard bay leaf. Cut ham into bite-size chunks and discard bone. Return ham to the pot, stirring well. Heat for 5 minutes.

> ### Tips
> This soup can also be made in 4½ hours. In step 2, press Adjust once to change the heat level to "More." Use the ➕ button to increase the time on the display to 4:30. Continue with step 3.
>
> In step 3, you can either press Cancel or keep the soup on the Keep Warm setting while you are serving.

Zuppa Toscana

This creamy, flavorful Italian soup with a mélange of vegetables and seasonings is the crowning glory of dinnertime favorites.

INSTANT POT FUNCTIONS

• Sauté •

• Slow Cook •

1 tbsp	virgin olive oil	15 mL
1 lb	Italian sausage (bulk or casings removed)	500 g
2	large russet potatoes, cut into 1-inch (2.5 cm) cubes	2
2	cloves garlic, minced	2
1	large onion, chopped	1
4 cups	water	1 L
2 cups	ready-to-use chicken broth	500 mL
2 cups	chopped Swiss chard	500 mL
1 cup	heavy or whipping (35%) cream	250 mL
4	slices bacon, cooked crisp and crumbled	4

Tips

This soup can also be made in 3$\frac{1}{2}$ hours. In step 2, press Adjust once to change the heat level to "More." Use the ➖ button to decrease the time on the display to 3:30. Continue with step 3.

If you like your soup a little creamier, you can mash the potatoes before adding the Swiss chard.

1. Press Sauté; the indicator will read "Normal." When the display says "Hot," add oil to the pot and heat until shimmering. Add sausage and cook, breaking it up with a spoon, for 5 to 7 minutes or until no longer pink. Press Cancel. Add potatoes, garlic, onion, water and broth, stirring well.

2. Close and lock the lid and turn the steam release handle to Venting. Press Slow Cook; the indicator will read "Normal." Press Adjust twice to change the heat level to "Less." Use the ➕ button to increase the time on the display to 7:00.

3. When the timer beeps, remove the lid. Using a fork, check to make sure the potatoes are tender. (If more cooking is needed, reset the slow cooker to "Less" for 30 minutes.) Press Cancel.

4. Stir in Swiss chard. Close the lid and let stand for 5 minutes. Add cream and stir gently to combine.

5. Ladle soup into serving bowls and serve garnished with bacon.

Coconut Curry Chicken Stew

Chicken thighs are served up moist and tender, swirling in a spicy, creamy coconut broth. This stew achieves a marriage of flavors that will leave you wanting more.

INSTANT POT FUNCTIONS

• Sauté •
• Slow Cook •

2 tbsp	virgin coconut oil	30 mL
4	boneless skinless chicken thighs, cut into 1-inch (2.5 cm) chunks	4
6	cloves garlic, minced	6
3 cups	chopped carrots	750 mL
2 cups	chopped onions	500 mL
1 tbsp	grated gingerroot	15 mL
1 cup	ready-to-use chicken broth	250 mL
1 cup	coconut milk	250 mL
1 tbsp	curry powder	15 mL
½ tsp	kosher salt	2 mL
¼ cup	chopped fresh cilantro	60 mL
1 tbsp	freshly squeezed lemon juice	15 mL

1. Press Sauté; the indicator will read "Normal." When the display says "Hot," add oil to the pot and heat until shimmering. Add chicken and cook, stirring, for 5 to 7 minutes or until lightly browned on all sides. Press Cancel. Add garlic, carrots, onions and ginger, stirring well.

2. In a medium bowl, whisk together broth, coconut milk, curry powder and salt. Pour into the pot.

3. Close and lock the lid and turn the steam release handle to Venting. Press Slow Cook; the indicator will read "Normal." Press Adjust twice to change the heat level to "Less." Use the ➕ button to increase the time on the display to 7:00.

4. When the timer beeps, remove the lid and test to make sure the chicken juices run clear when pierced with a fork. (If more cooking is needed, reset the slow cooker to "Less" for 1 hour.) Press Cancel and stir in cilantro and lemon juice before serving.

Tips

If you can only find bone-in chicken thighs, remove the skin and debone them by using a paring or boning knife to cut a line through the meat along either side of the bone. Expose the bone, scraping away any small pieces of meat. When the meat has been mostly scraped off the bone, separate the end of the bone from the meat. Trim off any leftover bone or gristle still on the thigh. Chicken can be very slippery, so curl your fingers when cutting to avoid exposing them to the knife.

This dish can also be made in 3½ hours. In step 3, press Adjust once to change the heat level to "More." Use the ➖ button to decrease the cooking time to 3:30. Continue with step 4.

Chuck Wagon Beef Stew

This hearty and savory stew is an all-time classic — the perfect crowd-pleasing dish. It's perfect for lazy days when everyone just wants to grab a bowl at their leisure, and for potlucks or any time you are asked to bring a dish.

MAKES 8 SERVINGS

INSTANT POT FUNCTIONS

• Sauté •
• Slow Cook •

⅔ cup	all-purpose flour, divided	150 mL
	Kosher salt	
2 tsp	Hungarian paprika, divided	10 mL
	Freshly ground black pepper	
2 lbs	beef stew meat, cut into 1-inch (2.5 cm) pieces	1 kg
	Virgin olive oil	
2 tbsp	tomato paste	30 mL
3	fresh thyme sprigs	3
1 cup	dry red wine	250 mL
2 cups	ready-to-use beef broth	500 mL
3	carrots, cut into 1-inch (2.5 cm) pieces	3
1 lb	small white potatoes, cut in half	500 g

Tips

If serving this stew for a party or taking it to a potluck, keep it in the pot on the Keep Warm setting. It can be kept warm for up to 2 hours.

Serve with cornbread or bread sticks for a warming, comforting meal.

1. In a medium bowl, combine ⅓ cup (75 mL) flour, 2 tsp (10 mL) salt, 1 tsp (5 mL) paprika and ½ tsp (2 mL) pepper, mixing well. Add beef, tossing to coat and shaking off any excess flour. Reserve excess flour mixture.

2. Press Sauté; the indicator will read "Normal." When the display says "Hot," add 2 tsp (10 mL) oil and heat until shimmering. Working in batches, add beef and cook, stirring, for 5 to 7 minutes or until browned on all sides, adding more oil as needed. Transfer beef to a plate.

3. Add 1 tbsp (15 mL) oil to the pot and heat until shimmering. Add tomato paste and cook, stirring, for 1 minute or until dark red. Add the remaining flour and flour mixture, whisking until combined. Add thyme, wine and broth; cook, whisking, for 4 to 5 minutes or until gravy is smooth and thickened. Press Cancel. Return beef and any accumulated juices to the pot and add carrots and potatoes, stirring well.

4. Close and lock the lid and turn the steam release handle to Venting. Press Slow Cook; the indicator will read "Normal." Press Adjust twice to change the heat level to "Less." Use the ➕ button to increase the time on the display to 7:00.

5. When the timer beeps, remove the lid and check to make sure the beef and vegetables are tender. (If more cooking is needed, reset the slow cooker to "Less" for 30 minutes.) Discard thyme sprigs. Season to taste with salt and pepper.

6. Ladle stew into serving bowls and serve garnished with the remaining paprika.

Main Courses

Pressure Cooker

continued on next page . . .

Main Courses *(continued)*

Slow Cooker

Cheesy Ziti Florentine

This rustic pasta dish will transport you to the Italian countryside with its hearty sauce of tomatoes and spinach blended with garlic and aromatic herbs. A surprise little ingredient adds depth of flavor and umami to this dish.

INSTANT POT FUNCTIONS

• Sauté •

• Manual Pressure •

2 tbsp	virgin olive oil	30 mL
1	onion, finely chopped	1
1	clove garlic, minced	1
4 cups	loosely packed trimmed spinach leaves	1 L
2 tbsp	chopped fresh basil (about 7 leaves)	30 mL
2½ cups	ready-to-use reduced-sodium chicken broth	625 mL
2 cups	chunky marinara sauce	500 mL
2½ cups	dried ziti pasta	625 mL
2 tsp	fish sauce	10 mL
1	large egg	1
1	container (15 oz/425 g) ricotta cheese	1
¼ cup	freshly grated Parmesan cheese	60 mL
½ tsp	garlic powder	2 mL
½ tsp	dried parsley	2 mL
½ tsp	dried thyme	2 mL
¼ tsp	ground sage	1 mL
1½ cups	shredded mozzarella cheese	375 mL
	Additional freshly grated Parmesan cheese	

Tip

Fish sauce, also called nam pla, can be found in the Asian section of the grocery store, in specialty markets or online.

1. Press Sauté; the indicator will read "Normal." When the display says "Hot," add oil to the pot and heat until shimmering. Add onion and cook, stirring, for 3 to 5 minutes or until softened. Add garlic and cook, stirring, for 1 minute or until fragrant.

2. Add spinach, basil, broth and marinara sauce; cook, stirring often, for 5 minutes or until spinach is wilted. Press Cancel. Add pasta and fish sauce, stirring well.

3. In a large bowl, whisk egg. Stir in ricotta, Parmesan, garlic powder, parsley, thyme and sage until combined. Drop by spoonfuls evenly over the mixture in the pot; do not stir.

4. Close and lock the lid and turn the steam release handle to Sealing. Press Manual; the indicator will read "High Pressure." Use the ⊖ button to decrease the time on the display to 6 minutes.

5. When the timer beeps, press Cancel and turn the steam release handle to Venting. When the float valve drops down, remove the lid.

6. Sprinkle top with mozzarella. Cover and let stand for 5 minutes or until mozzarella is melted. Uncover and let stand for 5 minutes before serving. Serve with additional Parmesan for garnish.

Fennel and Leek Halibut en Papillote

Fennel adds a whole new level of umami to this moist, delicate and flaky halibut. Cooking *en papillote* (in parchment paper) infuses the fish with even more flavor and moisture.

INSTANT POT FUNCTION

• Manual Pressure •

- **Two 15- by 12-inch (38 by 30 cm) sheets parchment paper**
- **Instant Pot steam rack**

1	stalk celery, thinly sliced	1
1	carrot, thinly sliced	1
1	small bulb fennel, thinly sliced	1
1	small leek (white part only), thinly sliced	1
2 tbsp	chopped fresh parsley	30 mL
1 tbsp	virgin olive oil	15 mL
2	skinless halibut fillets (each about 6 oz/175 g)	2
	Kosher salt and freshly ground black pepper	
	Lemon wedges (optional)	

Tips

Choose fillets that are about the same thickness throughout. This will help them cook evenly.

When using the Quick Release method to release pressure, keep your hands and face away from the hole on the top of the steam release handle so you don't get scalded by the escaping steam.

1. In a medium bowl, combine celery, carrot, fennel, leek, parsley and oil.

2. Fold parchment sheets in half lengthwise. Starting at the folded edge, use scissors to cut out a half heart shape. Open the paper (it will be a heart shape) and place a halibut fillet on one side, next to the center fold on each sheet. Season with salt and pepper. Add half of the vegetable mixture on top of each fish. Fold the opposite side of the paper over fish mixture to make a half heart shape again. Beginning with the top of the heart, fold the edges of the paper together, tucking it in as needed, working all the way along until the edges are tightly sealed.

3. Add 1 cup (250 mL) water to the inner pot and place the steam rack in the pot. Place the packets on the rack, without overlapping. Close and lock the lid and turn the steam release handle to Sealing. Press Manual; the indicator will read "High Pressure." Use the ⊖ button to decrease the time on the display to 5 minutes.

4. When the timer beeps, press Cancel and turn the steam release handle to Venting. When the float valve drops down, remove the lid. Carefully open a packet and check to make sure the fish is opaque and flakes easily when tested with a fork. (If more cooking is needed, close and lock the lid, turn the steam release handle to Sealing and let stand for 3 minutes.) Using tongs, transfer packets to the counter. Carefully open packets and, using a spatula, transfer fish fillets to plates. If desired, serve with lemon wedges.

Salmon Steaks in White Wine

If you are craving salmon, you'll be glad to indulge in a juicy, fork-tender salmon steak braised with mustard, thyme and wine.

MAKES 2 SERVINGS

INSTANT POT FUNCTIONS
- Sauté -
- Manual Pressure -

- **Instant Pot steam rack**

3 tbsp	Dijon mustard, divided	45 mL
2	1-inch (2.5 cm) thick skin-on salmon fillets (each about 6 oz/175 g)	2
2	sprigs fresh thyme	2
1 tbsp	virgin olive oil	15 mL
1	small onion, chopped	1
1	clove garlic, minced	1
1	bay leaf	1
1 cup	dry white wine (such as Sauvignon Blanc)	250 mL
1 tbsp	cornstarch	15 mL
	Kosher salt	

Tips

You can substitute ½ tsp (2 mL) dried thyme for the fresh thyme sprigs.

If you prefer not to use wine, you can substitute ready-to-use chicken broth. Add 2 tsp (10 mL) white vinegar with the broth.

1. Brush 1½ tbsp (22 mL) mustard over the tops of the fillets, dividing evenly. Top each fillet with a thyme sprig. Set aside.

2. Press Sauté; the indicator will read "Normal." When the display says "Hot," add oil to the pot and heat until shimmering. Add onion and cook, stirring, for 3 to 5 minutes or until translucent. Add garlic and cook, stirring, for 1 minute or until fragrant.

3. Stir in bay leaf and wine, scraping up any browned bits from the bottom of the pot. Press Cancel.

4. Place the steam rack in the pot. Using tongs, place fillets, skin side down, on rack. Close and lock the lid and turn the steam release handle to Sealing. Press Manual; the indicator will read "High Pressure." Use the ⊖ button to decrease the time on the display to 2 minutes.

5. When the timer beeps, press Cancel and turn the steam release handle to Venting. When the float valve drops down, remove the lid. Check to make sure the fish is opaque and flakes easily when tested with a fork. (If more cooking is needed, close and lock the lid, turn the steam release handle to Sealing and let stand for 2 minutes.) Using the handles on the steam rack, carefully remove rack with fillets. Transfer fillets to serving plates and cover with foil to keep warm.

6. Discard bay leaf. Transfer 3 tbsp (45 mL) liquid from the pot to a small bowl. Whisk in cornstarch and the remaining mustard; return to the pot. Press Sauté and boil, stirring, for 5 to 7 minutes or until thickened to your liking. Season to taste with salt. Spoon sauce over fillets.

Sumptuous Artichoke and Shrimp Risotto

It's a little bit of paradise in one dish when you serve this delectable combination of shrimp and artichokes with the tanginess of lemon, all wrapped up in a creamy risotto.

MAKES 4 SERVINGS

INSTANT POT FUNCTIONS

• Sauté •
• Manual Pressure •

1 tbsp	virgin olive oil	15 mL
1	large shallot, minced (about ⅓ cup/75 mL)	1
1	clove garlic, minced	1
1½ cups	Arborio rice	375 mL
½ cup	dry white wine	125 mL
1½ tsp	balsamic vinegar	7 mL
3½ cups	ready-to-use chicken broth	875 mL
12 oz	large shrimp (26 to 30 count), peeled and deveined	375 g
1	can (14 oz/398 mL) quartered artichoke hearts, drained	1
	Grated zest and juice of 1 lemon	
1 tbsp	butter (optional)	15 mL
⅓ cup	grated Parmigiano-Reggiano cheese	75 mL
	Kosher salt and freshly ground black pepper	

Tips

Using authentic, full-flavored Parmigiano-Reggiano creates a complex, yet subtle tango of flavors. If you can't find it, you can use regular Parmesan.

Serve with a fresh lettuce salad and a tangy vinaigrette for a complete meal.

1. Press Sauté; the indicator will read "Normal." When the display says "Hot," add oil to the pot and heat until shimmering. Add shallot and cook, stirring, for 2 to 3 minutes or until softened. Add garlic and cook, stirring, for 30 seconds or until fragrant.

2. Add rice, stirring to coat with oil. Add wine and vinegar; cook, stirring constantly, for 30 seconds or until wine is absorbed. Add broth, stirring well. Press Cancel.

3. Close and lock the lid and turn the steam release handle to Sealing. Press Manual; the indicator will read "High Pressure." Use the ⊖ button to decrease the time on the display to 4 minutes.

4. When the timer beeps, press Cancel and turn the steam release handle to Venting. When the float valve drops down, remove the lid.

5. Stir in shrimp, artichoke hearts, lemon zest and lemon juice. Press Sauté and cook, stirring, for 3 to 4 minutes or until shrimp are pink, firm and opaque and rice is done to your liking. If the rice becomes too thick before the shrimp are done, stir in butter. Press Cancel.

6. Stir in cheese until well combined. Season to taste with salt and pepper.

Shrimp Étouffée

This well-known dish from New Orleans, infused with sassy seasonings and a bounty of vegetables, borrows its profile from Cajun and Creole cuisines. Roughly translated, *étouffée* (pronounced "ay-too-fay") means "smothered," and the shrimp in this dish certainly get that divine treatment.

MAKES 6 SERVINGS

INSTANT POT FUNCTIONS
- Sauté -
- Manual Pressure -

⅓ cup	butter	75 mL
½ cup	all-purpose flour	125 mL
2 tsp	Cajun seasoning	10 mL
6	cloves garlic, minced	6
4	onions, chopped (about 3 cups/750 mL)	4
3	green bell peppers, chopped (about 2¼ cups/550 mL)	3
3	stalks celery, chopped (about 1½ cups/375 mL)	3
4 cups	shrimp stock (see tip, at right)	1 L
1	can (14 oz/398 mL) diced tomatoes, with juice	1
2	bay leaves	2
½ tsp	cayenne pepper	2 mL
	Kosher salt	
2 tsp	paprika	10 mL
	Freshly ground black pepper	
1½ tsp	dried oregano	7 mL
1½ tsp	dried thyme	7 mL
2 lbs	large shrimp (26 to 30 count), peeled and deveined	1 kg
¼ cup	chopped fresh parsley	60 mL
3 cups	hot cooked white rice	750 mL
	Hot pepper sauce (optional)	

1. Press Sauté; the indicator will read "Normal." When the display says "Hot," add butter to the pot and heat until melted. Add flour and Cajun seasoning; cook, stirring, for 3 minutes or until roux is light brown. Add garlic, onions, green peppers and celery; cook, stirring, for 5 to 7 minutes or until vegetables are softened.

2. Stir in shrimp stock, scraping up any browned bits from the bottom of the pot. Press Cancel. Add tomatoes, bay leaves, cayenne and ½ tsp (2 mL) salt, stirring well.

3. Close and lock the lid and turn the steam release handle to Sealing. Press Manual; the indicator will read "High Pressure." Use the ⊖ button to decrease the time on the display to 10 minutes.

4. When the timer beeps, press Cancel and let the pot stand, covered, for 15 minutes. After 15 minutes, turn the steam release handle to Venting and remove the lid. Discard bay leaves.

5. In a medium bowl, combine paprika, 1½ tsp (7 mL) black pepper, oregano and thyme. Add shrimp and toss to coat with seasoning.

6. Press Sauté and add shrimp to the pot. Cook, stirring, for 3 to 5 minutes or until shrimp are pink, firm and opaque. Stir in parsley. Season to taste with salt and pepper.

7. Divide rice among serving bowls, mounding it in the center, and distribute étouffée around rice. If desired, serve with hot pepper sauce on the side.

Tip
You can make simple shrimp stock by combining 1½ tbsp (22 mL) shrimp base with 4 cups (1 L) water. Shrimp base can be found in large grocery stores along with other flavored bases and bouillons.

Autumn Comfort Braised Chicken and Root Vegetables

You can take advantage of all of those beautiful fall harvest vegetables in this simple and rewarding braised chicken dish that will warm you up during the crisp breezes of autumn.

MAKES 6 SERVINGS

INSTANT POT FUNCTIONS

• Sauté •
• Manual Pressure •

1	whole chicken (about 3½ lbs/ 1.75 kg), cut into 6 sections	1
	Kosher salt and freshly ground black pepper	
2 tbsp	virgin olive oil (approx.), divided	30 mL
2	stalks celery, diced	2
1	onion, finely chopped	1
2 tsp	minced garlic	10 mL
1 tsp	chopped fresh thyme	5 mL
1 tbsp	tomato paste	15 mL
1 tbsp	chicken demi-glace (see tip, opposite)	15 mL
1 cup	dry white wine	250 mL
1 cup	ready-to-use chicken broth	250 mL
4	carrots, cut into 2-inch (5 cm) chunks	4
2	parsnips, cut into 2-inch (5 cm) chunks	2
2	turnips, cut into 1-inch (2.5 cm) wedges	2

1. Season chicken with salt and pepper. Press Sauté; the indicator will read "Normal." When the display says "Hot," add 1 tbsp (15 mL) oil to the pot and heat until shimmering. Working in batches, add chicken and cook, turning, for 5 to 7 minutes or until browned on all sides, adding more oil as needed between batches. Transfer chicken to a platter.

2. Add the remaining oil, celery and onion to the pot and cook, stirring, for 3 to 5 minutes or until onion is translucent and celery is softened. Add garlic, thyme, tomato paste and demi-glace; cook, stirring, for 1 minute or until fragrant.

3. Add wine and cook, scraping up any browned bits from the bottom of the pot, for 2 minutes. Stir in broth. Return chicken to the pot, along with any accumulated juices, and place carrots, parsnips and turnips on top of the chicken. Press Cancel.

4. Close and lock the lid and turn the steam release handle to Sealing. Press Manual; the indicator will read "High Pressure." Use the ⊖ button to decrease the time on the display to 12 minutes.

5. When the timer beeps, press Cancel and turn the steam release handle to Venting. When the float valve drops down, remove the lid. Check to make sure an instant-read thermometer inserted in the center of a chicken section registers 165°F (74°C). (If more cooking is needed, reset the manual pressure to "High Pressure" for 3 minutes.) Transfer chicken to a serving plate and arrange vegetables around it.

6. Separate any fat from the sauce. Drizzle some of the sauce over the chicken and serve the remaining sauce in a gravy boat.

Tip

Demi-glace is a thick, almost gel-like mixture that is added as a base to other sauces to give them a rich, deep taste and a glaze-like consistency. It is well worth having on hand, or you can make this substitute: In a small saucepan, bring 1 cup (250 mL) ready-to-use chicken broth and $1\frac{1}{2}$ tsp (7 mL) butter to a simmer over medium-low heat. Simmer, stirring often, for 5 minutes or until reduced by half. Meanwhile, combine $1\frac{1}{2}$ tbsp (22 mL) water, $\frac{1}{2}$ tsp (2 mL) cornstarch and a dash of balsamic vinegar. Add to broth and simmer, stirring, for 3 minutes or until mixture is a gel-like consistency. This will yield about $\frac{1}{2}$ cup (125 mL) demi-glace. Store it in a covered jar in the refrigerator for up to 2 weeks or in the freezer for up to 6 months.

Zesty Honey Garlic Chicken Leg Quarters

A flavor-infused sauce combines with moist and tender pressure-cooked chicken to make this dish one you will find yourself serving for many evening meals. The best part is that it is done in a snap.

INSTANT POT FUNCTIONS

- Manual Pressure -
- Sauté -

2	cloves garlic, minced	2
¾ cup	sweet tomato chili sauce (such as Heinz)	175 mL
¾ cup	liquid honey	175 mL
¼ cup	soy sauce	60 mL
2 tbsp	Worcestershire sauce	30 mL
1 tsp	Sriracha	5 mL
2	chicken leg quarters	2
1 tbsp	cornstarch	15 mL
2 tbsp	cold water	30 mL

Tips

Choose medium-size chicken leg quarters so they will both fit nicely in the bottom of the pot.

When using the Quick Release method to release pressure, keep your hands and face away from the hole on the top of the steam release handle so you don't get scalded by the escaping steam.

1. In the inner pot, combine garlic, chili sauce, honey, soy sauce, Worcestershire sauce and Sriracha. Add chicken.

2. Place the pot inside the cooker housing, close and lock the lid and turn the steam release handle to Sealing. Press Manual; the indicator will read "High Pressure." Use the ⊖ button to decrease the time on the display to 9 minutes.

3. When the timer beeps, press Cancel and turn the steam release handle to Venting. When the float valve drops down, remove the lid. Check to make sure an instant-read thermometer inserted in the center of a chicken leg registers 165°F (74°C). (If more cooking is needed, reset the manual pressure to "High Pressure" for 2 minutes.) Transfer chicken to a plate and cover with foil to keep warm.

4. In a small bowl, whisk together cornstarch and cold water. Press Sauté. Add the cornstarch mixture to the pot and cook, stirring, for 4 to 6 minutes or until sauce is thickened. Press Cancel.

5. Using tongs, return chicken to the pot and turn to coat with sauce. Transfer chicken to serving plates and serve with the remaining sauce.

Chicken Cacciatore

Add a little pizzazz to weeknight chicken dinners with this rustic, wholesome Italian dish that has at its heart the perfect trio of tomatoes, onions and bell pepper.

MAKES 4 SERVINGS

INSTANT POT FUNCTIONS
- Sauté -
- Manual Pressure -

4	bone-in skin-on chicken breasts (about 2 lbs/1 kg total)	4
	Kosher salt and freshly ground black pepper	
3 tbsp	virgin olive oil, divided	45 mL
1 lb	cremini mushrooms, sliced	500 g
3	onions, chopped	3
1	green bell pepper, chopped	1
3	cloves garlic, minced	3
½ tsp	hot pepper flakes	2 mL
1 cup	dry red wine	250 mL
2 tbsp	drained capers	30 mL
1½ tsp	dried oregano	7 mL
1 cup	ready-to-use reduced-sodium chicken broth	250 mL
1	can (28 oz/796 mL) plum (Roma) tomatoes, with juice	1
¼ cup	chopped fresh basil	60 mL
	Fresh basil leaves	

1. Season chicken with salt and pepper. Press Sauté; the indicator will read "Normal." When the display says "Hot," add 2 tbsp (30 mL) oil to the pot and heat until shimmering. Working in batches, add chicken and cook, turning once, for 3 to 4 minutes per side or until evenly browned. Transfer chicken to a plate.

2. Add mushrooms to the pot and cook, stirring occasionally, for 8 to 10 minutes or until mushrooms are browned and most of their liquid has evaporated. Transfer to a separate plate.

3. Add the remaining oil to the pot and heat until shimmering. Add onions and green pepper; cook, stirring, for 4 to 6 minutes or until softened. Add garlic and hot pepper flakes; cook, stirring, for 1 minute or until fragrant.

4. Add wine and cook, scraping up any browned bits from the bottom of the pot, for 5 minutes or until reduced by half. Stir in capers, oregano and broth. Return chicken to the pot, along with any accumulated juices. Scatter mushrooms over the chicken. Pour tomatoes over top; do not stir. Press Cancel.

5. Close and lock the lid and turn the steam release handle to Sealing. Press Manual; the indicator will read "High Pressure." Use the ⊖ button to decrease the time on the display to 10 minutes.

6. When the timer beeps, press Cancel and let the pot stand, covered, for 10 minutes. After 10 minutes, turn the steam release handle to Venting and remove the lid. Check to make sure an instant-read thermometer inserted in the center of a chicken breast registers 165°F (74°C). (If more cooking is needed, reset the manual pressure to "High Pressure" for 2 minutes.) Using tongs, transfer chicken to a serving plate. Tent with foil to keep warm.

7. Stir chopped basil into the sauce. Press Sauté and cook, stirring occasionally, for 5 minutes or until thickened.

8. Spoon sauce over chicken and serve garnished with basil leaves.

Tip
You can use bone-in skin-on chicken thighs if you prefer. Reduce the pressure cooking time to 8 minutes.

Salsa Lime Chicken Rollups

These delicate chicken rollups have just the right amount of zesty salsa and lime to make them delightful, but when wrapped around melted mozzarella, they truly rise to new heights.

MAKES 4 SERVINGS

INSTANT POT FUNCTION

• Manual Pressure •

• Kitchen string

4	boneless skinless chicken breasts (each about 4 oz/125 g)	4
8 oz	mozzarella cheese, cubed	250 g
1 cup	medium salsa	250 mL
1 cup	tomato sauce	250 mL
¼ cup	freshly squeezed lime juice	60 mL
½ tsp	kosher salt	2 mL

Tip

When using the Quick Release method to release pressure, keep your hands and face away from the hole on the top of the steam release handle so you don't get scalded by the escaping steam.

1. Place each chicken breast between two pieces of plastic wrap. Using a meat mallet or rolling pin, pound breasts to about ½ inch (1 cm) thick. Remove plastic wrap. Add cheese to the center of each breast and roll breast up. Tie rollups with kitchen string.

2. In the inner pot, combine salsa, tomato sauce, lime juice and salt, stirring to combine. Add chicken rollups, seam side down.

3. Place the pot inside the cooker housing, close and lock the lid and turn the steam release handle to Sealing. Press Manual; the indicator will read "High Pressure." Use the ⊖ button to decrease the time on the display to 6 minutes.

4. When the timer beeps, press Cancel and turn the steam release handle to Venting. When the float valve drops down, remove the lid. Check to make sure the chicken is no longer pink inside. (If more cooking is needed, cover the pot and let stand for 2 minutes or until chicken is fully cooked.)

5. Transfer chicken rollups to serving plates and remove string. Spoon sauce over top.

Chicken Alfredo with Mushrooms

This is one of my favorite dishes because it is satisfying on so many levels. The combination of chicken, pasta and mushrooms in a creamy, garlicky sauce just screams comfort food. It is also the perfect way to use up leftover chicken or turkey.

MAKES 6 SERVINGS

INSTANT POT FUNCTIONS

• Manual Pressure •
• Sauté •

8 oz	dried fettuccini pasta, broken in half	250 g
2 cups	ready-to-use chicken broth	500 mL
2 cups	cubed rotisserie chicken	500 mL
2	cloves garlic, minced	2
1/4 tsp	freshly ground black pepper	1 mL
1	can (4 oz/114 mL) mushroom pieces and stems, drained	1
1	jar (15 oz/425 mL) Alfredo sauce	1
1 tbsp	white wine (optional)	15 mL
1/4 cup	freshly grated Parmesan cheese	60 mL

Tips

A typical rotisserie chicken weighs about 2 1/2 lbs (1.25 kg) and will yield about 3 1/2 cups (875 mL) cubed chicken. The leftover chicken works well in Down-Home Chicken and Dumplings (page 82).

Pick up your rotisserie chicken at the end of your grocery shopping trip. Use it within 2 hours, or refrigerate it and use it within 3 days.

Leftover holiday turkey is a great substitute for chicken in this recipe and a nice alternative for using up leftovers.

1. In the inner pot, combine fettuccini and broth.
2. Place the pot inside the cooker housing, close and lock the lid and turn the steam release handle to Sealing. Press Manual; the indicator will read "High Pressure." Use the ⊖ button to decrease the time on the display to 2 minutes.
3. When the timer beeps, press Cancel and turn the steam release handle to Venting. When the float valve drops down, remove the lid. Stir pasta, then drain and return to the pot.
4. Stir in chicken, garlic, pepper, mushrooms, Alfredo sauce and wine (if using). Press Sauté and cook, stirring gently, for 3 to 4 minutes or until heated through. Serve garnished with Parmesan.

Down-Home Chicken and Dumplings

This mid-century favorite has been the cornerstone of family meals from the Midwest down through the South for decades. Quick, easy, delicious and budget-friendly — that is what a real cornerstone meal should be, and this recipe fits the bill.

MAKES 4 SERVINGS

INSTANT POT FUNCTIONS

• Sauté •

• Manual Pressure •

1½ cups	chopped cooked dark chicken meat (1-inch/2.5 cm chunks)	375 mL
	Kosher salt and freshly ground black pepper	
3 tbsp	butter	45 mL
3	carrots, cut crosswise into 1½-inch (4 cm) pieces	3
3	stalks celery, cut into ½-inch (1 cm) pieces	3
1	onion, chopped	1
2 tsp	ground sage	10 mL
1½ tsp	ground thyme	7 mL
1 tsp	ground marjoram	5 mL
1 tsp	dried rosemary	5 mL
½ tsp	ground nutmeg	2 mL
5 cups	ready-to-use chicken broth	1.25 L
1½ cups	frozen sweet peas	375 mL
1 cup	all-purpose baking mix (such as Bisquick)	250 mL
⅓ cup	milk	75 mL
	Paprika (optional)	

1. Season chicken with salt and pepper. Press Sauté; the indicator will read "Normal." When the display says "Hot," add butter to the pot and heat until melted. Add chicken and cook, stirring, for 2 minutes or until lightly browned on all sides. Press Cancel. Add carrots, celery, onion, sage, thyme, marjoram, rosemary, nutmeg and broth, stirring well.

2. Close and lock the lid and turn the steam release handle to Sealing. Press Manual; the indicator will read "High Pressure." Use the ⊖ button to decrease the time on the display to 4 minutes.

3. When the timer beeps, press Cancel and turn the steam release handle to Venting. When the float valve drops down, remove the lid. Stir in peas. Season to taste with salt.

4. In a small bowl, whisk together baking mix and milk. Press Sauté. Press Adjust twice to change the heat level to "Less." Drop rounded spoonfuls of dough on top of the chicken mixture, spacing evenly. Simmer, uncovered, for 8 minutes. Cover and simmer for 6 minutes or until dumplings are cooked through. If desired, serve garnished with paprika.

Tips

If you want to make this dish even easier, use 2 cups (500 mL) frozen chopped carrots instead of cleaning and cutting fresh carrots. Add the frozen carrots at the same time you add the peas in step 3. Or use 3½ cups (875 mL) frozen carrot and pea blend.

To test dumplings for doneness, remove one from the pot and cut through to the center to make sure it is evenly cooked and no soft batter remains. If necessary, return it to the pot and continue cooking until done.

South of the Border Pork Carnitas

These sassy carnitas are infused with citrus and smoky, spicy ancho chiles, then tucked into tortillas and topped with chopped onions and fresh cilantro.

2 lb	boneless pork shoulder blade roast, trimmed and cut into 1-inch (2.5 cm) chunks	1 kg
1 tbsp	kosher salt	15 mL
2 tsp	dried oregano	10 mL
1½ tsp	ground cumin	7 mL
1 tsp	freshly ground black pepper	5 mL
1 tsp	ground cloves	5 mL
2 tbsp	virgin olive oil, divided	30 mL
4	cloves garlic, minced	4
2	onions, chopped, divided	2
2	chipotle chiles in adobo sauce, drained and chopped	2
¾ cup	orange juice	175 mL
¼ cup	water	60 mL
6	taco-size (6-inch/15 cm) flour tortillas	6
	Fresh cilantro leaves	

Tips

Use kitchen gloves when rubbing the spices into the pork.

If you like your carnitas a bit spicier, use only 1 chipotle chile and add a chopped jalapeño pepper. Remove the seeds from the jalapeño for less heat, or keep them in for added heat. Use kitchen gloves when handling jalapeños.

1. In a large bowl, combine pork, salt, oregano, cumin, pepper, cloves and 1 tbsp (15 mL) oil. Using your hands, rub spice mixture into pork.

2. In the inner pot, combine pork, garlic, half the onions, chiles, orange juice and water.

3. Place the pot inside the cooker housing, close and lock the lid and turn the steam release handle to Sealing. Press Manual; the indicator will read "High Pressure." Use the − button to decrease the time on the display to 20 minutes.

4. When the timer beeps, press Cancel and let the pot stand, covered, for 10 minutes. After 10 minutes, turn the steam release handle to Venting and remove the lid. Check to make sure just a hint of pink remains in the pork. (If more cooking is needed, reset the manual pressure to "High Pressure" for 5 minutes.) Using a slotted spoon, transfer the pork to a plate. Remove ½ cup (125 mL) liquid from the pot and set aside. Discard the remaining liquid.

5. Press Sauté; the indicator will read "Normal." When the display says "Hot," add the remaining oil to the pot and heat until shimmering. Return the pork to the pot and cook, turning often, for 3 to 5 minutes or until lightly seared on all sides.

6. Transfer pork to a serving bowl and drizzle with the reserved liquid. Serve with tortillas. Top with the remaining onions and cilantro.

Moo Shu Pork in Lettuce Wraps

This dish is savory, sweet, salty and crunchy, all wrapped up in lettuce leaves for a mouthwatering dish that is hard to resist.

MAKES 4 SERVINGS

INSTANT POT FUNCTIONS

• Sauté •

• Manual Pressure •

1½ lbs	pork tenderloin, cut into thin strips	750 g
	Kosher salt and freshly ground black pepper	
2	cloves garlic, minced	2
3 tbsp	hoisin sauce	45 mL
3 tbsp	rice vinegar	45 mL
2 tbsp	sesame oil	30 mL
8 oz	shiitake mushrooms, stemmed and sliced	250 g
¼ cup	ready-to-use beef broth	60 mL
1	bag (14 oz/400 g) shredded coleslaw mix	1
3 tbsp	soy sauce	45 mL
1	bunch green onions (about 4), thinly sliced, divided	1
12	Bibb lettuce leaves	12
	Additional hoisin sauce (optional)	

Tips

Hoisin sauce can be found in the Asian food section of the grocery store. It is a full-flavored sauce that goes well in a variety of dishes.

For a crunchy and flavorful variation, substitute a broccoli slaw mix for the traditional coleslaw mix.

1. Season pork with salt and pepper. In a medium bowl, combine garlic, hoisin sauce and vinegar. Add pork and let stand for 10 minutes.

2. Press Sauté; the indicator will read "Normal." When the display says "Hot," add oil to the pot and heat until shimmering. Working in batches, use tongs to transfer marinated pork to the pot; reserve marinade. Cook pork, stirring, for 3 to 5 minutes or until just browned on all sides. Transfer pork to a plate.

3. Add mushrooms to the pot and cook, stirring, for 4 to 6 minutes or until lightly browned. Stir in broth, scraping up any browned bits from the bottom of the pot. Stir in coleslaw mix and soy sauce. Press Cancel.

4. Close and lock the lid and turn the steam release handle to Sealing. Press Manual; the indicator will read "High Pressure." Use the ⊖ button to decrease the time on the display to 3 minutes.

5. When the timer beeps, press Cancel and turn the steam release handle to Venting. When the float valve drops down, remove the lid.

6. Stir in the reserved marinade. Return pork to the pot, along with any accumulated juices and half the green onions. Press Sauté and cook, stirring, for 2 to 3 minutes or until just a hint of pink remains inside pork and sauce is slightly thickened.

7. Spoon pork mixture onto lettuce leaves and sprinkle with the remaining green onions. Serve with additional hoisin sauce, if desired.

Orange-Glazed Pork Chops

A delightful pairing of orange juice and marmalade blends to create a unique and tangy glaze for these succulent pork chops.

INSTANT POT FUNCTIONS

• Sauté •
• Manual Pressure •

4	boneless pork loin chops (about 1 inch/2.5 cm thick)	4
	Kosher salt and freshly ground black pepper	
1 tbsp	virgin olive oil	15 mL
1 cup	ready-to-use chicken broth	250 mL
1 tsp	fresh thyme leaves	5 mL
1 tsp	dry mustard	5 mL
	Grated zest and juice of ½ orange	
½ cup	orange marmalade	125 mL
1 tbsp	apple cider vinegar	15 mL
2 tsp	soy sauce	10 mL

Tip

You can zest and juice the remaining half orange to save for another recipe. Use an ice cube tray to freeze the zest and juice: Measure 1 tsp (5 mL) zest into each cube and fill with water. Measure 1 tsp (5 mL) juice into separate cubes. Freeze for later use.

1. Season pork with salt and pepper. Press Sauté; the indicator will read "Normal." When the display says "Hot," add oil to the pot and heat until shimmering. Add pork and cook, turning once, for 3 to 4 minutes per side or until browned. Transfer to a plate.

2. Stir broth into the pot, scraping up any browned bits from the bottom. Stir in thyme, mustard and orange zest. Return pork and any accumulated juices to the pot. Press Cancel.

3. Close and lock the lid and turn the steam release handle to Sealing. Press Manual; the indicator will read "High Pressure." Use the ⊖ button to decrease the time on the display to 11 minutes.

4. When the timer beeps, press Cancel and let the pot stand, covered, for 10 minutes. After 10 minutes, turn the steam release handle to Venting and remove the lid. Check to make sure just a hint of pink remains in the pork. (If more cooking is needed, reset the manual pressure to "High Pressure" for 2 minutes.) Transfer pork to a plate, cover with foil and let stand for 10 minutes. Discard liquid from the pot.

5. Add orange juice, marmalade, vinegar and soy sauce to the pot. Press Sauté and cook, whisking, for 3 to 4 minutes or until bubbling. Press Cancel. Return pork to the pot and turn to coat with glaze.

6. Transfer pork to a serving plate and serve with any remaining glaze, if desired.

Cheesy Macaroni with Prosciutto and Peas

When I first heard of making macaroni and cheese in a pressure cooker, my first reaction was "Why?" since it isn't that difficult to make. But when I tried it and realized I didn't have to wait for water to boil and then experience the uncertainty of knowing whether my pasta was perfectly done, I knew I would never go back to making pasta the old way. Try it for yourself.

MAKES 6 SERVINGS

INSTANT POT FUNCTIONS

• Manual Pressure •
• Sauté •

1 lb	dried elbow macaroni	500 g
2 tsp	kosher salt	10 mL
2 cups	water	500 mL
4 oz	finely chopped prosciutto	125 g
2 cups	shredded Cheddar cheese	500 mL
1 cup	frozen sweet peas	250 mL
1	can (12 oz or 370 mL) evaporated milk	1
1 tsp	dry mustard (optional)	5 mL
½ tsp	Worcestershire sauce	2 mL

Tips

You can substitute 4 oz (125 g) chopped cooked pancetta for the prosciutto.

For a spicier take, substitute pepper Jack cheese for the Cheddar.

Mac and cheese aficionados either love or hate adding mustard to this dish, which is why it is optional. If you have never had macaroni and cheese with mustard, you owe it to yourself to give it a try.

1. In the inner pot, combine macaroni, salt and water.

2. Place the pot inside the cooker housing, close and lock the lid and turn the steam release handle to Sealing. Press Manual; the indicator will read "High Pressure." Use the ⊖ button to decrease the time on the display to 4 minutes.

3. When the timer beeps, press Cancel and turn the steam release handle to Venting. When the float valve drops down, remove the lid.

4. Stir in prosciutto, cheese, peas, milk, mustard (if using) and Worcestershire sauce. Press Sauté and cook, stirring, for 2 to 3 minutes or until sauce is smooth and pasta is al dente.

Melt-in-Your-Mouth BBQ Baby Back Ribs

These tender ribs with their rich barbecue sauce are mouthwatering and fall-off-the-bone tender. Make them for guests or for a quick and easy family night dinner.

INSTANT POT FUNCTIONS

• Manual Pressure •
• Sauté •

1 tbsp	kosher salt	15 mL
1 tbsp	Hungarian paprika	15 mL
1 tsp	freshly ground black pepper	5 mL
2	slabs baby back ribs (about 4 lbs/2 kg)	2
4	cloves garlic, minced	4
2 tsp	dried onion flakes	10 mL
1½ cups	ready-to-use beef broth	375 mL
⅓ cup	ketchup	75 mL
3 tbsp	apple cider vinegar	45 mL
1 tbsp	Worcestershire sauce	15 mL
2 tsp	prepared mustard	10 mL
1 tbsp	cornstarch	15 mL
2 tbsp	cold water	30 mL
	Kosher salt and freshly ground black pepper	

Tip

Hungary produces some of the finest paprika in the world. It is classified into grades based on the quality of the peppers and the thoroughness of the grinding process.

1. In a small bowl, combine salt, paprika and pepper. Rub mixture evenly over ribs. Cut ribs into 4 sections per slab.

2. In the inner pot, combine garlic, onion flakes, broth, ketchup, vinegar, Worcestershire sauce and mustard, stirring well. Add ribs, tossing to coat in sauce, then stand ribs vertically in the pot.

3. Place the pot inside the cooker housing, close and lock the lid and turn the steam release handle to Sealing. Press Manual; the indicator will read "High Pressure." Use the ⊖ button to decrease the time on the display to 25 minutes.

4. When the timer beeps, press Cancel and let the pot stand, covered, for 10 minutes. After 10 minutes, turn the steam release handle to Venting and remove the lid. The ribs should be falling off the bone. (If more cooking is needed, reset the manual pressure to "High Pressure" for 5 minutes.) Transfer ribs to a serving platter and tent with foil to keep warm.

5. In a small bowl, whisk together cornstarch and cold water. Press Sauté. Add the cornstarch mixture to the pot and cook, stirring, for 4 minutes or until sauce is thickened. Season to taste with salt and pepper. Spoon sauce over ribs.

Cottage Pie with Lamb, Carrots and Potato Mash

This dish is Old World comfort food at its best. Make it on cold winter evenings when you want a hearty, satisfying all-in-one meal. You can even make it ahead and just pop it in the oven when you are ready for dinner.

MAKES 8 SERVINGS

INSTANT POT FUNCTIONS
• Sauté •
• Manual Pressure •

- **13- by 9-inch (33 by 23 cm) glass baking dish, sprayed with nonstick cooking spray**
- **Baking sheet, lined with parchment paper**

3 tbsp	butter, divided	45 mL
1	large onion, chopped	1
1½ lbs	ground lamb	750 g
2	carrots, finely chopped	2
2	sprigs fresh thyme	2
1	bay leaf	1
Pinch	freshly ground black pepper	Pinch
1 cup	ready-to-use beef broth	250 mL
1 tbsp	tomato paste	15 mL
1 tbsp	Worcestershire sauce	15 mL
1 tsp	red wine vinegar	5 mL
1 cup	frozen sweet peas	250 mL
6	russet potatoes (about 1½ lbs/ 750 g), peeled and cubed	6
1 tsp	kosher salt	5 mL
1 cup	water	250 mL
1	large egg yolk, beaten	1
¼ cup	half-and-half (10%) cream	60 mL

1. Press Sauté; the indicator will read "Normal." When the display says "Hot," add 1 tbsp (15 mL) butter to the pot and heat until melted. Add onion and cook, stirring, for 3 to 5 minutes or until translucent. Add lamb and cook, breaking the meat up with a spoon, for 5 to 7 minutes or until lamb is no longer pink. Add carrots, thyme sprigs, bay leaf, pepper, broth, tomato paste, Worcestershire sauce and vinegar, stirring well.

2. Close and lock the lid and turn the steam release handle to Sealing. Press Manual; the indicator will read "High Pressure." Use the ⊖ button to decrease the time on the display to 8 minutes.

3. When the timer beeps, press Cancel and turn the steam release handle to Venting. When the float valve drops down, remove the lid. Discard thyme sprigs and bay leaf. Stir in peas. Transfer mixture to prepared baking dish. Clean the inner pot.

4. Preheat the oven to 400°F (200°C), with the rack in the middle position.

5. Meanwhile, add potatoes, salt and water to the inner pot. Close and lock the lid and turn the steam release handle to Sealing. Press Manual; the indicator will read "High Pressure." Use the ⊖ button to decrease the time on the display to 9 minutes.

6. When the timer beeps, press Cancel and turn the steam release handle to Venting. When the float valve drops down, remove the lid. Drain potatoes, return to the pot and mash potatoes. Add egg yolk, cream and the remaining butter. Continue mashing until potatoes are smooth.

7. Add potatoes in spoonfuls to the top of the lamb mixture. Using the back of a spoon, spread potatoes evenly over top, spreading to the edges of the dish to completely seal in the lamb mixture. Place dish on prepared baking sheet.

8. Bake for 25 minutes or until potatoes are golden brown. Let cool for 10 minutes before serving.

Tips

This dish can be prepared through step 3 up to 2 days ahead. Cover and refrigerate. When ready to serve, continue with step 4. In step 8, bake for 35 minutes or until pie is heated through.

If you are making the dish ahead of time, do not prepare the mashed potatoes until you are ready to finish cooking.

You can substitute ground beef for the lamb, if you prefer.

For a fancier presentation, use a pastry bag to pipe the potatoes over the lamb mixture. You may want to leave little peaks when piping, for browner tips and more variation in color.

Leftover cottage pie can be stored in an airtight container in the refrigerator for up to 3 days. I do not recommend freezing this dish, as potatoes do not freeze well.

Karla's Sweet-and-Sour Beef Short Ribs

I have made the oven version of this family favorite recipe for years, even though it takes preplanning and more than 3 hours to cook. But now when everyone asks for my dear friend Karla's ribs, I can have this rich and hearty dish on the table in under an hour, start to finish.

MAKES 4 SERVINGS

INSTANT POT FUNCTION

• Manual Pressure •

4 lbs	beef short ribs, trimmed	2 kg
4 cups	sliced onions, separated into rings (about 3 large)	1 L
½ cup	granulated sugar	125 mL
¾ cup	ketchup	175 mL
½ cup	water	125 mL
¼ cup	soy sauce	60 mL
2 tbsp	apple cider vinegar	30 mL
2 tbsp	Worcestershire sauce	30 mL

Tips

The Potato and Celery Root Mash (page 122) is a fabulous accompaniment to these ribs.

Make the ribs a day ahead of time. When the inner pot is cool, remove it, cover with plastic wrap and refrigerate. When ready to reheat, remove any congealed fat from the top of the ribs and return the pot to the cooker housing. Press Sauté and heat, uncovered, stirring occasionally, for 7 to 9 minutes or until ribs are heated through.

1. Arrange ribs in the inner pot. Scatter onion rings over and around ribs.

2. In a medium bowl, combine sugar, ketchup, water, soy sauce, vinegar and Worcestershire sauce. Pour over ribs and onions.

3. Place the pot inside the cooker housing, close and lock the lid and turn the steam release handle to Sealing. Press Manual; the indicator will read "High Pressure." Use the ✚ button to increase the time on the display to 40 minutes.

4. When the timer beeps, press Cancel and turn the steam release handle to Venting. When the float valve drops down, remove the lid. The meat should be tender and ready to fall off the bone. (If more cooking is needed, reset the manual pressure to "High Pressure" for 5 minutes.) Using tongs, transfer ribs and onions to a serving platter and discard sauce.

Classic French Dip Sandwiches au Jus

Versatile and satisfying, these all-time-favorite sandwiches have a distinctive savory and salty flavor and are bursting with mouthwateringly tender sliced beef atop crusty French rolls.

MAKES 4 SERVINGS

INSTANT POT FUNCTION
• Manual Pressure •

2 cups	ready-to-use beef broth	500 mL
2½ tbsp	dried onion flakes	37 mL
2 tsp	beef bouillon granules	10 mL
1 tsp	onion powder	5 mL
½ tsp	garlic powder	2 mL
Pinch	freshly ground black pepper	Pinch
1½ lb	beef top round or round tip roast, thinly sliced	750 g
	Butter	
4	French rolls, sliced lengthwise	4

1. In the inner pot, combine broth, onion flakes, bouillon granules, onion powder, garlic powder and pepper. Add beef slices individually to the broth, so they do not stick together.

2. Place the pot inside the cooker housing, close and lock the lid and turn the steam release handle to Sealing. Press Manual; the indicator will read "High Pressure." Use the ⊖ button to decrease the time on the display to 10 minutes.

3. When the timer beeps, press Cancel and let the pot stand, covered, for 10 minutes. After 10 minutes, turn the steam release handle to Venting and remove the lid.

4. Meanwhile, preheat the broiler. Butter cut sides of rolls. Place rolls, buttered side up, on a baking sheet. Broil for 2 minutes or until lightly toasted.

5. Using tongs, transfer beef slices from broth and layer on bottom halves of rolls. Cover with top halves of rolls. Strain broth and skim off fat. Divide the broth among 4 small bowls and serve with the sandwiches for dipping.

Variation

Top the beef with 2 slices of provolone or another semisoft cheese in step 5. Transfer to the baking sheet and broil until the cheese is just melted. Remove from broiler and cover with top halves of rolls.

BBQ Brisket Lovers' Sandwiches and Slaw

Even the staunchest of brisket connoisseurs will find this barbecue brisket satisfying, tender and packed with flavor.

MAKES 6 SERVINGS

INSTANT POT FUNCTIONS
- Sauté •
- Manual Pressure •

- **13- by 9-inch (33 by 23 cm) baking dish**
- **Rimmed baking sheet**

Brisket

1 tbsp	Hungarian paprika	15 mL
1 tbsp	dry mustard	15 mL
1 tsp	chili powder	5 mL
3 tbsp	Worcestershire sauce	45 mL
	Virgin olive oil	
4 lb	piece beef brisket (see tip, opposite), cut into fourths	2 kg
2 tsp	kosher salt	10 mL
1	onion, finely chopped	1
5	cloves garlic, sliced	5
¼ cup	packed brown sugar	60 mL
1	bottle (12 oz/341 mL) lager beer	1
1 cup	barbecue sauce	250 mL

Coleslaw

½ cup	buttermilk	125 mL
½ cup	mayonnaise	125 mL
¼ cup	white vinegar	60 mL
1 tbsp	granulated sugar	15 mL
½ tsp	kosher salt	2 mL
1	package (14 oz/400 g) shredded coleslaw mix	1
6	kaiser rolls, sliced	6

1. *Brisket:* In the baking dish, combine paprika, mustard, chili powder, Worcestershire sauce and 2 tbsp (30 mL) oil. Add brisket and turn to coat. Cover dish with plastic wrap and marinate for 30 minutes.

2. Remove brisket from marinade, discarding marinade, and season with salt. Press Sauté; the indicator will read "Normal." When the display says "Hot," add 1 tbsp (15 mL) oil to the pot and heat until shimmering. Working in batches, add brisket and cook, turning often, for 3 to 5 minutes or until browned on all sides, adding more oil as needed. Transfer brisket to rimmed baking sheet.

3. Add onion to the pot and cook, stirring, for 5 minutes or until translucent. Add garlic and cook, stirring, for 1 minute or until fragrant. Press Cancel. Return the brisket to the pot, along with any accumulated juices, and add brown sugar, beer and barbecue sauce, stirring well.

4. Close and lock the lid and turn the steam release handle to Sealing. Press Manual; the indicator will read "High Pressure." Use the ⊕ button to increase the time on the display to 90 minutes.

5. When the timer beeps, press Cancel and turn the steam release handle to Venting. When the float valve drops down, remove the lid. Transfer the brisket to a cutting board and let cool slightly, then thinly slice across the grain.

6. Press Sauté. When the display says "Hot," return brisket slices and any juices to the pot. Simmer, uncovered, for 15 to 20 minutes or until brisket is done to your liking.

7. *Coleslaw:* Meanwhile, in a large bowl, combine buttermilk, mayonnaise, vinegar, sugar and salt. Add coleslaw mix and toss to combine.

8. Serve brisket slices on rolls, topped with coleslaw.

Tips

Your brisket should be "boneless," with deckle off. This cut of brisket is often called "cut 120." It has bones 1 to 4 removed and the hard fat, known as deckle, trimmed off. You can ask your butcher to trim your brisket to these specifications, if it's not already done.

The coleslaw can be served alongside the brisket sandwich instead of on top, if you prefer.

Sweet-and-Savory Beef and Broccoli

This take-out favorite is simple to make at home in your pressure cooker. You can make it with fresh, quality ingredients without ever having to leave the house or wait for delivery. Serve with cooked white rice.

MAKES 6 SERVINGS

INSTANT POT FUNCTIONS

• Sauté •
• Manual Pressure •

1½ lb	beef sirloin roast, cut into thin strips	750 g
	Kosher salt and freshly ground black pepper	
1 tbsp	virgin olive oil	15 mL
1	onion, finely chopped	1
4	cloves garlic, minced	4
⅓ cup	packed brown sugar	75 mL
2 tsp	minced gingerroot	10 mL
¾ cup	ready-to-use beef broth	175 mL
⅓ cup	soy sauce or liquid amino acids	75 mL
2 tbsp	sesame oil	30 mL
1 lb	broccoli florets	500 g
	Hot pepper flakes (optional)	

Tips

You can use frozen broccoli florets, but add 1 minute to the cooking time in step 5.

When using the Quick Release method to release pressure, keep your hands and face away from the hole on the top of the steam release handle so you don't get scalded by the escaping steam.

1. Season beef with salt and pepper. Press Sauté; the indicator will read "Normal." When the display says "Hot," add olive oil and heat until shimmering. Working in batches, add beef and cook, turning occasionally, for 3 to 5 minutes or until browned on all sides. Transfer beef to a plate.

2. Add onion to the pot and cook, stirring, for 2 to 3 minutes or until softened. Add garlic and cook, stirring, for 1 minute or until fragrant. Add brown sugar, ginger, broth, soy sauce and sesame oil, stirring until sugar is dissolved. Press Cancel. Return beef to the pot, along with any accumulated juices.

3. Close and lock the lid and turn the steam release handle to Sealing. Press Manual; the indicator will read "High Pressure." Use the ⊖ button to decrease the time on the display to 12 minutes.

4. When the timer beeps, press Cancel and turn the steam release handle to Venting. When the float valve drops down, remove the lid.

5. Stir in broccoli florets. Close and lock the lid and turn the steam release handle to Sealing. Press Manual; the indicator will read "High Pressure." Press Pressure once to adjust the pressure to "Low Pressure." Use the ⊖ button to decrease the time on the display to 2 minutes.

6. When the timer beeps, press Cancel and turn the steam release handle to Venting. When the float valve drops down, remove the lid. Test the broccoli to see if it is done to your liking. (If more cooking is needed, cover pot and let stand for 1 minute.) If desired, serve sprinkled with hot pepper flakes.

Classic Creamy Beef Stroganoff

This eastern European favorite has become a New World favorite for many people. With its tender beef chunks and mushrooms swooning in a deep, rich and savory gravy, it's no wonder this dish has earned the coveted spot on our dinner table.

MAKES 6 SERVINGS

INSTANT POT FUNCTIONS

• Sauté •

• Manual Pressure •

1½ tbsp	all-purpose flour, divided	22 mL
2 tsp	kosher salt	10 mL
1 tsp	garlic powder	5 mL
½ tsp	freshly ground black pepper	2 mL
1½ lb	boneless beef chuck roast, cut into 1½-inch (4 cm) pieces	750 g
1 tbsp	virgin olive oil	15 mL
¼ cup	butter	60 mL
1	large onion, cut in half, sliced and separated	1
1 lb	mushrooms, sliced	500 g
1 cup	dry white wine	250 mL
1 cup	ready-to-use beef broth	250 mL
1 tbsp	Dijon mustard	15 mL
12 oz	broad egg noodles	375 g
1 cup	sour cream	250 mL
¼ cup	chopped fresh chives	60 mL

Tips

The beef should be lightly coated in the flour and seasonings, not dredged in flour. It is not necessary to use all of the flour coating.

Instead of the sour cream, try Homemade Yogurt (page 212).

1. In a small bowl, combine 1 tbsp (15 mL) flour, salt, garlic powder and pepper. Place beef on a plate and sprinkle with flour mixture; toss to lightly coat.

2. Press Sauté; the indicator will read "Normal." When the display says "Hot," add oil to the pot and heat until shimmering. Working in batches, add beef and cook, stirring, for 3 to 5 minutes or until browned on all sides. Transfer beef to a plate. Discard excess flour mixture.

3. Add butter to the pot and heat until melted. Add onion and mushrooms; cook, stirring, for 5 to 7 minutes or until mushrooms are softened and onions are lightly browned.

4. Stir in wine, scraping up any browned bits from the bottom of the pot. Stir in the remaining flour and simmer, stirring, for 2 minutes or until liquid is reduced by half. Add broth and mustard. Return beef to the pot, along with any accumulated juices, stirring to combine. Press Cancel.

5. Close and lock the lid and turn the steam release handle to Sealing. Press Manual; the indicator will read "High Pressure." Use the ⊖ button to decrease the time on the display to 18 minutes.

6. Meanwhile, in a large pot of boiling salted water, cook egg noodles according to package directions. Drain and set aside.

7. When the timer beeps, press Cancel and turn the steam release handle to Venting. When the float valve drops down, remove the lid. Stir in sour cream.

8. Serve beef mixture over noodles, garnished with chives.

Zesty Beef Burritos

Indulge all of your senses with these tender beef cubes graced with sublime flavors, wrapped in tortillas and then covered in golden, bubbly cheese.

MAKES 8 SERVINGS

INSTANT POT FUNCTIONS
• Sauté •
• Manual Pressure •

- 13- by 9-inch (33 by 23 cm) baking dish, sprayed with nonstick cooking spray

1 tbsp	virgin olive oil	15 mL
1½ lb	boneless beef chuck roast, cut into ¾-inch (2 cm) cubes	750 g
3	cloves garlic, minced	3
2 tbsp	packed brown sugar	30 mL
1 cup	chunky medium salsa	250 mL
½ cup	ready-to-use beef broth	125 mL
1 tbsp	soy sauce	15 mL
¼ cup	chopped fresh cilantro	60 mL
1 tbsp	freshly squeezed lime juice	15 mL
8	burrito-size (10-inch/25 cm) flour tortillas	8
2 cups	shredded Monterey Jack cheese, divided	500 mL

Tip

You can prepare the burrito filling through step 5 up to 2 days ahead. When the inner pot is cool, remove the pot, cover it with plastic wrap and refrigerate. When ready to make burritos, return the pot to the cooker housing and press Sauté to reheat, stirring frequently until warm.

1. Press Sauté; the indicator will read "Normal." When the display says "Hot," add oil to the pot and heat until shimmering. Working in batches, add beef and cook, stirring, for 3 minutes or until browned on all sides. Transfer beef to a plate.

2. Press Cancel. Return beef to the pot, along with any accumulated juices. Add garlic, brown sugar, salsa, broth and soy sauce, stirring well.

3. Close and lock the lid and turn the steam release handle to Sealing. Press Manual; the indicator will read "High Pressure." Leave the time at 30 minutes.

4. When the timer beeps, press Cancel and let the pot stand, covered, for 10 minutes. After 10 minutes, turn the steam release handle to Venting and remove the lid. Check to make sure the beef is fork-tender. (If more cooking is needed, reset the manual pressure to "High Pressure" for 5 minutes.)

5. Stir in cilantro and lime juice. Press Sauté and cook, stirring, for 5 minutes or until sauce is thickened to your desired consistency.

6. Preheat the broiler. Place a tortilla on a plate. Add one-eighth of the beef mixture to the center of the tortilla. Sprinkle with 3 tbsp (45 mL) cheese. Fold in edges of tortilla and roll into a burrito. Transfer to prepared baking dish, seam side down. Repeat with the remaining tortillas and filling. Sprinkle the remaining cheese over the burritos. Broil for 3 to 4 minutes or until cheese is bubbly.

Crustless Bacon Broccoli Quiche (page 23)

Cherry and Coconut Granola (page 24)

Colombian Vegetable Soup (page 48)

Chuck Wagon Beef Stew
(page 68)

Salsa Lime Chicken Rollups (page 80)

Moo Shu Pork in
Lettuce Wraps (page 84)

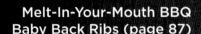

Melt-In-Your-Mouth BBQ
Baby Back Ribs (page 87)

Low and Slow Brisket with Carrots
and Brown Gravy (page 110)

Lusciously Layered Lasagna

If you love lasagna but hesitate to make it at home because of the time it takes, this version will delight you. From start to finish, homemade lasagna can be yours in under 40 minutes. Who wouldn't be excited about that?

INSTANT POT FUNCTIONS
- Sauté •
- • Manual Pressure •

1 tbsp	virgin olive oil	15 mL
1 lb	ground beef	500 g
1	large onion, finely chopped	1
1	clove garlic, minced	1
4 oz	mushrooms, sliced	125 g
Pinch	kosher salt	Pinch
3 cups	chunky marinara sauce	750 mL
1/4 cup	water	60 mL
2	large eggs	2
2	containers (each 15 oz/425 g) ricotta cheese	2
1/3 cup	freshly grated Parmesan cheese	75 mL
1 tsp	dried parsley	5 mL
1 tsp	dried thyme	5 mL
1/2 tsp	ground sage	2 mL
8 oz	oven-ready (no-boil) lasagna noodles	250 g
2 cups	shredded mozzarella cheese	500 mL

1. Press Sauté; the indicator will read "Normal." When the display says "Hot," add oil to the pot and heat until shimmering. Add beef and cook, breaking it up with a spoon, for 12 minutes or until no longer pink.

2. Add onion, garlic, mushrooms and salt; cook, stirring, for 3 to 5 minutes or until mushrooms are softened and onion is translucent. Add marinara sauce, stirring well. Press Cancel.

3. Transfer most of the sauce to a bowl, leaving 1/2 inch (1 cm) of sauce in the pot. Add water to the bowl, stirring well.

4. In a large bowl, whisk eggs. Stir in ricotta, Parmesan, parsley, thyme and sage.

5. Layer one-quarter of the noodles on top of the sauce in the pot, breaking noodles as needed to evenly cover sauce. Top with one-third of the cheese mixture, then one-quarter of the sauce. Continue with two more layers of noodles, cheese and sauce. Finish with a layer of noodles and a layer of sauce.

6. Close and lock the lid and turn the steam release handle to Sealing. Press Manual; the indicator will read "High Pressure." Use the ⊖ button to decrease the time on the display to 6 minutes.

7. When the timer beeps, press Cancel and turn the steam release handle to Venting. When the float valve drops down, remove the lid. Sprinkle with mozzarella. Cover and let stand for 10 minutes or until cheese is melted. Remove the lid and let stand for 15 minutes (this will help make the lasagna easier to cut).

Tips

Use a stainless steel potato masher instead of a spoon to break up the beef while cooking — it makes the process much easier.

For best results, cut the lasagna right in the pot (use a plastic knife so you don't damage the pot). You can also serve the lasagna out of the pot.

Leftover lasagna can be stored in an airtight container in the refrigerator for up to 3 days.

It's-Always-Better-with-Bacon Meatloaf

For the bacon lovers in your life, this meatloaf is not only packed with zesty flavor but is moist and swathed in the smoky, mouthwatering taste of bacon and a tangy barbecue sauce.

MAKES 6 SERVINGS

INSTANT POT FUNCTION

• Manual Pressure •

- **Instant Pot steam rack**
- **1 sheet heavy-duty foil, edges turned up and folded to form a loaf-like pan**

2	large eggs	2
1½ lbs	ground beef	750 g
½ cup	finely chopped onion	125 mL
½ cup	dry bread crumbs	125 mL
½ cup	freshly grated Parmesan cheese	125 mL
2 tsp	Hungarian paprika	10 mL
2 tsp	garlic powder	10 mL
1 tsp	onion powder	5 mL
1 tsp	granulated sugar	5 mL
1 tsp	kosher salt	5 mL
½ tsp	freshly ground black pepper	2 mL
½ tsp	chili powder	2 mL
4	slices bacon, cooked	4
5 tbsp	barbecue sauce, divided	75 mL

1. In a large bowl, whisk eggs. Add beef, onion, bread crumbs, cheese, paprika, garlic powder, onion powder, sugar, salt, pepper and chili powder. Using your hands, combine mixture, then shape into an oblong loaf that will fit in the inner pot.

2. Transfer loaf to prepared foil. Lay bacon slices across the top of the loaf, tucking the ends underneath. Brush top of loaf with 4 tbsp (60 mL) barbecue sauce.

3. Add 2 cups (500 mL) water to the inner pot. Use the foil to lift the loaf and place it on the steam rack. Lower the rack into the pot. Close and lock the lid and turn the steam release handle to Sealing. Press Manual; the indicator will read "High Pressure." Use the ⊖ button to decrease the time on the display to 12 minutes.

4. Meanwhile, preheat the broiler.

5. When the timer beeps, press Cancel and turn the steam release handle to Venting. When the float valve drops down, remove the lid. Check to make sure an instant-read thermometer inserted in the center of the loaf registers 165°F (74°C). (If more cooking is needed, cover pot, press Steam and cook for 3 minutes or until the center of the loaf is 165°F/74°C.)

6. Transfer loaf, in foil, to a baking sheet. Brush the remaining barbecue sauce over top of loaf. Broil for 3 to 5 minutes or until sauce begins to caramelize. Cover with foil and let rest for 5 minutes before slicing.

Variations

Use half ground beef and half ground pork.

Add 4 russet potatoes (about 1 lb/500 g), peeled and cubed, to the water under the steam rack. Cook along with the meatloaf. When you transfer the meatloaf to the broiler, use a slotted spoon to remove the potatoes. Mash the potatoes with milk to your desired consistency. Season with salt and pepper. Serve with the meatloaf.

Chicken Marsala

In this Italian-inspired dish, chicken thighs swoon in a sweet wine and mushroom sauce. You will be pleasantly surprised by the depth of flavor you can indulge in with just a few simple steps.

MAKES 4 SERVINGS

INSTANT POT FUNCTIONS

• Slow Cook •
• Sauté •

	Nonstick cooking spray	
1	clove garlic, chopped	1
2 tsp	virgin olive oil	10 mL
8	boneless skinless chicken thighs (about 1½ lbs/750 g)	8
	Kosher salt and freshly ground black pepper	
1 cup	thinly sliced cremini mushrooms	250 mL
1 cup	sweet Marsala	250 mL
¼ cup	cornstarch	60 mL
½ cup	cold water	125 mL
2 tbsp	chopped fresh parsley	30 mL

1. Spray the inner pot with cooking spray and add garlic and oil. Season chicken with salt and pepper; place on top of garlic. Add mushrooms and pour Marsala over chicken.

2. Place the pot inside the cooker housing, close and lock the lid and turn the steam release handle to Venting. Press Slow Cook; the indicator will read "Normal." Press Adjust twice to change the heat level to "Less." Press ➕ to increase the time on the display to 5:00.

3. When the timer beeps, remove the lid and check to make sure an instant-read thermometer inserted in the center of a thigh registers 165°F (74°C). (If more cooking is needed, reset the slow cooker to "Less" for 30 minutes.) Press Cancel. Transfer chicken to a plate and cover with foil to keep warm.

4. In a small bowl, whisk together cornstarch and cold water. Press Sauté. Add the cornstarch mixture to the pot, stirring well, and cook, stirring occasionally, for 10 minutes or until sauce is slightly thickened.

5. Return chicken to the pot, along with any accumulated juices. Simmer, uncovered, for 5 minutes, turning chicken to coat with sauce.

6. Transfer chicken to serving plates and spoon sauce over top. Sprinkle with parsley.

Tips

If you can only find bone-in chicken thighs, you will need about 2¾ lbs (1.375 kg). Remove the skin and debone them by using a paring or boning knife to cut a line through the meat along either side of the bone. Expose the bone, scraping away any small pieces of meat. When the meat has been mostly scraped off the bone, separate the end of the bone from the meat. Trim off any leftover bone or gristle still on the thigh. Chicken can be very slippery, so curl your fingers when cutting to avoid exposing them to the knife.

This recipe can be easily doubled.

Serve chicken Marsala over long-grain white rice or wide noodles.

Marsala comes in both sweet and dry versions. Make sure to use sweet in this recipe.

Chicken Mole

You will enjoy diving into the complex flavors of this traditional Mexican dish made with tender shredded chicken. When wrapped inside warm corn tortillas, these morsels get an added burst of flavor.

INSTANT POT FUNCTION

• Slow Cook •

3	cloves garlic, minced	3
1	onion, chopped	1
½ cup	raisins	125 mL
1½ tbsp	chili powder	22 mL
2 tsp	ground cumin	10 mL
1 tsp	ground coriander	5 mL
1 tsp	granulated sugar	5 mL
1	can (28 oz/796 mL) crushed tomatoes	1
1	chipotle pepper in adobo sauce, finely chopped	1
3 tbsp	creamy peanut butter	45 mL
	Grated zest and juice of 1 orange	
8	boneless skinless chicken thighs (about 1½ lbs/750 g total)	8
3 tbsp	grated Mexican chocolate (see tip, at right)	45 mL
Pinch	ground nutmeg	Pinch
8	taco-size (6-inch/15 cm) corn tortillas	8

1. In the inner pot, combine garlic, onion, raisins, chili powder, cumin, coriander, sugar, tomatoes, chipotles with sauce, peanut butter, orange zest and orange juice, stirring well. Place chicken on top of sauce.

2. Place the pot inside the cooker housing, close and lock the lid and turn the steam release handle to Venting. Press Slow Cook; the indicator will read "Normal." Press Adjust twice to change the heat level to "Less." Press ✚ to increase the time on the display to 5:00.

3. When the timer beeps, remove the lid and check to make sure an instant-read thermometer inserted in the center of a thigh registers 165°F (74°C). (If more cooking is needed, reset the slow cooker to "Less" for 30 minutes.)

4. Transfer thighs to a cutting board and, using a fork, shred the chicken. Return chicken to the pot and add chocolate and nutmeg, stirring to combine. Reset the slow cooker to "Less" and cook for 15 minutes.

5. Meanwhile, layer tortillas between sheets of parchment paper and arrange in two stacks. Wrap stacks tightly with foil. Place packets on top of ingredients in the pot for the last 7 minutes of cooking.

6. Remove packets from cooker and open carefully. Transfer warmed tortillas to serving plates and spoon chicken mole onto tortillas.

Tips

If you can only find bone-in chicken thighs, you will need about 2¾ lbs (1.375 kg). Remove the skin and debone them by using a paring or boning knife to cut a line through the meat along either side of the bone. Expose the bone, scraping away any small pieces of meat. When the meat has been mostly scraped off the bone, separate the end of the bone from the meat. Trim off any leftover bone or gristle still on the thigh. Chicken can be very slippery, so curl your fingers when cutting to avoid exposing them to the knife.

Mexican chocolate can be found in specialty grocery stores or online. You can substitute 3 tbsp (45 mL) unsweetened cocoa powder and 1 tsp (5 mL) ground cinnamon.

Cilantro Lime Chicken

This Mexican-inspired dish is bursting with flavor and incredibly versatile: you can serve it by itself with rice and beans, shred it for tacos or chili, or serve it on top of a salad. Simple ingredients and simple prep make it a go-to favorite.

INSTANT POT FUNCTIONS

• Sauté •

• Slow Cook •

4	cloves garlic, minced	4
¼ cup	chopped fresh cilantro	60 mL
2 tsp	hot pepper flakes	10 mL
1 tsp	ground cumin	5 mL
½ tsp	kosher salt	2 mL
2 tbsp	freshly squeezed lime juice	30 mL
2 tbsp	extra virgin olive oil, divided	30 mL
8	boneless skinless chicken thighs (about 1½ lbs/750 g total)	8
1	lime, cut into wedges	1
	Torn fresh cilantro leaves	

Tips

If you can only find bone-in chicken thighs, you will need about 2¾ lbs (1.375 kg). Remove the skin and debone them by using a paring or boning knife to cut a line through the meat along either side of the bone. Expose the bone, scraping away any small pieces of meat. When the meat has been mostly scraped off the bone, separate the end of the bone from the meat. Trim off any leftover bone or gristle still on the thigh. Chicken can be very slippery, so curl your fingers when cutting to avoid exposing them to the knife.

This dish can also be made in 4 hours. In step 3, press Adjust once to change the heat level to "More" and leave the time at 4:00. Continue with step 4.

1. In a large sealable plastic bag, combine garlic, chopped cilantro, hot pepper flakes, cumin, salt, lime juice and 1 tbsp (15 mL) oil. Add chicken, seal and turn bag to coat chicken in marinade. Seal and refrigerate for 2 hours.

2. Press Sauté; the indicator will read "Normal." When the display says "Hot," add the remaining oil to the pot and heat until shimmering. Using tongs, transfer chicken to the pot; reserve marinade. Cook chicken, turning once, for 5 to 6 minutes or until browned on both sides. Press Cancel. Pour marinade over chicken.

3. Close and lock the lid and turn the steam release handle to Venting. Press Slow Cook; the indicator will read "Normal." Press Adjust twice to change the heat level to "Less." Press ✚ to increase the time on the display to 6:00.

4. When the timer beeps, remove the lid and check to make sure an instant-read thermometer inserted in the center of a thigh registers 165°F (74°C). (If more cooking is needed, reset the slow cooker to "Less" for 30 minutes.)

5. Transfer chicken to serving plates and drizzle with some of the liquid from the pot, discarding the remainder. Garnish with lime wedges and torn cilantro.

Chinese Orange Chicken

This sweet and savory orange chicken is slow-cooked to perfection and ready when you are, with no need to run for takeout. Serve with cooked rice and steamed broccoli for a satisfying meal the whole family will enjoy.

INSTANT POT FUNCTIONS

• Slow Cook •
• Sauté •

1	clove garlic, minced	1
2 tbsp	packed brown sugar	30 mL
¾ cup	orange marmalade	175 mL
¼ cup	ready-to-use chicken broth	60 mL
2 tbsp	soy sauce	30 mL
1 tbsp	mirin	15 mL
1 tsp	sesame oil	5 mL
8	boneless skinless chicken thighs (about 1½ lbs/750 g total), cut into 1-inch (2.5 cm) pieces	8
2 tsp	cornstarch	10 mL
1½ tbsp	cold water	22 mL
2 tbsp	chopped green onions	30 mL
Pinch	hot pepper flakes (optional)	Pinch

1. In the inner pot, combine garlic, brown sugar, marmalade, broth, soy sauce, mirin and oil. Add chicken, stirring well.

2. Place the pot inside the cooker housing, close and lock the lid and turn the steam release handle to Venting. Press Slow Cook; the indicator will read "Normal." Press Adjust twice to change the heat level to "Less." Leave the time at 4:00.

3. When the timer beeps, remove the lid and check to make sure the chicken juices run clear when pierced with a fork. (If more cooking is needed, reset the slow cooker to "Less" for 30 minutes.) Using a slotted spoon, transfer chicken to a serving bowl.

4. In a small bowl, whisk together cornstarch and cold water. Press Sauté. Add cornstarch mixture to the pot, whisking well. Stir in green onions and cook, stirring, for 3 to 4 minutes or until sauce is slightly thickened. Pour sauce over chicken and sprinkle with hot pepper flakes (if using).

Tips

If you can only find bone-in chicken thighs, you will need about 2¾ lbs (1.375 kg). Remove the skin and debone them by using a paring or boning knife to cut a line through the meat along either side of the bone. Expose the bone, scraping away any small pieces of meat. When the meat has been mostly scraped off the bone, separate the end of the bone from the meat. Trim off any leftover bone or gristle still on the thigh. Chicken can be very slippery, so curl your fingers when cutting to avoid exposing them to the knife.

This dish can also be made in 2 to 3 hours. In step 2, press Adjust once to change the heat level to "More." Press ⊖ to decrease the time on the display to 2:00. Continue with step 3.

Slow Cooker Chicken Pot Pie

This down-home, made-from-scratch chicken pot pie is topped off with flaky biscuits. The result? Creamier chicken and vegetables and less worry about making the perfect crust.

MAKES 8 SERVINGS

INSTANT POT FUNCTIONS

• Sauté •
• Slow Cook •

3 tbsp	butter	45 mL
3	cloves garlic, minced	3
½ cup	all-purpose flour	125 mL
2 cups	ready-to-use chicken broth	500 mL
1 tsp	chopped fresh thyme	5 mL
1 tsp	chopped fresh oregano	5 mL
½ tsp	paprika	2 mL
4	bone-in skin-on chicken thighs (about 1½ lbs/750 g total)	4
	Kosher salt and freshly ground black pepper	
1 lb	red-skinned potatoes, diced	500 g
2	carrots, diced	2
2	stalks celery, diced	2
1	onion, finely chopped	1
2	bay leaves	2
1 cup	frozen corn	250 mL
1 cup	frozen sweet peas	250 mL
1	can (16 oz/500 g) refrigerated buttermilk biscuits	1
2 tbsp	chopped fresh parsley	30 mL

1. Press Sauté; the indicator will read "Normal." When the display says "Hot," add butter and heat until melted. Add garlic and cook, stirring, for 30 seconds or until fragrant. Whisk in flour and cook, whisking, for 1 to 2 minutes or until lightly browned. Gradually whisk in broth. Whisk in thyme, oregano and paprika; cook, whisking, for 3 to 5 minutes or until sauce starts to thicken. Press Cancel.

2. Season chicken with salt and pepper. Add chicken, potatoes, carrots, celery, onion and bay leaves to the pot.

3. Close and lock the lid and turn the steam release handle to Venting. Press Slow Cook; the indicator will read "Normal." Press Adjust twice to change the heat level to "Less." Press ⊖ to decrease the time on the display to 3:00.

4. When 30 minutes remains in the cooking time, stir in corn and peas, then relock the lid. When the timer beeps, remove the lid and check to make sure an instant-read thermometer inserted in the center of a thigh registers 165°F (74°C). (If more cooking is needed, reset the slow cooker to "Less" for 30 minutes.) Discard bay leaves.

5. Transfer the chicken to a cutting board and, using a fork, shred the meat and return it to the pot; discard bones and skin. Close and lock the lid and let stand on "Keep Warm" for 30 minutes.

6. Meanwhile, prepare biscuits according to package directions.

7. Spoon chicken mixture into bowls and season to taste with salt and pepper. Top with individual biscuits.

Tips

This dish can also be made in 1½ to 2 hours. In step 3, press Adjust once to change the heat level to "More." Press ⊖ to decrease the time on the display to 1:30. Continue with step 4.

Store leftover pot pie in an airtight container in the refrigerator for up to 3 days. The biscuits should be stored separately. They keep well in a waxed paper bag at room temperature for up to 3 days.

Sweet-and-Tangy Cranberry Chicken

These slow-cooked chicken breasts get their flavor from a sweet French-style dressing and cranberry sauce mixture, with an added boost of onion soup seasoning.

MAKES 4 SERVINGS

INSTANT POT FUNCTION

• Slow Cook •

	Nonstick cooking spray	
4	boneless skinless chicken breasts (about 2 lbs/1 kg total)	4
	Kosher salt and freshly ground black pepper	
1	clove garlic, minced	1
2 tbsp	packed brown sugar	30 mL
1 tsp	onion powder	5 mL
¼ cup	ketchup	60 mL
2 tbsp	white vinegar	30 mL
½ cup	extra virgin olive oil	125 mL
1	can (15 oz/425 mL) cranberry sauce	1
1	packet (1 oz/28 g) dry onion soup mix	1

Tips

This dish can also be made in 3 to 3½ hours. In step 3, press Adjust once to change the heat level to "More." Press ➖ to decrease the time on the display to 3:00. Continue with step 4.

Serve with a stovetop stuffing and mashed potatoes for the ultimate complete comfort meal.

1. Spray the inner pot with cooking spray. Season chicken lightly with salt and pepper and add to the pot.

2. In a medium bowl, whisk together garlic, brown sugar, onion powder, ketchup and vinegar. Gradually whisk in oil until blended. Stir in cranberry sauce and onion soup mix. Pour over chicken.

3. Place the pot inside the cooker housing, close and lock the lid and turn the steam release handle to Venting. Press Slow Cook; the indicator will read "Normal." Press Adjust twice to change the heat level to "Less." Press ➕ to increase the time on the display to 6:00.

4. When the timer beeps, remove the lid and check to make sure an instant-read thermometer inserted in the center of a breast registers 165°F (74°C). (If more cooking is needed, reset the slow cooker to "Less" for 30 minutes.) Serve chicken drizzled with sauce.

Asian-Style Chicken Lettuce Wraps

This variation of a restaurant favorite is not only easy to make at home in your Instant Pot, but I think it tastes better, too.

MAKES 6 SERVINGS		

INSTANT POT FUNCTION		
• Slow Cook •		

1½ lbs	ground chicken	750 g
2	cloves garlic, minced	2
1	onion, finely chopped	1
1	can (6 oz/170 mL) whole water chestnuts, drained and finely chopped	1
1 tbsp	ground ginger	15 mL
1 tbsp	packed brown sugar	15 mL
1 tsp	hot pepper flakes	5 mL
½ cup	hoisin sauce	125 mL
3 tbsp	soy sauce	45 mL
2 tbsp	rice vinegar	30 mL
6 to 12	Bibb or iceberg lettuce leaves	6 to 12
3	green onions, sliced	3
1	carrot, shredded	1

Tips

This dish can also be made in 3 to 4 hours. In step 2, press Adjust once to change the heat level to "More." Press ⊖ to decrease the time on the display to 3:00. Continue with step 3.

You can substitute ground turkey for the chicken, if you prefer.

1. In the inner pot, combine chicken, garlic, onion, water chestnuts, ginger, brown sugar, hot pepper flakes, hoisin sauce, soy sauce and vinegar, stirring well.

2. Place the pot inside the cooker housing, close and lock the lid and turn the steam release handle to Venting. Press Slow Cook; the indicator will read "Normal." Press Adjust twice to change the heat level to "Less." Press ⊕ to increase the time on the display to 6:00.

3. When the timer beeps, remove the lid and check to make sure the chicken is no longer pink. (If more cooking is needed, reset the slow cooker to "Less" for 1 hour.)

4. Spoon chicken mixture into lettuce leaves and garnish with green onions and carrot.

Sweet-and-Spicy Pork Tenderloin with Ginger Glaze

Just the right amounts of spicy and sweet are married together and rubbed into the tenderloin, which is then slow-cooked and finished with a tangy glaze.

MAKES 6 SERVINGS

INSTANT POT FUNCTION
• Slow Cook •

• **Baking sheet, lined with heavy-duty foil**

1 tbsp	packed brown sugar	15 mL
2 tsp	kosher salt	10 mL
1½ tsp	Chinese five-spice powder	7 mL
1 tsp	garlic powder	5 mL
½ tsp	hot pepper flakes	2 mL
2	pork tenderloins (each about 12 oz/375 g)	2

Ginger Glaze

1 tbsp	cornstarch	15 mL
½ cup	cold water	125 mL
½ cup	packed brown sugar	125 mL
¼ cup	white or rice vinegar	60 mL
2 tbsp	soy sauce	30 mL
1	1-inch (2.5 cm) piece gingerroot, minced	1

Tip

The tapered ends of the tenderloin will be more well done than the thicker part — ideal for those who like their pork medium-well or well done.

1. In a small bowl, combine brown sugar, salt, five-spice powder, garlic powder and hot pepper flakes. Rub spice mixture well into pork, covering all surfaces. Place pork in the inner pot.

2. Place the pot inside the cooker housing, close and lock the lid and turn the steam release handle to Venting. Press Slow Cook; the indicator will read "Normal." Press Adjust twice to change the heat level to "Less." Press ✚ to increase the time on the display to 6:00.

3. When the timer beeps, remove the lid and check to make sure an instant-read thermometer inserted in the thickest part of the tenderloin registers at least 160°F (71°C) for medium. (If more cooking is needed, reset the slow cooker to "Less" and cook for 30 to 60 minutes.) Transfer pork to prepared baking sheet, cover with foil and let stand for 10 minutes. Discard liquid in pot.

4. Meanwhile, preheat the broiler, with an oven rack in the top position.

5. *Glaze:* In a small saucepan over medium heat, whisk together cornstarch and cold water. Add brown sugar, vinegar and soy sauce; cook, whisking, for 4 to 5 minutes or until sauce is thickened to a glaze. Remove from heat and stir in ginger. Brush some of the glaze over tenderloin, coating it all over.

6. Broil for 2 to 3 minutes or until glaze is caramelized. Serve with the remaining glaze on the side.

Rustic Pork Chops with Mushroom Gravy

My mother made these pork chops on the stovetop, and they were always one of my favorites. I have updated her original recipe to include homemade mushroom gravy and a slow cooker method, for a ready-made dish at the end of the day.

INSTANT POT FUNCTIONS
- Sauté •
- Slow Cook •

1½ tbsp	virgin olive oil	22 mL
6	1-inch (2.5 cm) thick boneless pork loin chops (each about 5 oz/150 g)	6
½ cup	butter	125 mL
12 oz	cremini mushrooms, finely chopped	375 g
½ cup	finely chopped onion	125 mL
2	cloves garlic, minced	2
½ cup	all-purpose flour	125 mL
1 cup	heavy or whipping (35%) cream	250 mL
1 cup	ready-to-use chicken broth	250 mL
	Kosher salt and freshly ground black pepper	

Tip
You can use bone-in pork chops if you prefer, as they are often less expensive. You will need to make sure they are well covered with gravy as they cook.

1. Press Sauté; the indicator will read "Normal." When the display says "Hot," add oil to the pot and heat until shimmering. Working in batches, add pork chops and cook, turning once, for 4 to 6 minutes or until browned on both sides. Transfer pork to a plate. Drain off excess oil from pot.

2. Add butter to the pot and heat until melted, scraping up any browned bits from the bottom. Add mushrooms and onion; cook, stirring, for 6 to 8 minutes or until mushrooms are softened and onion is translucent. Add garlic and cook, stirring, for 30 seconds or until fragrant. Whisk in flour. Gradually whisk in cream and broth; simmer, whisking, for 2 minutes or until slightly thickened. Press Cancel. Season with salt and pepper. Add pork chops to sauce, turning to coat.

3. Close and lock the lid and turn the steam release handle to Venting. Press Slow Cook; the indicator will read "Normal." Press Adjust twice to change the heat level to "Less." Press ✚ to increase the time on the display to 4:30.

4. When the timer beeps, remove the lid and check to make sure an instant-read thermometer inserted in the thickest part of a pork chop registers at least 160°F (71°C) for medium. (If more cooking is needed, reset the slow cooker to "Less" and cook for 30 to 60 minutes.)

5. Using tongs, transfer pork to a serving platter. Spoon mushroom sauce into gravy boats and serve on the side.

Sweet-and-Tangy Hawaiian Pork Chops

Transport yourself to the carefree islands with the flavor and aroma of these juicy pork chops covered in a tangy sauce and paired with pineapple slices. Serve garnished with chopped cilantro, with a side of rice, if desired.

MAKES 6 SERVINGS		
INSTANT POT FUNCTION		
• Slow Cook •		
1	can (15 oz/425 mL) pineapple slices, with juice	1
3 tbsp	cornstarch	45 mL
½ cup	cold water	125 mL
1	clove garlic, minced	1
⅓ cup	packed brown sugar	75 mL
½ cup	soy sauce	125 mL
¼ cup	ketchup	60 mL
3 tbsp	rice vinegar	45 mL
	Nonstick cooking spray	
6	1-inch (2.5 cm) thick boneless pork loin chops (each about 5 oz/150 g)	6

Tip

This dish can also be made in 3 to 4 hours. In step 3, press Adjust once to change the heat level to "More." Press ➖ to decrease the time on the display to 3:00. Continue with step 4.

1. Drain juice from pineapple, reserving juice; set pineapple aside. In a medium bowl, whisk together cornstarch and cold water. Add garlic, brown sugar, pineapple juice, soy sauce, ketchup and vinegar, whisking well.

2. Spray the inner pot with cooking spray. Pour in half the sauce. Arrange pork chops and pineapple slices in pot. Pour the remaining sauce over top.

3. Place the pot inside the cooker housing, close and lock the lid and turn the steam release handle to Venting. Press Slow Cook; the indicator will read "Normal." Press Adjust twice to change the heat level to "Less." Press ➕ to increase the time on the display to 4:30.

4. When the timer beeps, remove the lid and check to make sure an instant-read thermometer inserted in the thickest part of a pork chop registers at least 160°F (71°C) for medium. (If more cooking is needed, reset the slow cooker to "Less" and cook for 30 to 60 minutes.) Using tongs, transfer pork and pineapple to a serving platter. Drizzle sauce over top.

Festa Italia Sausages with Peppers and Onions

One of my favorite festivals is the Feast of San Gennaro in New York City. The streets are teeming with colorful garb and festive music, and the air is swirling with the smell of these fabulous Italian sausages, piled high with grilled peppers and onions and nestled in a hearty Italian roll.

MAKES 6 SERVINGS

INSTANT POT FUNCTION

• Slow Cook •

¼ cup	packed brown sugar	60 mL
1	jar (26 oz/700 mL) marinara sauce	1
2	cloves garlic, minced	2
1	large sweet onion (such as Vidalia or Walla Walla)	1
1	green bell pepper, sliced	1
1	red bell pepper, sliced	1
6	Italian sausage links (about 3 lbs/ 1.5 kg total)	6
2	jars (each 4 oz/125 mL) pepperoncini peppers	2
6	large hoagie rolls, split	6
	Butter	
	Garlic powder	

1. In the inner pot, combine brown sugar and marinara sauce. Add garlic, onion, green pepper and red pepper, stirring well. Add sausages, pressing them down into the sauce.

2. Place the pot inside the cooker housing, close and lock the lid and turn the steam release handle to Venting. Press Slow Cook; the indicator will read "Normal." Press Adjust twice to change the heat level to "Less." Press ➕ to increase the time on the display to 8:00.

3. When 30 minutes remains in the cooking time, stir in pepperoncini, then relock the lid. When the timer beeps, remove the lid and check to make sure the sausages are no longer pink inside and the onion and peppers are tender. (If more cooking is needed, reset the slow cooker to "Less" and cook for 30 to 60 minutes.)

4. Preheat the broiler, with an oven rack in the top position.

5. Spread butter on inside of hoagie rolls and sprinkle with garlic powder. Broil, butter side up, on top rack for 1 to 3 minutes or until browned and slightly crisp. Using tongs, transfer sausages to buns. Top with peppers and onions. Discard sauce.

Low and Slow Brisket with Carrots and Brown Gravy

Brisket is one of those dishes that many of us love to eat and hate to make because it takes so much time. Well, this darling of a dish does take a bit of time, but it is all hands-off, and the result is tender and flavorful.

MAKES 8 SERVINGS

INSTANT POT FUNCTIONS

• Sauté •

• Slow Cook •

3 lb	piece beef brisket (see tip, opposite), cut into thirds	1.5 kg
	Kosher salt	
2 tbsp	virgin olive oil	30 mL
4	carrots, sliced	4
3	stalks celery, with leaves, chopped	3
2	onions, chopped	2
2	bay leaves	2
1 cup	chopped fresh parsley, divided	250 mL
3	cloves garlic, minced	3
2 tbsp	dried onion flakes	30 mL
2 tsp	horseradish powder	10 mL
2 cups	ready-to-use beef broth	500 mL
2 cups	dry red wine	500 mL
2 tbsp	tomato paste	30 mL
	Freshly ground black pepper	
2 tbsp	cornstarch	30 mL
1 cup	cold water	250 mL

1. Season brisket with salt. Press Sauté; the indicator will read "Normal." When the display says "Hot," add oil to the pot and heat until shimmering. Working in batches, add brisket and cook, turning often, for 3 to 5 minutes or until browned on all sides. Transfer brisket to a plate. Press Cancel.

2. Add carrots, celery, onions, bay leaves and ¾ cup (175 mL) parsley to the pot, stirring well. Return the brisket to the pot, along with any accumulated juices.

3. In a large bowl, combine garlic, onion flakes, horseradish, broth, wine and tomato paste. Pour over brisket. Season with salt and pepper.

4. Close and lock the lid and turn the steam release handle to Venting. Press Slow Cook; the indicator will read "Normal." Press Adjust twice to change the heat level to "Less." Press ➕ to increase the time on the display to 7:00.

5. When the timer beeps, remove the lid and check to make sure the brisket is tender and no longer pink inside. (If more cooking is needed, reset the slow cooker to "Less" and cook for 30 to 60 minutes.) Press Cancel. Discard bay leaves. Transfer the brisket to a cutting board and the vegetables to a serving bowl. Cover with foil and keep warm.

6. In a small bowl, whisk together cornstarch and cold water. Press Sauté. Add the cornstarch mixture to the pot and cook, stirring, for 2 to 4 minutes or until gravy is thickened to your liking.

7. Slice brisket crosswise against the grain and arrange slices on a serving platter. Drizzle with some of the gravy and garnish with the remaining parsley. Serve with the carrots and onions. Spoon the remaining gravy into a gravy boat and serve alongside.

Tips

Your brisket should be "boneless," with deckle off. This cut of brisket is often called "cut 120." It has bones 1 to 4 removed and the hard fat, known as deckle, trimmed off. You can ask your butcher to trim your brisket to these specifications, if it's not already done.

Cut the brisket into equal sections that will allow you to arrange them evenly in the pot, to aid with even cooking.

Any leftovers can be stored in an airtight container in the refrigerator for up to 3 days. To reheat, add brisket with gravy to an ovenproof dish large enough to accommodate laying the brisket flat without overlapping. Cover with heavy-duty foil and heat in a 250°F (120°C) oven for 20 minutes or until warmed through.

Three-Envelope Roast Beef

This pot roast recipe has been floating around local potlucks, fundraisers and on the Internet for a long time, and with good reason. It is easy to make, is incredibly tasty and can be transported to any social gathering with minimal effort in your Instant Pot.

INSTANT POT FUNCTIONS

• Slow Cook •

• Sauté •

1	packet (1 oz/28 g) dry onion soup mix	1
1	packet (1 oz/28 g) dry Italian dressing mix	1
1	packet (1 oz/28 g) dry brown gravy mix	1
1 cup	water	250 mL
1	boneless beef chuck roast (2½ to 3 lbs/1.25 to 1.5 kg)	1
1 tbsp	cornstarch	15 mL
½ cup	cold water	125 mL

Tip

This dish can also be made in 4 to 5 hours. In step 2, press Adjust once to change the heat level to "More." Leave the time at 4:00. Continue with step 3.

1. In a small bowl, whisk together onion soup mix, Italian dressing mix, gravy mix and 1 cup (250 mL) water. Pour ¼ cup (60 mL) of the mixture into the inner pot. Place roast in the pot and pour the remaining sauce mixture on top.

2. Close and lock the lid and turn the steam release handle to Venting. Press Slow Cook; the indicator will read "Normal." Press Adjust twice to change the heat level to "Less." Press ✚ to increase the time on the display to 7:00.

3. When the timer beeps, remove the lid and check to make sure the roast is tender and no longer pink inside. (If more cooking is needed, reset the slow cooker to "Less" and cook for 30 to 60 minutes.) Press Cancel. Transfer the roast to a serving plate and tent with foil.

4. In a small bowl, whisk together cornstarch and cold water. Press Sauté. Add the cornstarch mixture to the pot and cook, whisking, for 5 to 7 minutes or until gravy is thickened to your liking.

5. Slice roast against the grain and drizzle with gravy.

Variations

Add an 8-oz (227 mL) jar of picante sauce to the sauce mixture to add a little spiciness to your roast.

Mississippi Roast: Omit the onion soup mix and reduce the water in step 1 to ½ cup (125 mL). Sprinkle the dry mixes over the roast and dot with ½ cup (125 mL) butter. Top with 5 pepperoncini peppers from a jar. Continue with step 2.

No-Takeout Beef and Broccoli with Rice

This favorite Chinese dish is so easy to make at home using your slow cooker, you may never stop for takeout again. Head straight home and have a savory dish waiting for you.

MAKES 6 SERVINGS		
INSTANT POT FUNCTIONS		
• Slow Cook •		
• Sauté •		
3	cloves garlic, minced	3
¼ cup	packed brown sugar	60 mL
1 cup	ready-to-use beef broth	250 mL
¼ cup	tamari	60 mL
¼ cup	oyster sauce	60 mL
1 tbsp	sesame oil	15 mL
2 lbs	boneless beef sirloin, thinly sliced	1 kg
3 cups	frozen broccoli florets	750 mL
2 tbsp	cornstarch	30 mL
¼ cup	cold water	60 mL
3 cups	hot cooked white rice	750 mL

Tips

You can cook the white rice using the Rice function on your Instant Pot before making the beef and broccoli. Add 2 tbsp (30 mL) virgin olive oil or butter to the rice when cooking. Let the cooked rice cool, then cover and refrigerate until ready to use. Reheat and fluff with a fork before serving.

This dish can also be made in 3 to 4 hours. In step 2, press Adjust once to change the heat level to "More." Press ⊖ to decrease the time on the display to 3:00. Continue with step 3.

1. In the inner pot, combine garlic, brown sugar, broth, tamari, oyster sauce and oil, stirring well. Add beef and toss to coat with sauce.

2. Place the pot inside the cooker housing, close and lock the lid and turn the steam release handle to Venting. Press Slow Cook; the indicator will read "Normal." Press Adjust twice to change the heat level to "Less." Press ⊕ to increase the time on the display to 6:00.

3. When the timer beeps, remove the lid and check to make sure the beef is tender. (If more cooking is needed, reset the slow cooker to "Less" and cook for 1 to 2 hours.) Press Cancel.

4. Meanwhile, cook broccoli according to package directions. Drain and set aside.

5. In a small bowl, whisk together cornstarch and cold water. Gradually whisk into the pot until combined. Gently fold in broccoli. Press Sauté and cook, stirring occasionally, for 5 to 7 minutes or until sauce is thickened. Serve over rice.

Soul Food Oxtails with Tender Root Vegetables

This soul food staple is always worth the wait. If you have never tried oxtails, this is the perfect recipe to give them a true test. Succulent and flavorful, they are the ideal comfort food. And combined with root vegetables, they make a hearty one-pot meal.

MAKES 4 SERVINGS

INSTANT POT FUNCTIONS

- Sauté -
- Slow Cook -

3 lbs	sliced beef oxtails	1.5 kg
	Kosher salt and freshly ground black pepper	
1½ tbsp	virgin olive oil	22 mL
1 cup	dry red wine	250 mL
2 tbsp	tomato paste	30 mL
4	sprigs fresh thyme	4
2	bay leaves	2
2 cups	ready-to-use beef broth	500 mL
1 tbsp	Worcestershire sauce	15 mL
4	cloves garlic, minced	4
4	parsnips, coarsely chopped	4
3	carrots, coarsely chopped	3
2	onions, chopped	2

Tip

While braised oxtails are often served over rice, I especially like them with creamy mashed potatoes.

1. Season oxtails with salt and pepper. Press Sauté; the indicator will read "Normal." When the display says "Hot," add oil to the pot and heat until shimmering. Working in batches, add oxtails and cook, turning once, for 4 to 6 minutes or until browned on both sides. Transfer oxtails to a plate.

2. Add wine to the pot and cook for 1 minute, scraping up any browned bits from the bottom. Whisk in tomato paste. Stir in thyme sprigs, bay leaves, broth and Worcestershire sauce. Press Cancel. Add garlic, parsnips, carrots and onions, stirring well. Return oxtails to the pot, along with any accumulated juices.

3. Close and lock the lid and turn the steam release handle to Venting. Press Slow Cook; the indicator will read "Normal." Press Adjust twice to change the heat level to "Less." Press ✚ to increase the time on the display to 6:00.

4. When the timer beeps, remove the lid and check to make sure the oxtails are tender and no longer pink. (If more cooking is needed, reset the slow cooker to "Less" and cook for 30 to 60 minutes.) Discard thyme sprigs and bay leaves. Using a slotted spoon, transfer oxtails and vegetables to serving plates. Serve the remaining sauce in a gravy boat.

Side Dishes

Pressure Cooker

Slow Cooker

Quick and Easy Cook Functions

Chunky Picnic Potato Salad

A summertime party calls for a great potato salad that hits all the high notes. This version is easy to prepare, and the results are consistent every time.

- Instant Pot steam rack
- 3 canning jar screwbands

3	large eggs	3
	Cold water	
6	red-skinned potatoes (about 12 oz/375 g total)	6
1	stalk celery, chopped	1
¼ cup	chopped red onion	60 mL
	Kosher salt and freshly ground black pepper	
1 tbsp	chopped fresh dill	15 mL
½ cup	mayonnaise	125 mL
2 tsp	prepared yellow mustard	10 mL
1 tsp	apple cider vinegar	5 mL
2 tbsp	fresh parsley leaves	30 mL

Tips

If you prefer, you can substitute plain yogurt for the mayonnaise; increase the apple cider vinegar to 1¼ tsp (6 mL).

Eggs cooked in the pressure cooker do not need to be aged to make peeling them easier. Using fresh eggs will also help the whites keep their shape, without the typical indent on the end.

1. Add 1 cup (250 mL) water to the inner pot and place the steam rack in the pot. Place the screwbands on top of the rack. Place an egg in the middle of each screwband. Close and lock the lid and turn the steam release handle to Sealing. Press Manual; the indicator will read "High Pressure." Press Pressure once to adjust the pressure to "Low Pressure." Use the ⊖ button to decrease the time on the display to 6 minutes.

2. When the timer beeps, press Cancel. Let stand, covered, until the float valve drops down. Turn the steam release handle to Venting and remove the lid. Transfer eggs to a bowl of cold water to chill, refreshing water as necessary to keep cold. When cool enough to handle, peel and chop eggs and set aside. Drain water from the pot.

3. In the inner pot, combine potatoes and 1 cup (250 mL) cold water. Close and lock the lid and turn the steam release handle to Sealing. Press Manual; the indicator will read "High Pressure." Use the ⊖ button to decrease the time on the display to 4 minutes.

4. When the timer beeps, press Cancel and let the pot stand, covered, for 3 minutes. After 3 minutes, turn the steam release handle to Venting and remove the lid. Transfer potatoes to a cutting board. When cool enough to handle, cut potatoes into ½-inch (1 cm) cubes.

5. In a large bowl, combine potatoes, celery and onion. Season to taste with salt and pepper and toss gently. Add eggs and dill.

6. In a small bowl, combine mayonnaise, mustard and vinegar, mixing well. Gently fold into potato salad. Cover and refrigerate for at least 1 hour, until chilled, or for up to 1 day. Garnish with parsley before serving.

Tangy Black Bean and Heirloom Tomato Salad

Fresh, meaty heirloom tomatoes unite with sweet corn and black beans to make a simple, colorful dish that is highlighted by a tangy vinaigrette.

MAKES 6 SERVINGS

INSTANT POT FUNCTION
• Manual Pressure •

6	cloves garlic, minced	6
2	onions, chopped	2
1 lb	dried black beans, rinsed and soaked (see tip, below)	500 g
2 tsp	kosher salt, divided	10 mL
6 cups	water	1.5 L
2 tbsp	virgin olive oil	30 mL
4	heirloom tomatoes, chopped	4
1½ cups	frozen corn kernels, thawed and drained	375 mL
¼ cup	chopped fresh cilantro	60 mL
½ cup	lime juice	125 mL
½ cup	extra virgin olive oil	125 mL

1. In the inner pot, combine garlic, onions, beans, 1 tsp (5 mL) salt, water and virgin olive oil, stirring well.

2. Place the pot inside the cooker housing, close and lock the lid and turn the steam release handle to Sealing. Press Manual; the indicator will read "High Pressure." Use the ⊖ button to decrease the time on the display to 6 minutes.

3. When the timer beeps, press Cancel. Let stand, covered, until the float valve drops down. Turn the steam release handle to Venting and remove the lid. The beans should be evenly tender. (If more cooking is needed, cover the pot, press Sauté and cook, stirring occasionally, for 3 to 5 minutes or until tender.) Drain and rinse beans. Let stand until cool.

4. In a large bowl, combine beans, tomatoes and corn.

5. In a small bowl, combine cilantro, the remaining salt and lime juice. Gradually whisk in extra virgin olive oil. Pour over bean mixture and stir gently to combine. Let stand until beans are at room temperature before serving.

Tips

To soak the beans, place them in a large bowl and add at least 8 cups (2 L) cold water. Let stand for 8 to 12 hours, changing the water halfway through. Drain and rinse the beans.

For ½ cup (125 mL) lime juice, you will need about 4 limes.

For even more flavor and texture, add a cubed avocado to the salad with the tomatoes and corn.

When preparing beans of any type using the Manual Pressure function, make sure to fill the pot no more than halfway full. Do not attempt to double or triple the recipe; otherwise, the exhaust valve may become clogged as the beans froth up under pressure. Adding oil with the beans will help to reduce the amount of froth.

Chickpea, Kale and Sprout Salad

With its bounty of greens, punch of protein, light dressing and superpower sprouts, this salad makes for a fantastic midday meal.

MAKES 2 SERVINGS

INSTANT POT FUNCTIONS

• Manual Pressure•
• Steam •

- **Instant Pot steam rack**
- **Steamer basket**

1 cup	dried chickpeas (see tips, opposite), rinsed	250 mL
1	sprig fresh thyme	1
1 tsp	chopped fresh parsley	5 mL
2 cups	water	500 mL
1½ tsp	virgin olive oil	7 mL
8 cups	chopped trimmed kale	2 L
3	green onions, sliced	3
1 tsp	soy sauce	5 mL
	Juice of 1 lemon	
2 tbsp	extra virgin olive oil	30 mL
	Kosher salt and freshly ground black pepper	
¼ cup	lentil or bean sprouts	60 mL

1. In the inner pot, combine chickpeas, thyme sprig, parsley, water and virgin olive oil, stirring well.

2. Place the pot inside the cooker housing, close and lock the lid and turn the steam release handle to Sealing. Press Manual; the indicator will read "High Pressure." Use the ✚ button to increase the time on the display to 38 minutes.

3. When the timer beeps, press Cancel. Let stand, covered, until the float valve drops down. Turn the steam release handle to Venting and remove the lid. The chickpeas should be tender. (If more cooking is needed, cover the pot, press Sauté and cook, stirring occasionally, for 3 to 5 minutes or until tender.) Drain and rinse chickpeas, reserving 1 cup (250 mL) liquid. Discard thyme sprig. Transfer chickpeas to a large bowl and let stand until cool.

4. Return the reserved liquid to the pot and place the steam rack in the pot. Add kale to the steamer basket and place the basket on the rack. Close and lock the lid and turn the steam release handle to Sealing. Press Steam; the indicator will read "High Pressure." Use the ➖ button to decrease the time on the display to 1 minute.

5. When the timer beeps, press Cancel and turn the steam release handle to Venting. When the float valve drops down, remove the lid. Remove the steamer basket and let kale stand until cool. Add kale to chickpeas.

6. In a small bowl, combine green onions, soy sauce and lemon juice. Gradually whisk in extra virgin olive oil.

7. Pour dressing over chickpea mixture and toss gently to combine. Season to taste with salt and pepper. Garnish with sprouts.

Tips

To speed up the cooking process and reduce the gas in the chickpeas, you can presoak the chickpeas. Place the chickpeas in a medium bowl and cover with 2 cups (500 mL) cold water. Let stand for 8 to 12 hours, changing the water halfway through. Drain and rinse the chickpeas. In step 2, set the cooking time to 18 minutes.

When preparing beans of any type using the Manual Pressure function, make sure to fill the pot no more than halfway full. Do not attempt to double or triple the recipe; otherwise, the exhaust valve may become clogged as the beans froth up under pressure. Adding oil with the beans will help to reduce the amount of froth.

Brussels Sprouts with Bacon and Shallots

If you think you don't care for Brussels sprouts, your opinion of these oft-ignored green bundles will soon change when you taste this dish, infused with bacon, shallots and garlic.

MAKES 4 SERVINGS

INSTANT POT FUNCTIONS

- Sauté -
- Manual Pressure-

	Nonstick cooking spray	
4	slices thick-cut bacon, finely chopped	4
1	large shallot, thinly sliced	1
3	cloves garlic, minced	3
1 lb	Brussels sprouts, trimmed and cut in half	500 g
½ tsp	kosher salt	2 mL
¼ tsp	freshly ground black pepper	1 mL
½ cup	ready-to-use chicken broth	125 mL
1 tbsp	balsamic vinegar reduction (see tip, at right)	15 mL
½ cup	chopped pecans, toasted (see tip, at right)	125 mL

1. Spray the inner pot with cooking spray. Press Sauté; the indicator will read "Normal." When the display says "Hot," add bacon to the pot and cook, stirring, for 4 to 5 minutes or until medium-crisp. Using a slotted spoon, transfer bacon to a plate lined with paper towels.

2. Add shallot to the pot and cook, stirring, for 3 to 4 minutes or until softened. Add garlic and cook, stirring, for 1 minute or until fragrant. Press Cancel. Add Brussels sprouts, salt, pepper, broth and vinegar, stirring well.

3. Close and lock the lid and turn the steam release handle to Sealing. Press Manual; the indicator will read "High Pressure." Use the ⊖ button to decrease the time on the display to 2 minutes.

4. When the timer beeps, press Cancel and turn the steam release handle to Venting. When the float valve drops down, remove the lid. Check to make sure a fork inserted into the stem end pierces the Brussels sprouts easily. (If more cooking is needed, close and lock the lid and let stand for 2 minutes.) Transfer to a serving bowl and sprinkle with pecans and bacon.

Tips

Choose Brussels sprouts that are uniform in size, for even cooking.

You can purchase balsamic vinegar reduction or make your own. In a small saucepan, bring 1 cup (250 mL) balsamic vinegar and ¼ cup (60 mL) liquid honey or pure maple syrup to a boil over high heat. Reduce heat and simmer for 10 minutes or until reduced to about ⅓ cup (75 mL). Let cool. Leftover balsamic vinegar reduction can be drizzled over a Caprese salad, cut fruits or roasted vegetables.

You can toast the pecans in your Instant Pot before beginning step 1. Press Sauté; when the display says "Hot," add the pecans and cook, stirring, for 2 to 3 minutes or until fragrant. Press Cancel and transfer the pecans to a plate to cool. (They can also be toasted in a skillet over medium-high heat for 2 to 3 minutes.)

Root Vegetable Ratatouille

Ratatouille is a traditional French Provençal dish that is commonly served as an easy and light summertime dish. But with something so delicious, why stop there? With this version, you can continue to make this delightful dish with fall root vegetables.

MAKES 6 SERVINGS		

INSTANT POT FUNCTIONS		
• Sauté •		
• Manual Pressure •		

2 tbsp	virgin olive oil	30 mL
1	onion, thinly sliced	1
4	cloves garlic, thinly sliced	4
4	parsnips, cut into 1½-inch (4 cm) chunks	4
4	carrots, cut into 1-inch (2.5 cm) chunks	4
3	rutabagas, peeled and cut into 1-inch (2.5 cm) chunks	3
8 oz	cherry tomatoes	250 g
1½ tsp	herbes de Provence	7 mL
1 tsp	kosher salt	5 mL
Pinch	freshly ground black pepper	Pinch
1 cup	ready-to-use vegetable broth	250 mL
3 tbsp	butter, melted	45 mL
½ cup	fresh basil chiffonade (see tip, below)	125 mL

Tips

Cut each root vegetable into chunks of the same size, so they cook evenly and are done at the same time.

To chiffonade basil, remove the stems and stack 10 or more leaves. Roll the leaves up lengthwise into a fairly tight spiral, then cut crosswise into thin strips. Fluff the strips.

1. Press Sauté; the indicator will read "Normal." When the display says "Hot," add oil to the pot and heat until shimmering. Add onion and cook, stirring, for 4 to 5 minutes or until translucent. Add garlic and cook, stirring, for 1 minute or until fragrant. Press Cancel. Add parsnips, carrots, rutabagas, tomatoes, herbes de Provence, salt, pepper, broth and butter, stirring well.

2. Close and lock the lid and turn the steam release handle to Sealing. Press Manual; the indicator will read "High Pressure." Use the ⊖ button to decrease the time on the display to 4 minutes.

3. When the timer beeps, press Cancel and turn the steam release handle to Venting. When the float valve drops down, remove the lid. Check to make sure the vegetables are fork-tender. (If more cooking is needed, reset the pressure to "High Pressure" for 1 minute.) Serve garnished with basil.

Potato and Celery Root Mash

This new twist on mashed potatoes features an extra boost of vibrant flavor from the celery roots and garlic.

INSTANT POT FUNCTIONS

• Manual Pressure •

• Sauté •

2 lbs	gold-skinned potatoes, peeled and quartered	1 kg
2	medium celery roots, peeled and cut into ½-inch (1 cm) pieces	2
1 cup	water	250 mL
3	cloves garlic, minced	3
¾ cup	heavy or whipping (35%) cream	175 mL
¼ cup	butter	60 mL
1 tbsp	tahini (optional)	15 mL
	Kosher salt and freshly ground black pepper	

Tips

The easiest way to peel a celery root is to trim the ends and place it cut end down on a cutting board. Cut off the remaining skin in a vertical motion, making squared off edges. If any small nooks of skin remain, trim them with a knife.

When using the Quick Release method to release pressure, keep your hands and face away from the hole on the top of the steam release handle so you don't get scalded by the escaping steam.

1. In the inner pot, combine potatoes, celery roots and water.

2. Place the pot inside the cooker housing, close and lock the lid and turn the steam release handle to Sealing. Press Manual; the indicator will read "High Pressure." Use the ⊖ button to decrease the time on the display to 6 minutes.

3. When the timer beeps, press Cancel and turn the steam release handle to Venting. When the float valve drops down, remove the lid. Check to make sure the vegetables are fork-tender. (If more cooking is needed, reset the manual pressure to "High Pressure" for 2 minutes.) Drain potatoes and celery roots.

4. Press Sauté. Add garlic, cream, butter and tahini (if using) to the pot. Cook, stirring, for 3 to 4 minutes or until butter melts and cream is bubbling around the edges. Add potatoes and celery roots, mashing until well combined and your desired consistency. Season to taste with salt and pepper.

Rustic Boston Not-Baked Beans

My mother was always asked to bring her version of this dish to any get-together. I have been trying to recreate it for many years, and I have finally succeeded! I hope you enjoy it as much as I do.

MAKES 6 SERVINGS

INSTANT POT FUNCTIONS

• Manual Pressure •
• Sauté •

2 cups	dried navy beans (see tip, below), rinsed	500 mL
2 tsp	kosher salt	10 mL
11 cups	water, divided	2.75 L
6	slices thick-cut bacon, finely chopped	6
1	yellow onion, finely chopped	1
1 tsp	dry mustard	5 mL
½ tsp	ground cloves	2 mL
1 tbsp	virgin olive oil	15 mL
½ cup	packed brown sugar	125 mL
3 tbsp	tomato paste	45 mL
¼ cup	dark (cooking) molasses	60 mL
2 tbsp	bourbon (optional)	30 mL
2 tbsp	prepared yellow mustard	30 mL

Tips

Instead of pressure-soaking the beans in steps 1 to 3, you can presoak them in 8 cups (2 L) water at room temperature for 8 to 12 hours.

When preparing beans of any type using the Manual Pressure function, make sure to fill the pot no more than halfway full. Do not attempt to double or triple the recipe; otherwise, the exhaust valve may become clogged as the beans froth up under pressure.

1. In the inner pot, combine beans, salt and 8 cups (2 L) water.

2. Place the pot inside the cooker housing, close and lock the lid and turn the steam release handle to Sealing. Press Manual; the indicator will read "High Pressure." Use the ⊟ button to decrease the time on the display to 2 minutes.

3. When the timer beeps, press Cancel and let the pot stand, covered, for 10 minutes. After 10 minutes, turn the steam release handle to Venting and remove the lid. Drain and rinse beans. Rinse and dry the pot.

4. Press Sauté; the indicator will read "Normal." When the display says "Hot," add bacon and onion to the pot and cook, stirring, for 4 to 5 minutes or until bacon is medium-crisp. Press Cancel. Return beans to the pot and stir in dry mustard, cloves, the remaining water and oil, stirring well.

5. Close and lock the lid and turn the steam release handle to Sealing. Press Manual; the indicator will read "High Pressure." Use the ⊟ button to decrease the time on the display to 20 minutes.

6. When the timer beeps, press Cancel and let the pot stand, covered, for 10 minutes. After 10 minutes, turn the steam release handle to Venting and remove the lid. Check to make sure the beans are al dente. (If more cooking is needed, reset the manual pressure to "High Pressure" for 4 minutes.)

7. Press Sauté. Add brown sugar, tomato paste, molasses, bourbon (if using) and yellow mustard; cook, stirring often, for 5 to 7 minutes or until thickened to your liking.

Old-Fashioned Rice Pilaf

You have likely been making this type of rice pilaf from a box for years. Now you can make it just as quickly, but with fresh ingredients and no preservatives.

INSTANT POT FUNCTIONS

• Sauté •

• Manual Pressure •

2 tbsp	butter	30 mL
1 tbsp	virgin olive oil	15 mL
2 cups	basmati rice	500 mL
½ cup	broken dried angel hair pasta (1-inch/2.5 cm lengths)	125 mL
2	carrots, finely julienned (see tip, below)	2
1	onion, finely chopped	1
1 cup	frozen petite green peas	250 mL
4 cups	ready-to-use chicken or vegetable broth	1 L

Tips

To julienne carrots, first cut them into 2-inch (5 cm) lengths, then cut off the sides of the carrots to make a rectangle. (You do not need to cut the small tip.) Cut the rectangle into ¹⁄₁₆-inch (2 mm) slabs. Stack the slabs and cut them into ¹⁄₁₆-inch (2 mm) strips.

This recipe can be doubled, but make sure to fill the pot no more than halfway; otherwise, the exhaust valve may become clogged, resulting in excess pressure.

For a simpler rice pilaf, you can omit the peas and carrots.

For an added dimension, stir in ½ cup (125 mL) raisins before serving.

1. Press Sauté; the indicator will read "Normal." When the display says "Hot," add butter and oil to the pot and heat until butter is melted. Add rice and pasta; cook, stirring, for 1 to 2 minutes or until pasta turns golden and rice is lightly toasted. Add carrots, onion and peas; cook, stirring, for 3 minutes or until onion is softened. Stir in broth. Press Cancel.

2. Close and lock the lid and turn the steam release handle to Sealing. Press Manual; the indicator will read "High Pressure." Use the ⊖ button to decrease the time on the display to 3 minutes.

3. When the timer beeps, press Cancel and let the pot stand, covered, for 10 minutes. After 10 minutes, turn the steam release handle to Venting and remove the lid. Stir rice vigorously before serving.

Spiced Millet Pilaf with Raisins

This lightly spiced pilaf works very well with a variety of dishes, but particularly Indian fare. The millet adds a nice crunchy texture.

MAKES 4 SERVINGS

INSTANT POT FUNCTIONS

• Sauté •

• Manual Pressure •

1 tbsp	ghee (see tip, below)	15 mL
1 tbsp	cumin seeds	15 mL
½ tsp	ground cardamom	2 mL
1	onion, halved and thinly sliced	1
2 cups	millet, rinsed	500 mL
1	bay leaf	1
1 tsp	kosher salt	5 mL
3 cups	water	750 mL
¼ cup	golden raisins	60 mL

Tips

Ghee is a type of clarified butter used in Indian cuisine. It is commonly believed to have many health benefits. Ghee can be found in the Indian cooking section of most well-stocked grocery stores. You can substitute butter or virgin olive oil for the ghee.

This recipe can be doubled, but make sure to fill the pot no more than halfway; otherwise, the exhaust valve may become clogged, resulting in excess pressure.

1. Press Sauté; the indicator will read "Normal." When the display says "Hot," add ghee to the pot and heat until melted. Add cumin seeds and cardamom; cook, stirring, for 1 minute or until seeds begin to sputter. Add onion and cook, stirring, for 3 to 5 minutes or until softened. Add millet, stirring to coat with ghee. Add bay leaf, salt and water. Press Cancel.

2. Close and lock the lid and turn the steam release handle to Sealing. Press Manual; the indicator will read "High Pressure." Use the ● button to decrease the time on the display to 1 minute.

3. When the timer beeps, press Cancel and let the pot stand, covered, for 10 minutes. After 10 minutes, turn the steam release handle to Venting and remove the lid. Discard bay leaf. Stir in raisins and fluff millet with a fork.

Easy Moroccan Couscous

These tiny pearls of wheat pasta are a staple throughout North Africa. Here, they get an infusion of spices, for a delightful side dish to accompany lamb or salmon.

MAKES 2 SERVINGS

INSTANT POT FUNCTIONS
• Sauté •
• Manual Pressure •

⅓ cup	sliced almonds	75 mL
1 tbsp	virgin olive oil	15 mL
1	small red onion, finely chopped	1
1 cup	couscous	250 mL
½ tsp	ground coriander	2 mL
¼ tsp	freshly ground black pepper	1 mL
Pinch	saffron threads	Pinch
1 cup	ready-to-use vegetable broth	250 mL
¾ cup	dry white wine	175 mL
⅓ cup	golden raisins	75 mL
	Kosher salt	

Tip

This recipe can be doubled, but make sure to fill the pot no more than halfway; otherwise, the exhaust valve may become clogged, resulting in excess pressure.

1. Press Sauté; the indicator will read "Normal." When the display says "Hot," add almonds and cook, stirring, for 2 to 3 minutes or until just golden. Transfer almonds to a plate.

2. Add oil to the pot and heat until shimmering. Add onion and cook, stirring, for 3 to 5 minutes or until softened. Press Cancel. Add couscous, coriander, pepper, saffron, broth and wine, stirring well.

3. Close and lock the lid and turn the steam release handle to Sealing. Press Manual; the indicator will read "High Pressure." Use the ⊖ button to decrease the time on the display to 3 minutes.

4. When the timer beeps, press Cancel. Let stand, covered, until the float valve drops down. Turn the steam release handle to Venting and remove the lid. Check to make sure the couscous is tender with a bit of texture. (If more cooking is needed, cover pot and let stand for 2 minutes.) Stir in almond and raisins, then fluff couscous with a fork. Season to taste with salt.

Mediterranean Lentil Salad

While I like to serve this divine lentil salad as a side dish, it would definitely work as a main course for vegetarians and anyone looking for a new idea for meatless Mondays.

1½ cups	dried chickpeas (see tips, page 119), rinsed	375 mL
1	sprig fresh thyme	1
1 tsp	chopped fresh parsley	5 mL
3 cups	water	750 mL
5 tbsp	virgin olive oil, divided	75 mL
1 cup	dried French green (Puy) lentils, rinsed	250 mL
1 tsp	herbes de Provence	5 mL
½ tsp	kosher salt	2 mL
1¾ cups	ready-to-use vegetable broth	425 mL
4 tbsp	dry white wine, divided	60 mL
1	clove garlic, minced	1
½ cup	chopped fresh mint	125 mL
12 oz	cherry tomatoes, quartered	375 g
¼ cup	chopped black olives	60 mL
½ cup	crumbled feta cheese	125 mL

Tip

You can substitute a 15-oz (425 mL) can of chickpeas for the dried chickpeas. You can then eliminate steps 1 to 3 and the thyme, parsley, water and 1 tbsp (15 mL) oil.

1. In the inner pot, combine chickpeas, thyme, parsley, water and 1 tbsp (15 mL) oil, stirring well.

2. Place the pot inside the cooker housing, close and lock the lid and turn the steam release handle to Sealing. Press Manual; the indicator will read "High Pressure." Use the ✛ button to increase the time on the display to 38 minutes.

3. When the timer beeps, press Cancel. Let stand, covered, until the float valve drops down. Turn the steam release handle to Venting and remove the lid. The chickpeas should be tender. (If more cooking is needed, cover the pot and press Sauté. Cook, stirring, for 3 to 5 minutes or until tender.) Drain and rinse chickpeas and set aside. Rinse and dry inner pot.

4. In the inner pot, combine chickpeas, lentils, herbes de Provence, salt, broth and 1 tbsp (15 mL) wine. Place the pot inside the cooker housing, close and lock the lid and turn the steam release handle to Venting. Press Slow Cook; the indicator will read "Normal." Press Adjust twice to change the heat level to "Less." Press ➖ to decrease the time on the display to 3:00.

5. When the timer beeps, remove the lid and check to make sure the lentils are firm-tender. (If more cooking is needed, reset the slow cooker to "More" for 15 minutes.) Press Cancel.

6. In a small bowl, whisk together garlic, mint and the remaining wine. Gradually whisk in the remaining oil until emulsified. Drizzle over mixture in pot. Gently stir in tomatoes and olives.

7. Transfer salad to a serving dish and garnish with feta.

Tangy Beets with Feta and Walnuts

I love beets just about any way they are prepared, but this is one of my favorites. You eliminate some of the spattering red mess that comes with boiling them, and the nuts and feta add a unique tang and texture.

INSTANT POT FUNCTIONS		
• Sauté •		
• Slow Cook •		

¼ cup	chopped walnuts	60 mL
	Nonstick cooking spray	
2	cloves garlic, minced	2
4½ cups	sliced peeled beets (about 7 medium)	1.125 L
1 tsp	kosher salt	5 mL
1 cup	white grape juice	250 mL
½ cup	balsamic vinegar	125 mL
1 tbsp	cornstarch	15 mL
1 tbsp	cold water	15 mL
¼ cup	crumbled feta cheese	60 mL

Tips

Use kitchen gloves while peeling and slicing the beets to avoid staining your hands.

The beet leaves can be used in salads with other lettuces.

1. Press Sauté; the indicator will read "Normal." When the display says "Hot," add walnuts and cook, stirring, for 4 to 5 minutes or until browned and fragrant. Transfer walnuts to a plate.

2. Spray the inner pot with cooking spray. Add garlic, beets, salt, grape juice and vinegar to the pot, stirring well.

3. Place the pot inside the cooker housing, close and lock the lid and turn the steam release handle to Venting. Press Slow Cook; the indicator will read "Normal." Press Adjust once to change the heat level to "More." Press ⊖ to decrease the time on the display to 3:00.

4. When the timer beeps, remove the lid and check to make sure the beets are fork-tender. (If more cooking is needed, reset the slow cooker to "More" for 30 minutes.) Press Cancel.

5. In a small bowl, whisk together cornstarch and cold water. Press Sauté. Add the cornstarch mixture to the pot and cook, stirring occasionally, for 7 to 9 minutes or until sauce is thickened. Serve sprinkled with feta and walnuts.

Root Vegetable Ratatouille (page 121)

Mediterranean Lentil Salad (page 127)

Quinoa and Edamame Salad (page 138)

Thai Crazy Meatballs (page 162)

Lamb Shanks with Red Wine and Mushrooms (page 174)

Pork and Shrimp Wontons (page 179)

Classic Petite Cheesecake (page 187)

Lemon Mousse with
Mixed Berries (page 195)

Curried Spinach

If you love creamed spinach, the infusion of spicy Middle Eastern seasonings in this dish will make you swoon. The flavors are truly intoxicating.

INSTANT POT FUNCTION
• Slow Cook •

3	packages (each 10 oz/300 g) frozen spinach, thawed and drained	3
4	cloves garlic, minced	4
1	onion, chopped	1
1	2-inch (5 cm) piece gingerroot, grated	1
2 tsp	curry powder	10 mL
1 tsp	ground cumin	5 mL
½ tsp	ground turmeric	2 mL
½ tsp	kosher salt	2 mL
¼ cup	ghee (see tip, below)	60 mL
¼ cup	ready-to-use chicken or vegetable broth	60 mL
¼ cup	plain yogurt	60 mL
2 tsp	freshly squeezed lemon juice	10 mL

Tips

Ghee can be found in the Indian cooking section of most well-stocked grocery stores. You can substitute butter, if you prefer.

You can use 2 tbsp (30 mL) chopped or minced ginger from a jar in place of the grated gingerroot. Look for small glass jars of ginger at specialty markets and well-stocked grocery stores. Once opened, they must be refrigerated. I love to keep them on hand, as it makes it so much easier to add ginger to recipes.

1. In the inner pot, combine spinach, garlic, onion, ginger, curry powder, cumin, turmeric, salt, ghee and broth, stirring well.

2. Place the pot inside the cooker housing, close and lock the lid and turn the steam release handle to Venting. Press Slow Cook; the indicator will read "Normal." Press Adjust twice to change the heat level to "Less." Press ⊖ to decrease the time on the display to 3:00.

3. When 30 minutes remains in the cooking time, stir in yogurt and lemon juice, then relock the lid. When the timer beeps, remove the lid, stir the spinach and check to make sure the flavors are melded and spinach is cooked to desired tenderness. (If more cooking is needed, reset the slow cooker to "Less" for 30 minutes.)

Creamy Scalloped Potatoes and Parsnips

Classic scalloped potatoes get new life when paired with sweet and nutty parsnips. This dish is an easy way to add more vegetables to your arsenal.

MAKES 6 SERVINGS

INSTANT POT FUNCTIONS

• Sauté •
• Slow Cook •

⅓ cup	butter	75 mL
3 tbsp	all-purpose flour	45 mL
1½ cups	heavy or whipping (35%) cream	375 mL
1 tbsp	dry mustard	15 mL
1½ tsp	kosher salt	7 mL
Pinch	freshly ground black pepper	Pinch
2	russet potatoes (about 12 oz/375 g), peeled, cut in half lengthwise, then cut into ¼-inch (0.5 cm) slices	2
2	parsnips, cut into ¼-inch (0.5 cm) slices	2
1	onion, chopped	1
2 cups	shredded sharp (old) Cheddar cheese	500 mL
	Hungarian paprika	

> **Tip**
> This dish can also be made in 3½ hours. In step 2, press Adjust once to change the heat level to "More." Press ⊖ to decrease the time on the display to 3:30. Continue with step 3.

1. Press Sauté; the indicator will read "Normal." When the display says "Hot," add butter to the pot and heat until melted. Whisk in flour and cook, whisking, for 2 minutes or until flour is incorporated and the floury smell has cooked off. Slowly whisk in cream until smooth. Stir in mustard, salt and pepper. Press Cancel. Add potatoes, parsnips and onions, tossing to coat with sauce.

2. Close and lock the lid and turn the steam release handle to Venting. Press Slow Cook; the indicator will read "Normal." Press Adjust twice to change the heat level to "Less." Press ⊕ to increase the time on the display to 7:00.

3. When the timer beeps, remove the lid and check to make sure the vegetables are fork-tender. (If more cooking is needed, reset the slow cooker to "More" for 30 minutes.) Press Cancel.

4. Add cheese, stirring well. Cover and let stand for 5 minutes or until cheese is melted. Sprinkle with paprika.

Sweet Potato Casserole

Creamy and sweet, these potatoes are taken up a notch with hints of cinnamon, nutmeg and vanilla. This is a wonderful option for a small holiday gathering, because it frees up your oven for other dishes.

MAKES 4 SERVINGS

INSTANT POT FUNCTION

• Slow Cook •

2 lbs	sweet potatoes, peeled and cut into 1/2-inch (1 cm) chunks	1 kg
1/4 cup	packed brown sugar	60 mL
1 tsp	ground cinnamon	5 mL
1/2 tsp	ground nutmeg	2 mL
1/4 tsp	kosher salt	1 mL
2 tbsp	butter, cut into pieces	30 mL
1 tsp	vanilla extract	5 mL

Tip

This dish can also be made in 3 1/2 hours. In step 2, press Adjust once to change the heat level to "More." Press ⊖ to decrease the time on the display to 3:30. Continue with step 3.

1. In the inner pot, combine sweet potatoes, brown sugar, cinnamon, nutmeg and salt.

2. Place the pot inside the cooker housing, close and lock the lid and turn the steam release handle to Venting. Press Slow Cook; the indicator will read "Normal." Press Adjust twice to change the heat level to "Less." Press ⊕ to increase the time on the display to 7:00.

3. When the timer beeps, remove the lid. Check to make sure the potatoes are fork-tender. (If more cooking is needed, reset the slow cooker to "Less" for 30 minutes.) Gently stir in butter and vanilla.

Mexican Refried Beans

This seasoned bean dish is a staple in Mexican, Tex-Mex and Latin American cuisines. The name is somewhat misleading, as the beans are rarely fried at all, let alone more than once. Instead, the Spanish term *refritos* simply implies well cooked. The dish is so versatile it can be served as a side dish with breakfast, lunch or dinner or as a great dip for tortilla chips.

MAKES 6 SERVINGS

INSTANT POT FUNCTION

• Slow Cook •

3 cups	dried borlotti beans	750 mL
	Water	
6	cloves garlic, minced	6
1	onion, cut in half	1
1	small jalapeño pepper, seeded and chopped	1
2 tbsp	kosher salt	30 mL
1½ tsp	freshly ground black pepper	7 mL
¼ tsp	ground cumin	1 mL
1 cup	shredded sharp (old) Cheddar cheese	250 mL

Tips

You can substitute pinto beans or cannellini (white kidney) beans for the borlotti beans, if desired.

Do not use the pressure-soaking method for these beans, as the amount of beans and water would fill the pot above the recommended level for safe cooking under pressure.

1. Place beans in a large bowl and cover with water. Let stand for 8 to 12 hours, draining and changing water once halfway through. Drain and rinse beans.

2. In the inner pot, combine beans, garlic, onion, jalapeño, salt, pepper, cumin and 9 cups (2.25 L) water, stirring well.

3. Place the pot inside the cooker housing, close and lock the lid and turn the steam release handle to Venting. Press Slow Cook; the indicator will read "Normal." Press ✚ to increase the time on the display to 8:00. Check the beans periodically, in case you need to add more water to keep them moist and covered.

4. When the timer beeps, remove the lid and check to make sure the beans are very tender and easy to mash. (If more cooking is needed, reset the slow cooker to "Normal" for 1 hour.) Drain beans, reserving the cooking liquid.

5. Using a potato masher, mash beans to your desired consistency, adding the reserved cooking liquid as needed. Serve sprinkled with cheese.

Cajun Red Beans and Rice

This classic Louisiana dish brings together cuisines from the Spanish, Italian and Arcadian settlers in that region. The red beans, rice and okra coalesce for a rustic, spicy side dish.

INSTANT POT FUNCTIONS

- Sauté -
- Slow Cook -

1 tbsp	virgin olive oil	15 mL
3	cloves garlic, minced	3
	Kosher salt	
1 tsp	cayenne pepper	5 mL
1 tsp	garlic powder	5 mL
1/2 tsp	onion powder	2 mL
1/2 tsp	sweet paprika	2 mL
1/2 tsp	dried oregano	2 mL
1/4 tsp	dried thyme	1 mL
	Freshly ground black pepper	
8 oz	dried small red beans, rinsed and soaked (see tip, at right)	250 g
1	green bell pepper, chopped	1
4 cups	ready-to-use chicken or vegetable broth	1 L
2 cups	frozen okra, thawed	500 mL
2 cups	cooked rice	500 mL
2	tomatoes, cut into 1/2-inch (1 cm) pieces	2

1. Press Sauté; the indicator will read "Normal." When the display says "Hot," add oil to the pot and heat until shimmering. Add garlic, 1 1/2 tsp (7 mL) salt, cayenne, garlic powder, onion powder, paprika, oregano, thyme and 1/4 tsp (1 mL) black pepper; cook, stirring, for 1 to 2 minutes or until fragrant. Add beans, green pepper and broth, stirring well. Press Cancel.

2. Close and lock the lid and turn the steam release handle to Venting. Press Slow Cook; the indicator will read "Normal." Press Adjust twice to change the heat level to "Less." Press ➕ to increase the time on the display to 9:00.

3. When the timer beeps, remove the lid and check to make sure the beans are tender. (If more cooking is needed, reset the slow cooker to "Less" for 1 hour.)

4. Add okra and rice to the pot, stirring well. Cover and let stand for 10 minutes or until okra and rice are heated through. Stir in tomatoes and season to taste with salt and pepper.

Tips

To soak the beans, place them in a large bowl and add at least 4 cups (1 L) cold water. Let stand for 8 to 12 hours, changing the water halfway through. Drain and rinse the beans.

When cutting tomatoes, use a sharp chef's knife to avoid squashing the tomatoes.

This dish can also be made in 5 hours. In step 2, press Adjust once to change the heat level to "More." Press ➕ to increase the time on the display to 5:00. Continue with step 3.

Butternut Squash Risotto with Peas

Risotto is one of those dishes that is so appealing to eat, yet so completely frustrating to make. I've taken away the frustrating part of the equation with this slow cooker version that yields creamy rice highlighted by sweet butternut squash and tender sweet peas.

MAKES 6 SERVINGS

INSTANT POT FUNCTIONS

- Sauté -
- Slow Cook -

6 cups	ready-to-use chicken or vegetable broth, divided	1.5 L
3 tbsp	butter, divided	45 mL
1	onion, finely chopped	1
2 cups	Arborio rice	500 mL
½ cup	dry white wine	125 mL
2 cups	cubed butternut squash (½-inch/1 cm cubes)	500 mL
	Kosher salt	
1 cup	frozen sweet peas, thawed	250 mL
1 cup	freshly grated Parmesan cheese	250 mL
1 tbsp	chopped fresh thyme	15 mL
	Freshly ground black pepper	

Tips

If your risotto is not creamy enough for your liking, stir in more hot chicken broth as desired.

Do not substitute another type of rice for the Arborio rice in this recipe. Arborio rice gives this dish the right amount of texture and starch for a perfect risotto.

1. In a small saucepan, heat 4 cups (1 L) broth over medium-high heat for 4 minutes or until steaming. Set aside and keep hot.

2. Press Sauté; the indicator will read "Normal." When the display says "Hot," add 1 tbsp (15 mL) butter and heat until melted. Add onion and rice; cook, stirring, for 3 to 5 minutes or until ends of rice are transparent and onion is softened. Press Cancel.

3. Add wine, stirring well, and let stand for 2 minutes or until wine is almost completely absorbed. Add squash, ½ tsp (2 mL) salt and hot broth, stirring well.

4. Close and lock the lid and turn the steam release handle to Venting. Press Slow Cook; the indicator will read "Normal." Press Adjust once to change the heat level to "More." Press ⊖ to decrease the time on the display to 2:00.

5. When the timer beeps, remove the lid and check to make sure the risotto is tender. (If more cooking is needed, reset the slow cooker to "More" for 30 minutes.) Press Cancel.

6. Heat the remaining broth as in step 1 and pour over risotto, stirring gently for about 1 minute or until rice is creamy and liquid is absorbed. Gently stir in peas, cover and let stand for 5 minutes. Gently stir in Parmesan, thyme and the remaining butter. Season to taste with salt and pepper.

Green Beans and Toasted Slivered Almonds

Here, French green beans float gracefully in a lemony butter sauce and are garnished with delicate toasted slivered almonds.

INSTANT POT FUNCTIONS

• Steam •

• Sauté •

- **Instant Pot steam rack**
- **Steamer basket**

1½ lbs	thin French green beans, trimmed	750 g
2 tbsp	butter	30 mL
2 tbsp	virgin olive oil	30 mL
½ cup	slivered almonds	125 mL
1	clove garlic, minced	1
	Juice of 1 lemon	
	Kosher salt and freshly ground black pepper	

Tips

At the market, pick out each bean individually to make sure you have the best quality and even size and shape.

You can use regular green beans, but increase the steaming time in step 1 to 6 minutes.

1. Add 1 cup (250 mL) water to the inner pot and place the steam rack in the pot. Add beans to the steamer basket and place on the rack. Close and lock the lid and turn the steam release handle to Sealing. Press Steam; the indicator will read "High Pressure." Use the ⊖ button to decrease the time on the display to 3 minutes.

2. When the timer beeps, press Cancel and turn the steam release handle to Venting. When the float valve drops down, remove the lid. The beans should be just tender-crisp. (If more cooking is needed, reset the steamer for 1 minute.) Press Cancel.

3. Remove the steamer basket and plunge beans into cold water to quickly cool them. Drain and spread on paper towels to dry. Remove the steam rack, drain the water from the pot and wipe the pot dry.

4. Press Sauté; the indicator will read "Normal." Press Adjust twice to decrease the heat level to "Less." When the display says "Hot," add butter and oil to the pot and heat until butter is melted. Add almonds and cook, stirring, for 3 to 5 minutes or until golden brown all over. Using a slotted spoon, transfer almonds to a plate.

5. Add garlic to the pot and cook, stirring, for 1 minute or until fragrant. Add beans and cook, stirring occasionally, for 6 to 8 minutes or until beans are lightly browned. Stir in lemon juice and season to taste with salt and pepper. Serve sprinkled with almonds.

Creamy Polenta with Sun-Dried Tomatoes and Olives

A bubbling pot of polenta is so tantalizing it is hard to resist. When you cook it using the Instant Pot, you are assured a creamy, soothing dish that belies its grainy, mushy roots.

MAKES 6 SERVINGS

INSTANT POT FUNCTIONS
• Sauté •
• Rice •

2 tbsp	virgin olive oil	30 mL
1	small onion, finely chopped	1
2	cloves garlic, minced	2
⅓ cup	finely diced dry-packed sun-dried tomatoes	75 mL
¼ cup	chopped drained green olives with pimentos	60 mL
1	bay leaf	1
3 tbsp	chopped fresh basil, divided	45 mL
2 tbsp	chopped fresh parsley, divided	30 mL
2 tsp	chopped fresh oregano	10 mL
1 tsp	chopped fresh rosemary	5 mL
1 tsp	kosher salt	5 mL
4 cups	ready-to-use chicken or vegetable broth	1 L
1 cup	yellow cornmeal (polenta)	250 mL

Tip
You can serve the creamy polenta after step 3 or, for a crispier finish, let it cool and transfer it to a cast-iron pan to bake or cook on the stovetop.

1. Press Sauté; the indicator will read "Normal." When the display says "Hot," add oil and heat until shimmering. Add onion and cook, stirring, for 3 to 5 minutes or until softened. Add garlic and cook, stirring, for 30 seconds or until fragrant. Add tomatoes, olives, bay leaf, 1½ tbsp (22 mL) basil, 1 tbsp (15 mL) parsley, oregano, rosemary, salt and broth, stirring well. Add cornmeal on top; do not stir. Press Cancel.

2. Close and lock the lid and turn the steam release handle to Sealing. Press Rice; the indicator will read "Low Pressure." Leave the time at 12 minutes.

3. When the timer beeps, press Cancel and turn the steam release handle to Venting. When the float valve drops down, remove the lid. Check to make sure the polenta is done to your liking. (If more cooking is needed, cover the pot and let stand for 5 minutes.) Discard bay leaf. Add the remaining basil and parsley, whisking until smooth.

Pomegranate and Quinoa Salad

Sweet and tangy pomegranate seeds are paired with nutty and crunchy quinoa for a salad that is colorful and oh-so inviting. It's the ideal refreshing side dish for a spring or summer meal.

MAKES 8 SERVINGS

INSTANT POT FUNCTIONS

- Sauté -
- Rice -

½ cup	pine nuts	125 mL
3 tbsp	virgin olive oil, divided	45 mL
2 cups	quinoa, rinsed	500 mL
	Kosher salt	
3 cups	water	750 mL
½ tsp	ground cinnamon	2 mL
½ tsp	ground cloves	2 mL
Pinch	ground nutmeg	Pinch
	Juice of 1 lemon	
1 cup	pomegranate seeds	250 mL
½ cup	chopped fresh mint	125 mL
	Freshly ground black pepper	

1. Press Sauté; the indicator will read "Normal." When the display says "Hot," add pine nuts and cook, stirring, for 2 to 3 minutes or until golden and fragrant. Transfer pine nuts to a plate.

2. Add 1 tbsp (15 mL) oil to the pot and heat until shimmering. Add quinoa and cook, stirring, for 2 to 3 minutes or until lightly toasted. Press Cancel. Add ½ tsp (2 mL) salt and water, stirring well.

3. Close and lock the lid and turn the steam release handle to Sealing. Press Rice; the indicator will read "Low Pressure." Leave the time at 12 minutes.

4. When the timer beeps, press Cancel and turn the steam release handle to Venting. When the float valve drops down, remove the lid. Check to make sure the quinoa is tender with a bit of texture. (If more cooking is needed, cover the pot and let stand for 2 minutes.) Fluff quinoa with a fork.

5. Add cinnamon, cloves, nutmeg and lemon juice, stirring well. Let cool to room temperature. Stir in pomegranate seeds, mint and the remaining oil, fluffing quinoa. Season to taste with salt and pepper.

Tips

To easily separate pomegranate seeds from their shell, cut the pomegranate in half, turn it seed side down over a bowl and tap the top with a wooden spoon. The seeds will drop out readily into the bowl.

You can purchase pomegranate seeds in the produce section of well-stocked grocery stores.

This recipe can be doubled, but make sure to fill the pot no more than halfway; otherwise, the exhaust valve may become clogged, resulting in excess pressure. The Rice function adjusts the cooking time based on the amount of ingredients in the pot. If you double the recipe, leave the timer at whatever time it adjusts to, for best results.

Quinoa and Edamame Salad

Take quinoa and edamame to a new level by combining them with cucumbers, onions, cabbage and a zesty ginger soy dressing that explodes in your mouth.

MAKES 4 SERVINGS

INSTANT POT FUNCTIONS

- Sauté •
- Rice •

2 tsp	virgin olive oil	10 mL
1/2 cup	quinoa, rinsed	125 mL
3/4 cup	water	175 mL
1/4 tsp	kosher salt	1 mL
1/2 cup	frozen shelled edamame	125 mL
3	green onions, thinly sliced	3
1	small carrot, shredded	1
1	small cucumber, chopped	1
1 cup	shredded red cabbage	250 mL
1/4 cup	chopped peanuts	60 mL
2 tbsp	chopped fresh cilantro	30 mL
1 tbsp	chopped fresh basil	15 mL

Ginger Soy Dressing

1 1/2 tbsp	grated gingerroot	22 mL
1 tbsp	granulated sugar	15 mL
2 tsp	hot pepper flakes	10 mL
3 tbsp	sesame oil	45 mL
2 tbsp	freshly squeezed lime juice	30 mL
1 1/2 tsp	soy sauce	7 mL

> ## Tip
> One fresh lime will yield 2 tbsp (30 mL) juice. You can also zest the lime before squeezing the juice. Add measured amounts of zest to ice cube trays, cover with water and freeze for later use.

1. Press Sauté; the indicator will read "Normal." When the display says "Hot," add oil to the pot and heat until shimmering. Add quinoa and cook, stirring, for 2 to 3 minutes or until lightly toasted. Press Cancel. Add water and salt, stirring well.

2. Close and lock the lid and turn the steam release handle to Sealing. Press Rice; the indicator will read "Low Pressure." Leave the time at 12 minutes.

3. Meanwhile, cook edamame according to package directions. Drain and set aside.

4. When the timer beeps, press Cancel and turn the steam release handle to Venting. When the float valve drops down, remove the lid. Check to make sure the quinoa is tender with a bit of texture. (If more cooking is needed, cover the pot and let stand for 2 minutes.)

5. Fluff quinoa with a fork and transfer to a large bowl. Add edamame, green onions, carrot, cucumber and cabbage, tossing to combine.

6. *Dressing:* In a small bowl, whisk together ginger, sugar, hot pepper flakes, oil, lime juice and soy sauce.

7. Pour dressing over salad, tossing to combine. Sprinkle peanuts, cilantro and basil over top.

Zesty Spanish Rice

Every fabulous Mexican or Spanish main dish needs an equally tantalizing rice dish to complement it, and this zesty dish is not only a great pairing but is so easy to make.

MAKES 6 SERVINGS		

INSTANT POT FUNCTION		
• Multigrain •		
2 cups	long-grain brown rice, rinsed	500 mL
2 cups	canned diced tomatoes, with juice	500 mL
2½ cups	ready-to-use chicken or vegetable broth	625 mL
1	onion, finely chopped	1
3 tbsp	chili powder	45 mL
1 tsp	ground cumin	5 mL
1 tsp	garlic powder	5 mL
1 tsp	kosher salt	5 mL

Tips

This rice works well as a filling for burritos and tacos.

You can also use long-grain white rice in this recipe, but I prefer the texture and added nutrients of brown rice. For white rice, use an additional ½ cup (125 mL) broth. In step 2, press Rice and use the ⊖ button to decrease the time on the display to 4 minutes.

1. In the inner pot, combine rice, tomatoes and broth. Add onion, chili powder, cumin, garlic powder and salt, stirring to dissolve.

2. Place the pot inside the cooker housing, close and lock the lid and turn the steam release handle to Sealing. Press Multigrain; the indicator will read "Low Pressure." Press Adjust twice to adjust the temperature to "Low." Leave the time at 20 minutes.

3. When the timer beeps, press Cancel and let the pot stand, covered, for 10 minutes. After 10 minutes, turn the steam release handle to Venting and remove the lid. Check to make sure the rice is done to your liking. (If more cooking is needed, cover the pot and let stand for 2 minutes.) Fluff rice with a fork.

Brown Rice Tabbouleh

The marriage of brown rice, tomatoes, cucumbers and herbs in this Arabic dish is an experience you will want to enjoy again and again.

MAKES 6 SERVINGS

INSTANT POT FUNCTION
• Rice •

2½ cups	medium-grain brown rice, rinsed	625 mL
	Kosher salt	
5 cups	water	1.25 L
3	tomatoes, diced	3
3	seedless cucumbers, cut into small cubes	3
¼ cup	minced green onions	60 mL
1 cup	minced fresh parsley	250 mL
¼ cup	chopped fresh mint	60 mL
½ tsp	paprika	2 mL
¼ cup	virgin olive oil	60 mL
	Juice of 1 lemon	
	Freshly ground black pepper	

Tip

Seedless cucumbers are often called English cucumbers. If you cannot find them, regular cucumbers also work well. You can either remove the seeds or use them with the seeds, depending on your preference.

1. In the inner pot, combine rice, 1 tsp (5 mL) salt and water, stirring well.

2. Place the pot inside the cooker housing, close and lock the lid and turn the steam release handle to Sealing. Press Rice; the indicator will read "Low Pressure." Leave the time at 12 minutes.

3. When the timer beeps, press Cancel and turn the steam release handle to Venting. When the float valve drops down, remove the lid. Check to make sure the rice is done to your liking. (If more cooking is needed, cover the pot and let stand for 2 minutes.) Fluff rice with a fork, transfer to a large plate and let cool for 30 minutes.

4. Meanwhile, in a large bowl, gently combine tomatoes, cucumbers, green onions, parsley, mint, paprika, oil and lemon juice. Gently stir in rice. Season to taste with salt and pepper.

Entertaining and Special Occasions

Pressure Cooker

Slow Cooker

continued on next page . . .

Entertaining and Special Occasions *(continued)*

Creamy Spinach and Artichoke Dip

This restaurant favorite appetizer is so easy to make at home using your pressure cooker, you can enjoy it anytime. With loads of cheese, creamy spinach, artichoke hearts and a little bit of spiciness, it's no wonder this dish is so popular.

MAKES 8 TO 10 SERVINGS

INSTANT POT FUNCTIONS
- Sauté •
- Manual Pressure •

- **6-cup (1.5 L) round casserole dish, sprayed with nonstick cooking spray**
- **Instant Pot steam rack**

1	package (10 oz/300 g) frozen chopped spinach, thawed	1
1	can (14 oz/398 mL) artichoke hearts, drained	1
2 tbsp	butter	30 mL
3	cloves garlic, minced	3
¾ cup	shredded mozzarella cheese	175 mL
½ cup	freshly grated Parmesan cheese	125 mL
½ cup	shredded pepper Jack cheese	125 mL
¼ cup	crumbled feta cheese	60 mL
1 cup	mayonnaise	250 mL
½ cup	sour cream	125 mL
¼ tsp	freshly ground black pepper	1 mL
	Sliced French bread	

Tips

This dip can also be served with crackers, tortilla chips or pita wedges, or with baby carrots, celery, cauliflower and broccoli florets.

When using the Quick Release method to release pressure, keep your hands and face away from the hole on the top of the steam release handle so you don't get scalded by the escaping steam.

1. Gently squeeze spinach to remove excess moisture. Coarsely chop artichoke hearts. Add spinach and artichokes to a large bowl. Set aside.

2. Press Sauté; the indicator will read "Normal." When the display says "Hot," add butter to the pot and heat until melted. Add garlic and cook, stirring, for 30 seconds or until fragrant. Press Cancel. Add garlic mixture to spinach and artichokes. Clean the pot.

3. Add mozzarella, Parmesan, pepper Jack, feta, mayonnaise, sour cream and pepper to the spinach mixture, stirring well. Spoon into prepared casserole dish and cover with foil.

4. Add 2 cups (500 mL) water to the pot and place the steam rack in the pot. Place casserole dish on the rack. Close and lock the lid and turn the steam release handle to Sealing. Press Manual; the indicator will read "High Pressure." Use the ⊖ button to decrease the time on the display to 10 minutes.

5. When the timer beeps, press Cancel and turn the steam release handle to Venting. When the float valve drops down, remove the lid. The cheese should be melted and the dip hot. (If more cooking is needed, reset the manual pressure to "High Pressure" for 3 minutes.) Using the handles on the steam rack, carefully lift the casserole from the pot. Serve with French bread.

Roasted Garlic Hummus

The best hummus uses dried chickpeas cooked to creamy perfection, then blended with generous amounts of garlic, tahini and extra virgin olive oil. The Manual Pressure function on your Instant Pot gets it done quickly. Serve the delectable results with pita chips or tortilla chips.

MAKES 8 SERVINGS

INSTANT POT FUNCTION
• Manual Pressure •

• Food processor

2 cups	dried chickpeas, rinsed	500 mL
1½ tbsp	virgin olive oil	22 mL
	Water	
3	cloves garlic, roasted (see tip, below)	3
1½ tbsp	ground cumin, divided	22 mL
½ tsp	kosher salt	2 mL
	Freshly ground black pepper	
½ cup	tahini	125 mL
⅓ cup	extra virgin olive oil, divided	75 mL
2 tbsp	freshly squeezed lemon juice	30 mL

Tips

To roast garlic, cut off the top of a head of garlic, exposing the tops of the cloves but leaving the outer skin intact. Place garlic on a sheet of heavy-duty foil and drizzle olive oil over the cloves. Seal foil around garlic. Bake in a 350°F (180°C) oven for 50 minutes or until cloves are soft when pierced with a knife. Squeeze out cloves. Store extra cloves in an airtight container in the refrigerator for up to 5 days. They are a great addition to other dips and sauces.

The hummus can be covered and refrigerated for up to 3 days.

1. In the inner pot, combine chickpeas, virgin olive oil and enough water to cover chickpeas by 2 inches (5 cm).

2. Place the pot inside the cooker housing, close and lock the lid and turn the steam release handle to Sealing. Press Manual; the indicator will read "High Pressure." Use the ➕ button to increase the time on the display to 35 minutes.

3. When the timer beeps, press Cancel and let the pot stand, covered, for 15 minutes. After 15 minutes, turn the steam release handle to Venting and remove the lid. The chickpeas should give almost no resistance when pressed between your fingers. (If more cooking is needed, reset the manual pressure to "High Pressure" for 5 minutes.) Drain chickpeas.

4. In food processor, combine chickpeas, garlic, 1 tbsp (15 mL) cumin, salt, pepper to taste, tahini, ¼ cup (60 mL) extra virgin olive oil and lemon juice. Process until smooth and creamy, adding water if necessary to reach the desired consistency.

5. Transfer hummus to a serving bowl. Using the back of a spoon, make a depression in the hummus and drizzle with the remaining extra virgin olive oil. Garnish with the remaining cumin.

Perfectly Devilish Eggs

Walk into a room with a plate of deviled eggs, and you suddenly become the most popular person there. And with their seemingly endless variations, it's no wonder these creamy, tangy filled eggs are so adored. Pressure cooking the eggs makes this appetizer even easier: they come out perfect every time, and the shells practically fall right off the eggs.

MAKES 6 SERVINGS

INSTANT POT FUNCTION
• Manual Pressure •

- **Instant Pot steam rack**
- **6 canning jar screwbands**

6	large eggs	6
½ cup	mayonnaise	125 mL
1 tbsp	prepared yellow or Dijon mustard	15 mL
Pinch	kosher salt	Pinch
	Hungarian paprika	

1. Add 2 cups (500 mL) water to the inner pot and place the steam rack in the pot. Place the screwbands on top of the rack. Place an egg in the middle of each screwband. Close and lock the lid and turn the steam release handle to Sealing. Press Manual; the indicator will read "High Pressure." Press Pressure once to adjust the pressure to "Low Pressure." Use the ⊖ button to decrease the time on the display to 6 minutes.

2. When the timer beeps, press Cancel. Let stand, covered, until the float valve drops down. Turn the steam release handle to Venting and remove the lid. Transfer eggs to a bowl of cold water. When cool enough to handle, peel eggs.

3. Slice eggs in half lengthwise. Remove the yolks and add them to a medium bowl. Using a fork, mash yolks until finely crumbled. Add mayonnaise, mustard and salt, mixing well. Spoon mixture into egg white halves, dividing evenly. Garnish with paprika.

Variations

Add 1 tsp (5 mL) white vinegar to the yolk mixture for a tangier flavor.

Substitute ½ tsp (2 mL) truffle oil for the mustard.

Instead of paprika, garnish with sliced green onions; minced cooked bacon and minced fresh chives; Sriracha and minced fresh cilantro; smoked salmon and drained capers; kalamata olives and chopped fresh parsley; sun-dried tomatoes and chopped fresh parsley; prosciutto, freshly grated Parmesan cheese and chopped fresh chives; taco seasoning and torn fresh cilantro; diced cooked ham and shredded Cheddar cheese.

Tips

For a creamier consistency, use an immersion blender to blend the yolks in step 3.

Add the yolk mixture to a piping bag with the tip of your choice and pipe the mixture into the egg white halves for a pretty presentation.

The eggs can be served immediately or refrigerated in an airtight container for up to 3 days.

Spicy Maple Chicken Wings

Who doesn't love to dive into savory wings on game day? These wings get so tender in the pressure cooker, and the sweet-and-spicy sauce adds just the right amount of zing. Talk about a party starter!

MAKES 2 TO 6 SERVINGS

INSTANT POT FUNCTION

• Manual Pressure •

- **Steamer basket**
- **Instant Pot steam rack**
- **Baking sheet, lined with heavy-duty foil and sprayed with nonstick cooking spray**

Blue Cheese Dressing

2 oz	blue cheese (preferably Roquefort), crumbled	60 g
¼ cup	buttermilk	60 mL
¼ cup	mayonnaise	60 mL
¼ cup	sour cream	60 mL
	Juice of ½ lemon	
Pinch	kosher salt	Pinch

Chicken Wings

12	chicken wings, sections split apart, wing tips removed	12
1	clove garlic, minced	1
1 tsp	dry mustard	5 mL
1 tsp	smoked paprika	5 mL
¼ tsp	cayenne pepper	1 mL
⅓ cup	chili sauce	75 mL
3 tbsp	pure maple syrup	45 mL
2 tsp	soy sauce	10 mL
5	stalks celery, cut into 3-inch (7.5 cm) sections	5

1. *Blue Cheese Dressing:* In a medium bowl, whisk together blue cheese, buttermilk, mayonnaise, sour cream, lemon juice and salt. Cover and refrigerate until ready to serve or for up to 7 days.

2. *Chicken Wings:* Arrange chicken wings in the steamer basket with as much of their surface exposed as possible. Add 1 cup (250 mL) water to the inner pot and place the steam rack in the pot. Place the steamer basket on the rack. Close and lock the lid and turn the steam release handle to Sealing. Press Manual; the indicator will read "High Pressure." Use the ⊖ button to decrease the time on the display to 10 minutes.

3. Meanwhile, preheat the broiler, with an oven rack in the top position.

4. In a medium bowl, combine garlic, mustard, paprika, cayenne, chili sauce, maple syrup and soy sauce.

5. When the timer beeps, press Cancel and turn the steam release handle to Venting. When the float valve drops down, remove the lid. Using tongs, transfer wings to the sauce and toss to coat. Arrange wings on prepared baking sheet.

6. Broil for 4 to 5 minutes or until wings are caramelized and juices run clear when chicken is pierced. Transfer wings to a serving platter and serve with blue cheese dressing and celery sticks.

Tips

If this is the only appetizer you are serving, allow for 6 wing sections per person. If you are serving more appetizers, allow for 2 wing sections per person.

If you want to double this recipe, you can place 24 more wing sections in a separate steamer basket and stack the baskets in the inner pot. Do not add them to the same steamer basket, as they will not get done evenly.

Teriyaki Chicken Strips

These teriyaki chicken strips are sure to be a hit at your next event. With just the right amount of sweetness and tanginess, they make an inviting appetizer.

MAKES 12 SERVINGS

INSTANT POT FUNCTIONS

- Manual Pressure -
- Sauté -

- **24 bamboo skewers (6 inches/15 cm long), soaked for 10 to 20 minutes**

3	cloves garlic, minced	3
1 tbsp	packed brown sugar	15 mL
2/3 cup	water, divided	150 mL
1 tbsp	teriyaki sauce	15 mL
2 tsp	rice vinegar	10 mL
2 tsp	dark (cooking) molasses	10 mL
6	boneless skinless chicken thighs (about 2 lbs/1 kg), cut into 1/2-inch (1 cm) strips	6
1 tbsp	cornstarch	15 mL
2 tbsp	cold water	30 mL
3	green onions (green part only), sliced	3
1 1/2 tbsp	sesame seeds, toasted	22 mL

Tips

If you are making this as an appetizer, allow for 2 strips per person. If you are making it as a main dish, allow for 4 strips per person.

Soaking the bamboo skewers while you prepare the rest of your ingredients will make it easier to skewer the chicken strips.

1. In the inner pot, combine garlic, brown sugar, 2/3 cup (150 mL) water, teriyaki sauce, vinegar and molasses, stirring well. Add chicken and toss to coat.

2. Place the pot inside the cooker housing, close and lock the lid and turn the steam release handle to Sealing. Press Manual; the indicator will read "High Pressure." Use the ⊖ button to decrease the time on the display to 4 minutes.

3. When the timer beeps, press Cancel and let the pot stand, covered, for 4 minutes. After 4 minutes, turn the steam release handle to Venting and remove the lid. Check to make sure juices run clear when chicken is pierced. (If more cooking is needed, reset the manual pressure to "High Pressure" for 1 minute.) Using tongs, transfer chicken to a plate.

4. In a small bowl, whisk together cornstarch and cold water. Press Sauté. Add the cornstarch mixture to the pot and cook, stirring, for 4 minutes or until sauce is reduced by one-third and thickened to a glaze.

5. When chicken is cool enough to handle, thread the strips onto the skewers, twisting them slightly. Pour glaze over skewered chicken, turning to coat. Arrange skewers on a serving platter and garnish with green onions and sesame seeds.

Party-Perfect Meatballs

So simple, yet so tantalizing, these meatballs make an ideal appetizer for any holiday gathering or game day event. They can even be used in meatball sandwiches.

MAKES 12 SERVINGS

INSTANT POT FUNCTIONS

• Manual Pressure •
• Sauté •

- **Instant Pot steam rack**
- **Steamer basket**
- **36 toothpicks**

1	package (3 lbs/1.5 kg) frozen fully cooked beef meatballs	1
2¼ cups	barbecue sauce	550 mL
2 cups	grape jelly	500 mL
¼ cup	apple cider vinegar	60 mL

Tips

Press Keep Warm at the end of step 3 to keep the meatballs warm until you are ready to serve, for up to 2 hours.

As an appetizer, this recipe allows for about 3 meatballs per person.

For a meatball sandwich, add 3 meatballs to a toasted hoagie roll and drizzle with sauce.

1. Add 1 cup (250 mL) water to the inner pot and place the steam rack in the pot. Stack meatballs in the steamer basket, alternating the spacing, and place the basket on the rack. Close and lock the lid and turn the steam release handle to Sealing. Press Manual; the indicator will read "High Pressure." Use the ⊖ button to decrease the time on the display to 5 minutes.

2. When the timer beeps, press Cancel and turn the steam release handle to Venting. When the float valve drops down, remove the lid. Check to make sure the meatballs are heated through. (If more cooking is needed, reset the manual pressure to "High Pressure" for 2 minutes.) Carefully remove the steamer basket and rack. Discard water.

3. Add barbecue sauce, jelly and vinegar to the pot, stirring well. Press Sauté and cook, stirring often, for 5 to 7 minutes or until sauce is smooth. Add meatballs and cook, stirring to coat, for 2 minutes.

4. Skewer meatballs with toothpicks and transfer to a serving platter. Serve sauce in small bowls for dipping.

Lemon Tarragon Salmon

This delicate dish is indeed company-worthy. The salmon retains its moist, buttery flavor, and the lemon and tarragon meld in a creamy, tangy sauce. It's so elegant, yet so simple that you will have more time to enjoy visiting with your guests.

MAKES 4 SERVINGS

INSTANT POT FUNCTION
• Manual Pressure •

- **Two 18- by 12-inch (45 by 30 cm) sheets heavy-duty foil, sprayed with nonstick cooking spray**
- **Instant Pot steam rack**

2 tsp	finely chopped fresh tarragon	10 mL
1 cup	crème fraîche	250 mL
3 tbsp	freshly squeezed lemon juice	45 mL
4	skin-on salmon fillets (each about 6 oz/175 g)	4
	Kosher salt and freshly ground black pepper	
2 tbsp	butter	30 mL
1	small shallot, minced (about 2 tbsp/30 mL)	1
½ cup	dry white wine	125 mL
1 tbsp	chopped fresh chives	15 mL
	Lemon wedges (optional)	

Tips

Choose salmon fillets that are about 1 inch (2.5 cm) thick for best results.

One medium lemon will yield about 3 tbsp (45 mL) juice.

When using the Quick Release method to release pressure, keep your hands and face away from the hole on the top of the steam release handle so you don't get scalded by the escaping steam.

1. In a small bowl, combine tarragon, crème fraîche and lemon juice.

2. Place 2 salmon fillets, skin side down, in the center of each prepared foil sheet. Season with salt and pepper. Divide crème fraîche mixture evenly on top of salmon. Bring the long ends of the foil together over the salmon and fold the foil down until the top of the packet is sealed tightly but there is a substantial gap between the salmon and the top of the packet. Fold up the open ends of the foil until they are close to the salmon and the sides of the packet are sealed tightly.

3. Add 1 cup (250 mL) water to the inner pot and place the steam rack in the pot. Place packets on steam rack; do not overlap. Close and lock the lid and turn the steam release handle to Sealing. Press Manual; the indicator will read "High Pressure." Use the ⊖ button to decrease the time on the display to 6 minutes.

4. Meanwhile, in a small saucepan, melt butter over medium heat. Add shallot and cook, stirring, for 3 to 4 minutes or until softened and lightly browned. Add wine and cook, stirring, for 5 minutes or until reduced by about half and the consistency of a glaze.

5. When the timer beeps, press Cancel and turn the steam release handle to Venting. When the float valve drops down, remove the lid. Using tongs, transfer packets to the counter and carefully open packets.

6. Using a spatula, transfer fish fillets and sauce to plates. Drizzle glaze over top and sprinkle with chives. Serve with lemon wedges, if desired.

Holiday-Worthy Stuffed Turkey Breast

Not all holiday celebrations require food for a crowd. Sometimes it's nice to celebrate with the traditional parade of ingredients, but on a smaller scale.

MAKES 4 SERVINGS

INSTANT POT FUNCTIONS

• Sauté •
• Manual Pressure •

• Kitchen string

1 tbsp	butter	15 mL
1	stalk celery, chopped	1
1	small red onion, chopped	1
1	clove garlic, minced	1
2 tbsp	chopped fresh sage	30 mL
1 cup	dry bread crumbs	250 mL
2 tbsp	chopped fresh parsley	30 mL
2 tbsp	dried cranberries, coarsely chopped	30 mL
1 tsp	kosher salt, divided	5 mL
½ cup	milk	125 mL
2 lb	boneless skinless turkey breast	1 kg
Pinch	freshly ground black pepper	Pinch
2 tsp	virgin olive oil	10 mL
1 cup	ready-to-use chicken broth	250 mL

1. Press Sauté; the indicator will read "Normal." When the display says "Hot," add butter to the pot and heat until melted. Add celery and onion; cook, stirring, for 3 to 5 minutes or until softened. Add garlic and sage; cook, stirring, for 30 seconds or until fragrant. Press Cancel.

2. In a medium bowl, combine bread crumbs, parsley, cranberries and ½ tsp (2 mL) salt. Gradually pour in milk, using a fork to mix the ingredients until blended and crumbly. Add the celery mixture to the bread crumb mixture, mixing well.

3. Butterfly the turkey breast and pound it evenly to about ½ inch (1 cm) thick. Season with pepper and the remaining salt. Spread bread crumb mixture over cut side of the breast in an even layer, starting in the center and leaving ½ inch (1 cm) uncovered at the edges. Starting at the narrowest part of the breast, tightly roll up the breast like a jelly roll, tucking in edges. Tie the roll with kitchen string.

4. Press Sauté. When the display says "Hot," add oil to the pot and heat until shimmering. Add turkey roll and cook, turning often, for 8 to 10 minutes or until well browned. Press Cancel. Add broth.

5. Close and lock the lid and turn the steam release handle to Sealing. Press Manual; the indicator will read "High Pressure." Use the ⊖ button to decrease the time on the display to 20 minutes.

6. When the timer beeps, press Cancel. Let stand, covered, until the float valve drops down. Turn the steam release handle to Venting and remove the lid. Check to make sure an instant-read thermometer inserted in the center of the turkey roll registers 165°F (74°C). (If more cooking is needed, reset the manual pressure to "High Pressure" for 5 minutes.)

7. Transfer roast to a cutting board, remove string and carve into slices. Serve with cooking juices drizzled over top.

Tip
To butterfly a turkey breast, place it on a cutting board with the smooth (skinless) side down. Using a paring knife or chef's knife, cut horizontally from the narrowest part of the breast to about $^3/_4$ inch (2 cm) from the thickest end. Open the breast to form a large flat piece.

Hasselback Pork Roast with Apples and Prosciutto

This pork roast is a riff on the Hasselback potato, a baked potato with numerous tiny slices that make the outside crisp and the inside tender. The slices in this pork roast are stuffed with apples and prosciutto, for tender and charming results.

MAKES 6 SERVINGS

INSTANT POT FUNCTIONS

• Sauté •

• Manual Pressure •

• **Kitchen string**

3 lb	pork single loin roast (less than 8 inches/20 cm long), untied	1.5 kg
1	tart apple (such as Granny Smith), cut into 12 thin slices	1
12	thin slices prosciutto	12
	Kosher salt	
2 tbsp	herbes de Provence	30 mL
2 tbsp	virgin olive oil	30 mL
1 cup	ready-to-use chicken broth	250 mL

1. Cutting only about three-quarters of the way to the bottom, cut roast crosswise into twelve ½-inch (1 cm) slices. Add an apple slice and a prosciutto slice to each cut, folding and arranging them so they fit evenly in the cuts. Tie the roast horizontally with kitchen string so it retains its shape. Season roast with salt and herbes de Provence.

2. Press Sauté; the indicator will read "Normal." When the display says "Hot," add oil to the pot and heat until shimmering. Add roast and cook, turning carefully, for 8 to 10 minutes or until browned on all sides. Press Cancel. Position the roast with the cut side up and add broth to the pot.

3. Close and lock the lid and turn the steam release handle to Sealing. Press Manual; the indicator will read "High Pressure." Use the ⊖ button to decrease the time on the display to 15 minutes.

4. When the timer beeps, press Cancel. Let stand, covered, until the float valve drops down. Turn the steam release handle to Venting and remove the lid. Check to make sure an instant-read thermometer inserted in the center of the roast registers at least 160°F (71°C) for medium. (If more cooking is needed, reset the manual pressure to "High Pressure" for 5 minutes.)

5. Transfer roast to a serving platter and remove string. Drizzle cooking juices over top. Cut through to the bottom of each slice to serve.

Tips

You can also use a Cortland, Empire or Honeycrisp apple. The best varieties for this recipe are apples that hold their shape when baking and have a tart flavor.

You can substitute round slices of pancetta for the prosciutto.

Sunday Pot Roast

This dish was one of my favorite meals when I was growing up. The aromas wafting from the kitchen while the roast is cooking are intoxicating. This version takes much less time, but the end result is still a family favorite.

MAKES 6 SERVINGS

INSTANT POT FUNCTIONS

• Sauté •

• Manual Pressure •

3 lb	boneless beef chuck roast (less than 8 inches/20 cm in diameter)	1.5 kg
	Kosher salt and freshly ground black pepper	
2 tbsp	virgin olive oil	30 mL
1 tbsp	horseradish powder (see tip, below)	15 mL
2	bay leaves	2
1½ cups	ready-to-use beef broth	375 mL
8	carrots, cut into 4-inch (10 cm) lengths (see tip, below)	8
6	red-skinned potatoes, cut in half	6
2	onions, cut into ½-inch (1 cm) wedges	2
2	stalks celery, chopped	2
1 tsp	celery salt	5 mL

Tips

Look for horseradish powder in the spice section of well-stocked grocery stores and specialty shops. If you can't find it, you can substitute 2 tbsp (30 mL) prepared horseradish or 1 tbsp (15 mL) dry mustard.

Make sure your carrot sticks are of roughly equal width, for even cooking. If your carrots are more than ¾ inch (2 cm) in diameter, cut them lengthwise. Or use 4 cups (1 L) baby carrots to make preparation easier.

1. Season roast with salt and pepper. Press Sauté; the indicator will read "Normal." When the display says "Hot," add oil to the pot and heat until shimmering. Add roast and cook, turning occasionally, for 8 to 10 minutes or until browned on all sides. Press Cancel. Sprinkle roast with horseradish powder. Add bay leaves and broth.

2. Close and lock the lid and turn the steam release handle to Sealing. Press Manual; the indicator will read "High Pressure." Use the ➕ button to increase the time on the display to 75 minutes.

3. When the timer beeps, press Cancel and turn the steam release handle to Venting. When the float valve drops down, remove the lid. Add carrots, potatoes, onions and celery to the pot. Sprinkle celery salt over the vegetables. Reset the manual pressure to "High Pressure" for 5 minutes.

4. When the timer beeps, press Cancel and let the pot stand, covered, for 10 minutes. After 10 minutes, turn the steam release handle to Venting and remove the lid. Check to make sure an instant-read thermometer inserted in the center of the roast registers at least 160°F (71°C) for medium and the vegetables are fork-tender. (If more cooking is needed, reset the manual pressure to "High Pressure" for 15 minutes.) Discard bay leaves. Transfer roast to a cutting board, cover with foil and let stand for 5 minutes.

5. Slice roast across the grain and transfer to a serving platter. Using a slotted spoon, remove vegetables from pot and arrange around roast. Drizzle roast with some of the juices from the pot.

Osso Buco

This Northern Italian classic features fall-off-the-bone veal shanks that have been braised in a sumptuous tomato sauce bursting with umami. Although it's often thought of as a dish that takes hours to make, you can now enjoy osso buco in far less time with your pressure cooker.

MAKES 6 SERVINGS

INSTANT POT FUNCTIONS
• Sauté •
• Manual Pressure •

- **Kitchen string**

6	slices veal shank (about 1½ inches/4 cm thick)	6
	Kosher salt and freshly ground black pepper	
½ cup	all-purpose flour	125 mL
¼ cup	virgin olive oil (approx.)	60 mL
2	onions, finely chopped	2
2	stalks celery, diced	2
2	small carrots, diced	2
6	cloves garlic, minced, divided	6
1	bay leaf	1
2 tsp	dried thyme, divided	10 mL
2 tsp	dried rosemary, divided	10 mL
1 tsp	dried oregano	5 mL
3 tbsp	tomato paste	45 mL
¾ cup	dry red wine	175 mL
4 cups	ready-to-use beef broth	1 L
2	anchovy fillets, minced (optional)	2
3 tbsp	chopped fresh parsley	45 mL
1 tbsp	grated lemon zest	15 mL
1 tbsp	cornstarch	15 mL
1 tbsp	cold water	15 mL

1. Tie the veal shanks around the center with kitchen string. Season with salt and pepper. Add the flour to a bowl and dredge the veal shanks lightly in flour, shaking off excess. Discard any excess flour.

2. Press Sauté; the indicator will read "Normal." When the display says "Hot," add 2 tbsp (30 mL) oil to the pot and heat until shimmering. Working in batches, add shanks and cook, turning occasionally, for 8 to 10 minutes or until browned on all sides, adding the remaining oil as needed. Transfer shanks to a plate.

3. Add onions, celery and carrots to the pot and cook, stirring, for 5 to 6 minutes or until lightly browned. Add two-thirds of the garlic, bay leaf, 1 tsp (5 mL) thyme, 1 tsp (5 mL) rosemary, oregano, 1 tsp (5 mL) salt and tomato paste; cook, stirring, for 1 to 2 minutes or until fragrant.

4. Add wine and cook for 2 minutes, scraping up any browned bits from the bottom of the pot. Return shanks to the pot, along with any accumulated juices. Add broth and bring to a boil. Press Cancel.

5. Close and lock the lid and turn the steam release handle to Sealing. Press Manual; the indicator will read "High Pressure." Use the ➕ button to increase the time on the display to 65 minutes.

6. Meanwhile, in a small bowl, combine the remaining garlic, anchovies (if using), parsley and lemon zest.

7. When the timer beeps, press Cancel and turn the steam release handle to Venting. When the float valve drops down, remove the lid. Check to make sure the shanks are tender and ready to fall off of the bone. (If more cooking is needed, reset the manual pressure to "High Pressure" for 10 minutes.) Transfer the shanks to a platter and cover loosely with foil. Discard bay leaf.

8. In a small bowl, whisk together cornstarch and cold water. Press Sauté. Add the cornstarch mixture to the pot, along with half the parsley mixture and the remaining rosemary and thyme; cook, stirring occasionally, for 7 to 9 minutes or until sauce is thickened. Return shanks to the pot, along with any accumulated juices, and cook, spooning sauce over the top, until shanks are warmed through.

9. Transfer shanks to a serving platter and spoon sauce over top. Dollop the remaining parsley mixture on top.

Tip

Osso buco is one of those dishes that seems to taste even better the next day. After step 8, cover and refrigerate. Remove any congealed fat from the top and reheat before serving.

Lamb Shanks in Ginger Plum Sauce

Lamb is one of those dishes we typically think of eating only at a fine restaurant. This recipe gives you all the tools to make fall-off-the-bone exceptional lamb at home with ease.

INSTANT POT FUNCTIONS

- Sauté •
- Manual Pressure •

4	small lamb shanks (about 7 lbs/3.5 kg)	4
	Kosher salt and freshly ground black pepper	
1 tsp	ground nutmeg	5 mL
¼ cup	virgin olive oil (approx.)	60 mL
1	red onion, finely chopped	1
2	cloves garlic, minced	2
1½ cups	dry red wine	375 mL
2	sprigs fresh thyme	2
1	sprig fresh rosemary	1
2 tbsp	packed brown sugar	30 mL
½ tsp	minced gingerroot	2 mL
2 cups	ready-to-use beef broth	500 mL
½ cup	plum jam	125 mL

Tip

A rice pilaf or risotto and steamed asparagus are ideal accompaniments for these lamb shanks.

---

1. Season lamb with salt, pepper and nutmeg. Press Sauté; the indicator will read "Normal." When the display says "Hot," add 2 tbsp (30 mL) oil to the pot and heat until shimmering. Working in batches if necessary, add shanks and cook, turning occasionally, for 8 to 10 minutes or until browned on all sides, adding the remaining oil as needed. Transfer shanks to a plate.

2. Add onion to the pot and cook, stirring, for 4 to 5 minutes or until translucent. Add garlic and cook, stirring, for 30 seconds or until fragrant.

3. Add wine and cook for 3 minutes, scraping up any browned bits from the bottom of the pot. Add thyme and rosemary sprigs; cook, stirring occasionally, for 7 to 9 minutes or until wine is reduced by half. Press Cancel. Add brown sugar, ginger, broth and jam, stirring well.

4. Close and lock the lid and turn the steam release handle to Sealing. Press Manual; the indicator will read "High Pressure." Press Pressure once to adjust the pressure to "Low." Use the ⊖ button to decrease the time on the display to 22 minutes.

5. When the timer beeps, press Cancel. Let stand, covered, until the float valve drops down. Turn the steam release handle to Venting and remove the lid. Check to make sure the lamb is fall-off-the-bone tender. (If more cooking is needed, reset the manual pressure to "Low Pressure" for 2 minutes.) Discard thyme and rosemary sprigs. Transfer shanks to a serving plate and cover with foil.

6. Skim fat from sauce. Press Sauté and cook sauce, stirring frequently, for 5 minutes or until sauce is thickened to your liking. Pour sauce over shanks.

Beer and Cheese Fondue

A simple beer and cheese fondue allows the slow cooker to really shine. This version, served with soft pretzels, is intended as an appetizer, but you could also serve it as a main dish for 5 people, with vegetables, mini sausages and breads for dipping.

MAKES 8 SERVINGS

INSTANT POT FUNCTION
• Slow Cook •

1 tbsp	cornstarch	15 mL
1 tsp	dry mustard	5 mL
½ tsp	ground nutmeg	2 mL
1	sweet onion, finely chopped	1
1	clove garlic, minced	1
2 cups	shredded Cheddar cheese	500 mL
1 cup	shredded Gruyère cheese	250 mL
1	bottle (12 oz/341 mL) beer (any type)	1
	Kosher salt and freshly ground black pepper	
	Soft pretzels, warmed	

Tips

Gruyère cheese is the classic cheese for fondues, as it melts well and has a slightly nutty flavor. If you can't find a good Gruyère, you can substitute Emmental or Jarlsberg.

The fondue can be kept on Keep Warm for up to 2 hours before serving.

1. In the inner pot, combine cornstarch, mustard and nutmeg, mixing well. Stir in onion, garlic, Cheddar and Gruyère until coated. Add beer, stirring well.

2. Place the pot inside the cooker housing, close and lock the lid and turn the steam release handle to Venting. Press Slow Cook; the indicator will read "Normal." Press Adjust twice to adjust the heat level to "Less." Use the ⊖ button to decrease the time on the display to 2:00. Stir twice during the cooking time.

3. When the timer beeps, press Cancel. The cheese should be melted. (If more cooking is needed, reset the slow cooker to "Less" for 30 minutes.)

4. Stir the fondue, close and lock the lid and reset the slow cooker to "More" for 1 hour. Stir occasionally during the cooking time. Remove the lid and check to make sure the cheese is thickened to your desired consistency. (If more cooking is needed, reset the slow cooker to "Less" for 30 minutes.) Stir and season with salt and pepper. Serve with pretzels.

Caramelized Onion and Asiago Cheese Dip

I just love the aroma of cooking onions, and caramelizing them gives me extra time to experience that heady smell. The sweet little gems are then slow-cooked with Asiago cheese for a dip that will be a guest favorite. Serve with crackers.

MAKES 8 SERVINGS

INSTANT POT FUNCTIONS

• Sauté •
• Slow Cook •

1 tbsp	butter	15 mL
4	onions, chopped	4
1 tsp	granulated sugar	5 mL
¼ tsp	baking soda	1 mL
	Water	
2	cloves garlic, minced	2
½ tsp	dried thyme	2 mL
½ tsp	kosher salt	2 mL
1 lb	brick-style cream cheese, softened	500 g
1 cup	grated Asiago cheese	250 mL
⅓ cup	mayonnaise	75 mL
2 tsp	Worcestershire sauce	10 mL
2 tsp	chopped fresh chives (optional)	10 mL

Tip

This dip is also fantastic spread on toasted French bread or served with thick pretzel sticks for dipping.

1. Press Sauté; the indicator will read "Normal." When the display says "Hot," add butter and heat until melted. Add onions, sugar and baking soda; cook, stirring often, for 7 to 9 minutes or until the bottom of the pot is covered in a pale brown coating. Add 2 tbsp (30 mL) water, scraping up browned bits with a wooden spoon, and cook, stirring often, for 2 minutes or until coating has built up again. Continue cooking, adding water and scraping up browned bits every 3 minutes, for 25 minutes or until onions are softened and dark brown. Press Cancel.

2. Add garlic, thyme, salt, cream cheese, Asiago, mayonnaise and Worcestershire sauce to the pot, stirring well.

3. Close and lock the lid and turn the steam release handle to Venting. Press Slow Cook; the indicator will read "Normal." Press Adjust once to adjust the heat level to "More." Use the ⊖ button to decrease the time on the display to 2:00. Stir well every 30 minutes during the cooking time.

4. When the timer beeps, press Cancel. The dip should be well combined and the flavors melded. (If more cooking is needed, reset the slow cooker to "More" for up to 1 hour, stirring every 30 minutes.)

5. Transfer dip to a serving bowl and garnish with chives, if desired.

Zesty Crab Party Dip

This is one dip that will consistently please a large gathering, especially those guests who like a little bit of a kick. The crabmeat and artichokes contribute delicious substance to the creamy, spicy cheese. Serve with assorted crackers.

MAKES 30 SERVINGS

INSTANT POT FUNCTION
• Slow Cook •

8 oz	brick-style cream cheese, cut into cubes	250 g
2 cups	shredded mozzarella cheese	500 mL
¾ cup	freshly grated Parmesan cheese	175 mL
1 cup	mayonnaise	250 mL
½ cup	sour cream	125 mL
½ cup	milk	125 mL
Dash	Sriracha	Dash
2	cloves garlic, minced	2
2	cans (each 6 oz/170 g) backfin (lump) crabmeat, drained	2
1	can (14 oz/398 mL) artichoke hearts, drained and chopped	1
1 tsp	kosher salt	5 mL
½ tsp	freshly ground black pepper	2 mL
	Grated zest and juice of 1 lemon	
	Assorted crackers (optional)	

Tips

Do not increase the amount of Sriracha or make any other adjustments to the seasonings until the last 45 minutes of cooking. Spices intensify during long cooking times.

The dip can be kept on Keep Warm for up to 2 hours before serving.

1. In the inner pot, combine cream cheese, mozzarella, Parmesan, mayonnaise, sour cream, milk and Sriracha, stirring well.

2. Place the pot inside the cooker housing, close and lock the lid and turn the steam release handle to Venting. Press Slow Cook; the indicator will read "Normal." Press Adjust twice to adjust the heat level to "Less." Use the ⊖ button to decrease the time on the display to 1:30. Stir halfway through the cooking time.

3. When the timer beeps, press Cancel. The cheese should be melted. (If more cooking is needed, reset the slow cooker to "Less" for 30 minutes.)

4. Fold in garlic, crabmeat, artichoke hearts, salt, pepper, lemon zest and lemon juice. Close and lock the lid and reset the slow cooker to "More" for 45 minutes or until heated through. Stir occasionally during the cooking time.

Variation

For a spicier dip, replace half the mozzarella with pepper Jack cheese. Do not add the Sriracha in step 1. You can add it to taste, if desired, with the lemon juice in step 4.

Sweet-and-Spicy Dipping Wings

The blend of spices on these wings gives them a kick that is balanced by a sweet and cooling marinade. Serve them with celery stalks and ranch or blue cheese dressing for dipping, and this will become one of your go-to party recipes.

MAKES 12 SERVINGS

INSTANT POT FUNCTION

• Slow Cook •

- **Preheat broiler, with rack placed 6 inches (15 cm) from the heat source**
- **Baking sheet, lined with heavy duty foil and sprayed with nonstick cooking spray**

18	chicken wings, sections split apart, wing tips removed	18
2 tsp	Montreal steak seasoning	10 mL
2	cloves garlic, minced	2
1 tsp	smoked paprika	5 mL
¼ tsp	cayenne pepper	1 mL
¼ tsp	hot pepper flakes	1 mL
½ cup	chili sauce	125 mL
3 tbsp	pure maple syrup	45 mL
2 tbsp	Worcestershire sauce	30 mL

1. Season wings with steak seasoning and arrange on prepared baking sheet. Broil, turning often, for 8 to 12 minutes or until skin is browned and juices run clear when wings are pierced with a fork.

2. In the inner pot, combine garlic, paprika, cayenne, hot pepper flakes, chili sauce, maple syrup and Worcestershire sauce, stirring well. Add wings and stir to coat with sauce.

3. Place the pot inside the cooker housing, close and lock the lid and turn the steam release handle to Venting. Press Slow Cook; the indicator will read "Normal." Press Adjust twice to adjust the heat level to "Less." Use the ⊖ button to decrease the time on the display to 3:00. Stir occasionally during the cooking time.

4. When the timer beeps, remove the lid and check to make sure the wings are heated through and well coated with sauce. (If more cooking is needed, reset the slow cooker to "Less" for 30 minutes.)

Variation

To give the wings a firmer, glazed texture, after step 4, return wings to the prepared baking sheet and broil, turning occasionally, for 3 to 5 minutes or until browned and slightly caramelized.

Chipotle Chicken Nachos

These nachos make a great addition to a Cinco de Mayo party or any festive event. Honestly, I could eat a good Mexican dish just about anytime, and this one comes together beautifully.

INSTANT POT FUNCTION

• Slow Cook •

2 tbsp	garlic powder	30 mL
1 tbsp	seasoning salt	15 mL
1 tbsp	ground cumin	15 mL
1 tsp	freshly ground black pepper	5 mL
8	bone-in chicken thighs, skin removed	8
1	onion, chopped	1
1	can (4½ oz/127 mL) chopped green chiles	1
1	canned chipotle pepper, chopped	1
4 cups	ready-to-use chicken broth	1 L
¼ cup	ranch dressing	60 mL
1 tbsp	water	15 mL
1	bag (18 oz/560 g) tortilla chips	1
2 cups	shredded Mexican cheese blend	500 mL
2	jalapeño peppers, seeded and sliced	2

Tips

This dish can also be made in 4 hours. In step 3, press Adjust once to change the heat level to "More" and leave the time at 4:00. Continue with step 4.

Sliced black olives, sliced canned jalapeños and diced tomatoes are great toppings for these nachos.

---

1. In a small bowl, combine garlic powder, seasoning salt, cumin and pepper. Rub chicken with 1 tbsp (15 mL) of this seasoning. Reserve the remaining seasoning.

2. In the inner pot, combine chicken, onion, green chiles and chipotle pepper. Pour broth over top.

3. Place the pot inside the cooker housing, close and lock the lid and turn the steam release handle to Venting. Press Slow Cook; the indicator will read "Normal." Press Adjust twice to change the heat level to "Less." Use the ➕ button to increase the time on the display to 6:00.

4. Meanwhile, in a small bowl, combine ranch dressing, water and the reserved seasoning, stirring well.

5. When the timer beeps, remove the lid and check to make sure an instant-read thermometer inserted in the center of a thigh registers 165°F (74°C). (If more cooking is needed, reset the slow cooker to "Less" for 30 minutes.) Transfer chicken to a cutting board and, using a fork, shred meat. Discard bones and liquid from pot.

6. Arrange tortilla chips on a large serving platter, overlapping them two to three layers deep. Arrange shredded chicken over top. Sprinkle with Mexican cheese blend. Garnish with jalapeños. Drizzle with ranch dressing mixture.

Thai Crazy Meatballs

Take a package of prepared meatballs, drop them in your slow cooker with Thai-inspired flavorings, and you will have a crazy-fun appetizer bursting with umami to serve to your guests. Serve with toothpicks or bamboo spears for spearing the meatballs.

MAKES 12 SERVINGS

INSTANT POT FUNCTIONS

- Steam -
- Sauté -
- Slow Cook -

- **Instant Pot steam rack**
- **Steamer basket**

2 tsp	packed brown sugar	10 mL
½ cup	coconut milk	125 mL
¼ cup	ready-to-use chicken broth	60 mL
2 tsp	mirin (optional)	10 mL
1 tsp	fish sauce	5 mL
1 tsp	Thai red curry paste	5 mL
1	bag (3 lbs/1.5 kg) frozen fully cooked meatballs, thawed	1
1 tbsp	virgin olive oil	15 mL
2 tsp	freshly squeezed lime juice	10 mL
1 tbsp	cornstarch	15 mL
2 tbsp	cold water	30 mL

1. In a medium bowl, combine brown sugar, coconut milk, broth, mirin (if using), fish sauce and curry paste, mixing well. Set aside.

2. Add 1 cup (250 mL) water to the inner pot and place the steam rack in the pot. Add meatballs to the steamer basket and place the basket on the rack. Close and lock the lid and turn the steam release handle to Sealing. Press Steam; the indicator will read "High Pressure." Use the ⊖ button to decrease the time on the display to 5 minutes.

3. When the timer beeps, press Cancel and turn the steam release handle to Venting. When the float valve drops down, remove the lid. The meatballs should be heated through. (If more cooking is needed, reset the steamer to "High Pressure" for 2 minutes.) Carefully remove the steamer basket and rack. Discard water.

4. Press Sauté; the indicator will read "Normal." When the display says "Hot," add oil and heat until shimmering. Working in batches, add meatballs and cook, turning, for 2 to 3 minutes or until browned on all sides. Transfer to a plate. Press Cancel.

5. Return meatballs and any accumulated juices to the pot and add the coconut milk mixture. Close and lock the lid and turn the steam release handle to Venting. Press Slow Cook; the indicator will read "Normal." Press Adjust once to change the heat level to "More." Use the ⊖ button to decrease the time on the display to 3:30.

6. When the timer beeps, remove the lid and check to make sure the meatballs are heated through. (If more cooking is needed, reset the slow cooker to "Less" for 30 minutes.) Press Cancel. Stir in lime juice.

7. In a small bowl, whisk together cornstarch and cold water. Press Sauté. Add the cornstarch mixture to the pot and cook, uncovered, stirring occasionally, for 10 to 12 minutes or until sauce is slightly thickened.

Tips

You can press Keep Warm instead of Cancel in step 6 to keep the meatballs warm for up to 2 hours, until about 15 minutes before you are ready to serve. Complete step 7 just before serving.

As an appetizer, this recipe allows for about 3 meatballs per person.

Quinoa-Stuffed Bell Peppers

These stuffed peppers, full of flavor and fiber, make a tantalizing, filling main dish or side.

INSTANT POT FUNCTIONS
- Sauté •
- Manual Pressure •
- Slow Cook •

1 tbsp	virgin olive oil	15 mL
1½ cups	quinoa, rinsed	375 mL
3 cups	water	750 mL
	Kosher salt	
4	bell peppers (any color)	4
1	can (14 oz/398 mL) black beans, drained and rinsed (see tip, below)	1
1 cup	frozen corn kernels	250 mL
1 cup	salsa	250 mL
1 cup	shredded Monterey Jack cheese, divided	250 mL
½ cup	shredded mozzarella cheese	125 mL
2 tbsp	chopped fresh cilantro	30 mL
1 tsp	ground cumin	5 mL
½ tsp	hot pepper flakes	2 mL
	Freshly ground black pepper	
	Nonstick cooking spray	

Tips

If you cannot find a 14-oz (398 mL) can of black beans, purchase a larger can, drain and rinse the beans, then measure out 1⅔ cups (400 mL) for this recipe.

This dish can also be made in 2 to 3 hours. In step 5, press Adjust once to change the heat level to "More." Use the ➖ button to decrease the time on the display to 2:00. Continue with step 6.

1. Press Sauté; the indicator will read "Normal." When the display says "Hot," add oil to the pot and heat until shimmering. Add quinoa and cook, stirring constantly, for 4 to 6 minutes or until golden brown. Press Cancel. Add water and a pinch of salt.

2. Close and lock the lid and turn the steam release handle to Sealing. Press Manual; the indicator will read High Pressure. Select the ➖ button to decrease the time on the display to 1 minute.

3. When the timer beeps, press Cancel and let the pot stand, covered, for 10 minutes. After 10 minutes, turn the steam release handle to Venting and remove the lid. Transfer quinoa to a large bowl and fluff with a fork. Wash and dry the pot.

4. Cut the tops off the peppers and remove the seeds and ribs. Finely chop the tops. To the quinoa, add finely chopped bell pepper, beans, corn, salsa, ½ cup (125 mL) Monterey Jack, mozzarella, cilantro, cumin and hot pepper flakes. Season with salt and black pepper, stirring well. Spoon mixture into bell pepper shells, dividing evenly.

5. Spray the pot with cooking spray. Arrange stuffed peppers upright in pot. Close and lock the lid and turn the steam release handle to Venting. Press Slow Cook; the indicator will read "Normal." Press Adjust twice to change the heat level to "Less." Use the ➕ button to increase the time on the display to 5:00.

6. When the timer beeps, remove the lid and check to make sure the bell peppers are tender and the stuffing is heated through. (If more cooking is needed, reset the slow cooker to "Less" for 30 minutes.)

7. Top peppers with the remaining Monterey Jack. Reset the slow cooker to "Less," close and lock the lid and cook for 10 minutes or until cheese is melted.

Cheesy Vegetarian Baked Ziti

There is something glorious about little tubes of pasta swimming in a zesty marinara sauce and loaded with cheese — just about anyone would swoon with delight. For color and a bit of snap, this version also includes tender-crisp green beans.

MAKES 8 SERVINGS

INSTANT POT FUNCTIONS

• Steam •

• Slow Cook •

- Instant Pot steam rack
- Steamer basket

8 oz	green beans, trimmed and cut into 3-inch (7.5 cm) lengths	250 g
2	large eggs	2
3	cloves garlic, minced	3
1	package (15 oz/425 g) ricotta cheese	1
1 tbsp	freshly squeezed lemon juice	15 mL
½ cup	chopped fresh basil	125 mL
1 tbsp	chopped fresh sage	15 mL
	Nonstick cooking spray	
2	jars (each 26 oz/700 mL) marinara sauce	2
1 lb	dried ziti pasta	500 g
3 cups	shredded Italian cheese blend	750 mL
	Kosher salt and freshly ground black pepper	

1. Add 1 cup (250 mL) water to the inner pot and place the steam rack in the pot. Add beans to the steamer basket and place on the rack. Close and lock the lid and turn the steam release handle to Sealing. Press Steam; the indicator will read "High Pressure." Use the ⊖ button to decrease the time on the display to 5 minutes.

2. Meanwhile, in a medium bowl, whisk eggs. Add garlic, ricotta and lemon juice, mixing well. Fold in basil and sage.

3. When the timer beeps, press Cancel and turn the steam release handle to Venting. When the float valve drops down, remove the lid. Remove the steamer basket and rack from the pot. The beans should be tender-crisp. (Do not continue cooking, as they will soften more while slow-cooking.) Plunge beans into a bowl of cold water, then drain. Discard water from pot, rinse the pot and wipe it dry.

4. Spray the pot with cooking spray. Add 2 cups (500 mL) marinara sauce to the pot, followed by layers of one-third of the pasta, half the ricotta mixture, half the beans and one-third of the Italian cheese blend. Repeat layers, then top with remaining pasta and marinara sauce.

5. Close and lock the lid and turn the steam release handle to Venting. Press Slow Cook; the indicator will read "Normal." Press Adjust once to change the heat level to "More." Use the ⊖ button to decrease the time on the display to 3:00.

6. When the timer beeps, remove the lid and check to make sure the pasta is al dente. (If more cooking is needed, reset the slow cooker to "More" for 30 minutes.)

7. Sprinkle with the remaining Italian cheese blend. Reset the slow cooker to "More," close and lock the lid and cook for 30 minutes or until cheese is melted. Season to taste with salt and pepper.

Variation

Substitute 2 cups (500 mL) loosely packed baby spinach for the green beans. In step 1, adjust the pressure on the Steam setting to "Low Pressure" and the time to 1 minute. Continue with step 2. In step 3, the spinach should be wilted.

Coq au Vin

The inimitable Julia Child introduced her updated take on this traditional French dish to American cooks decades ago, and it retains its glory on many a table. The slow cooker makes this classic even easier.

INSTANT POT FUNCTIONS
- Sauté -
- Slow Cook -

4	chicken leg quarters	4
	Kosher salt and freshly ground black pepper	
1 tbsp	virgin olive oil	15 mL
10	slices thick-cut bacon, coarsely chopped	10
12 oz	cremini mushrooms, quartered	375 g
3	carrots, chopped	3
3	stalks celery, minced	3
2	cloves garlic, minced	2
1	onion, minced	1
1 cup	dry red wine, divided	250 mL
½ cup	tomato paste	125 mL
12	sprigs fresh thyme	12
6	sprigs fresh rosemary	6
3½ cups	ready-to-use chicken broth	875 mL

Tip

For added depth of flavor, you can use 12 oz (375 g) salted pork belly in place of the bacon.

1. Season chicken with salt and pepper. Press Sauté; the indicator will read "Normal." When the display says "Hot," add oil to the pot and heat until shimmering. Working in batches, add chicken and cook, turning once, for 5 to 7 minutes or until browned on both sides. Transfer chicken to a plate.

2. Add bacon to the pot and cook, stirring, for 4 to 5 minutes or until just crisp and fat is rendered. Transfer bacon to a plate lined with paper towels and let cool, then crumble.

3. Add mushrooms to the pot and cook, stirring, for 5 minutes or until lightly browned. Add carrots, celery, garlic and onion; cook, stirring, for 5 to 7 minutes or until onion is translucent.

4. Stir in ½ cup (125 mL) wine and tomato paste; cook, stirring, for 3 minutes or until combined. Add the remaining wine and cook, stirring occasionally, for 15 minutes or until wine is reduced by half. Return chicken to pot, along with any accumulated juices. Sprinkle with bacon. Add thyme sprigs, rosemary sprigs and broth, stirring well.

5. Close and lock the lid and turn the steam release handle to Venting. Press Slow Cook; the indicator will read "Normal." Press Adjust twice to change the heat level to "Less." Use the ➕ button to increase the time on the display to 6:00.

6. When the timer beeps, remove the lid and check to make sure an instant-read thermometer inserted in the center of a leg registers 165°F (74°C) and chicken is falling off the bone. (If more cooking is needed, reset the slow cooker to "Less" for 1 hour.) Season to taste with salt and pepper. Transfer chicken to serving platter and drizzle juices over top.

Slow-Braised Ham with Maple Mustard Glaze

I love this ham for holidays and large gatherings because it is so hands-off, and it frees up my oven for other dishes to serve with it.

MAKES 10 SERVINGS

INSTANT POT FUNCTION

• Slow Cook •

	Nonstick cooking spray	
1	fully cooked bone-in ham (about 5 lbs/2.5 kg)	1
¾ cup	packed brown sugar	175 mL
¾ cup	pure maple syrup	175 mL
½ cup	Dijon mustard	125 mL
¼ cup	unsweetened apple juice	60 mL

Tips

The bone-in ham should be about 7 by 5 inches (18 by 12.5 cm) to fit inside the pot.

Reserve the ham bone to make the perfect Hearty Ham and Split Pea Soup (page 65). The ham bone can be frozen for up to 3 months.

1. Spray the inner pot with cooking spray. Cut slits across the top surface of the ham about ¼ inch (0.5 cm) deep and 1 inch (2.5 cm) apart, making a diamond pattern. Place ham in the pot with the slits up.

2. In a small bowl, combine brown sugar, maple syrup, mustard and apple juice, stirring well. Brush ham with some of the glaze, working it into the slits, then pour the remaining glaze over top.

3. Close and lock the lid and turn the steam release handle to Venting. Press Slow Cook; the indicator will read "Normal." Press Adjust twice to change the heat level to "Less." Use the ✚ button to increase the time on the display to 8:00.

4. When the timer beeps, remove the lid and check to make sure an instant-read thermometer inserted in the center of the ham registers 140°F (60°C). (If more cooking is needed, reset the slow cooker to "Less" for 30 minutes.) Remove ham from pot and slice. Drizzle some of the sauce over the ham and serve the remaining sauce in a gravy boat.

Jamaican Jerk Pork with Mango Salsa

You will need to plan ahead to allow this rustic dish its marinating and slow-cooking time, but it will be well worth the wait for the fiery taste of jerk paired with the cooling sensation of mangos.

INSTANT POT FUNCTION

• Slow Cook •

• Mortar and pestle

Jerk Pork

3 lb	boneless pork shoulder blade roast, trimmed	1.5 kg
6	cloves garlic, sliced	6
3 tbsp	dry Jamaican jerk seasoning	45 mL
1 tsp	kosher salt	5 mL
	Juice of 2 small oranges	
	Juice of 1½ limes, divided	

Mango Salsa

2	large ripe mangos, chopped	2
1	avocado, diced	1
2 tbsp	chopped red onion	30 mL
2 tbsp	chopped fresh cilantro	30 mL
	Kosher salt and freshly ground black pepper	

1. *Jerk Pork:* Cut small slits over the entire roast and push half of the sliced garlic into the slits.

2. Using the mortar and pestle, crush the remaining garlic, jerk seasoning and salt together to form a coarse paste. Using kitchen gloves, rub mixture all over roast. Transfer roast to a large sealable bag. Add orange juice and one-third of the lime juice. Seal bag and refrigerate for 8 hours, turning two or three times to keep pork coated.

3. Transfer pork and marinade to the inner pot. Close and lock the lid and turn the steam release handle to Venting. Press Slow Cook; the indicator will read "Normal." Press Adjust twice to change the heat level to "Less." Use the ✚ button to increase the time on the display to 9:00.

4. *Mango Salsa:* Meanwhile, in a medium bowl, combine mangos, avocado, onion, cilantro and the remaining lime juice. Cover and refrigerate until ready to use.

5. When the timer beeps, remove the lid and check to make sure an instant-read thermometer inserted in the thickest part of the roast registers 165°F (74°C) for medium-well. (If more cooking is needed, reset the slow cooker to "Less" and cook for 30 to 60 minutes.)

6. Transfer pork to a cutting board, cover with foil and let rest for 10 minutes. Carve into coarse pieces. Transfer to a serving platter and garnish with mango salsa.

Tip

This dish is excellent served with sweet potatoes prepared in any style. My favorite is to braise sliced sweet potatoes: In a skillet, melt 2 tbsp (30 mL) butter over medium-high heat. Add 1½ lbs (750 g) sliced peeled sweet potatoes, a pinch of kosher salt and 1 cup (250 mL) water; cover and bring to a boil. Boil, shaking pan occasionally, for 10 minutes or until a knife inserted in the sweet potatoes meets a little resistance. Add 1½ tbsp (22 mL) pure maple syrup and boil, uncovered, shaking pan occasionally, until sweet potatoes are lightly browned and the liquid forms a glaze. Season to taste with kosher salt.

Carnitas Tacos

Celebrate Cinco de Mayo with these flavorful, tender pork tacos. They make for the perfect taco bar for any occasion.

MAKES 12 SERVINGS		

INSTANT POT FUNCTIONS		
• Slow Cook •		
• Sauté •		

3½ lb	boneless pork shoulder blade roast, trimmed and cut in half	1.75 kg
1	onion, quartered	1
5	cloves garlic, minced	5
1 cup	ready-to-use chicken broth	250 mL
1	orange	1
	Juice of 1 lime	
2 tsp	ground cumin	10 mL
1 tsp	dried oregano	5 mL
2	bay leaves	2
	Kosher salt and freshly ground black pepper	
12	taco-size (6-inch/15 cm) flour tortillas	12

Suggested Toppings

Sour cream

Shredded cheese

Diced avocado

Diced tomatoes

Minced red onion

Salsa

Tip

This dish can also be made in 4 hours. In step 2, press Adjust once to change the heat level to "More" and leave the time at 4:00. Continue with step 3.

1. Place roast in the inner pot. Arrange onion over roast and sprinkle with garlic. Add broth. Cut orange in half and squeeze juice into a small bowl. Add squeezed halves to pot. Add lime juice, cumin and oregano to the orange juice, mixing well, then pour into the pot. Add bay leaves. Season well with salt and pepper.

2. Close and lock the lid and turn the steam release handle to Venting. Press Slow Cook; the indicator will read "Normal." Press Adjust twice to change the heat level to "Less." Use the ➕ button to increase the time on the display to 8:00.

3. When the timer beeps, remove the lid and check to make sure an instant-read thermometer inserted in the thickest part of the roast registers 165°F (74°C) for medium-well and pork is fork-tender. (If more cooking is needed, reset the slow cooker to "Less" for 30 minutes.) Discard bay leaves. Transfer pork to a cutting board, cover with foil and let rest for 10 minutes, then cut into ½-inch (1 cm) chunks.

4. Meanwhile, strain the pot juices, discarding solids, skim off the fat and return juices to the pot. Press Sauté and bring juices to a simmer. Simmer, stirring occasionally, for 12 to 15 minutes or until juices are reduced to about ½ inch (1 cm) deep in the pot.

5. Return pork to the pot, along with any accumulated juices. Simmer for 5 minutes or until flavors are blended. Season to taste with salt and pepper.

6. Press Keep Warm. Add a slotted spoon to the pot for serving. Serve buffet-style with tortillas and the suggested toppings.

Mississippi Delta Baby Back Pork Ribs

Inspired by the jazz music and sassy style of the Lower Delta, these ribs sing in a sweet and spicy barbecue sauce. When you want to reminisce about dinner in your favorite jazz club, serve these ribs and dive right in.

MAKES 10 SERVINGS

INSTANT POT FUNCTION
• Slow Cook •

	Nonstick cooking spray	
6 lbs	baby back pork ribs	3 kg
¾ cup	packed brown sugar	175 mL
2 tbsp	Cajun seasoning	30 mL
1 tbsp	garlic powder	15 mL
1 tbsp	onion powder	15 mL
5 cups	barbecue sauce	1.25 L
¼ cup	dark (cooking) molasses	60 mL

Tip

Any of your favorite barbecue sauces will work well in this recipe. Keep in mind that you will be adding sugar and molasses for sweetness and seasonings for spiciness, so select your sauce accordingly.

1. Spray the inner pot with cooking spray. Cut ribs into 3 to 4 sections and arrange in pot.

2. In a large bowl, combine brown sugar, Cajun seasoning, garlic powder, onion powder, barbecue sauce and molasses, stirring well. Transfer 1 cup (250 mL) sauce to a small bowl, cover and refrigerate. Pour the remaining sauce over ribs.

3. Close and lock the lid and turn the steam release handle to Venting. Press Slow Cook; the indicator will read "Normal." Press Adjust twice to change the heat level to "Less." Use the ✚ button to increase the time on the display to 8:00.

4. When the timer beeps, remove the lid and check to make sure the meat is no longer pink and falls easily off the bone. (If more cooking is needed, reset the slow cooker to "Less" and cook for 30 to 60 minutes.) Using tongs, transfer ribs to a serving plate.

5. Skim any fat from sauce. Drizzle sauce over ribs. Serve with the reserved sauce.

Spicy Chipotle Beef Brisket

For a truly fine brisket, the process needs to be low and slow. This one is no exception, but is hands-free once you close the slow cooker lid. The results are tender, packed with flavor and ready to feed a crowd.

MAKES 10 SERVINGS

INSTANT POT FUNCTIONS
- Slow Cook -
- Sauté -

	Nonstick cooking spray	
3 tbsp	packed brown sugar	45 mL
2 tsp	ground cumin	10 mL
2 tsp	horseradish powder (see tip, page 153)	10 mL
1 tsp	celery powder	5 mL
1 tsp	garlic powder	5 mL
1 tsp	kosher salt	5 mL
½ tsp	freshly ground black pepper	2 mL
4½ lb	beef brisket	2.25 kg
2	cloves garlic, minced	2
2	chipotle peppers in adobo sauce, chopped	2
¼ cup	finely chopped onion	60 mL
1	can (15 oz/425 mL) tomato sauce, divided	1
¾ cup	ready-to-use beef broth	175 mL
¼ cup	apple cider vinegar	60 mL
1 tbsp	Worcestershire sauce	15 mL

1. Spray the inner pot with cooking spray. In a small bowl, combine brown sugar, cumin, horseradish powder, celery powder, garlic powder, salt and pepper. Rub all over brisket. Place brisket in the pot.

2. In a medium bowl, combine garlic, chipotles and adobo sauce, onion, 1 cup (250 mL) tomato sauce, broth, vinegar and Worcestershire sauce, mixing well. Pour sauce over brisket.

3. Close and lock the lid and turn the steam release handle to Venting. Press Slow Cook; the indicator will read "Normal." Press Adjust once to change the heat level to "More." Use the ✚ button to increase the time on the display to 7:00.

4. When the timer beeps, remove the lid and check to make sure an instant-read thermometer inserted in the thickest part of the brisket registers at least 160°F (71°C) for medium. (If more cooking is needed, reset the slow cooker to "More" for 30 minutes.) Transfer brisket to a cutting board, cover loosely with foil and let rest for 10 minutes.

5. Meanwhile, skim the fat from the liquids in the pot and add the remaining tomato sauce. Press Sauté and cook, stirring often, for 5 to 7 minutes or until sauce is slightly thickened.

6. Slice brisket across the grain and arrange slices on a serving platter. Spoon sauce over top.

Tips

Your brisket should be "boneless," with deckle off. This cut of brisket is often called "cut 120." It has bones 1 to 4 removed and the hard fat, known as deckle, trimmed off. You can ask your butcher to trim your brisket to these specifications, if it's not already done.

Your brisket may need to be cut into smaller sections to fit inside the cooker. Arrange the pieces as needed so they will be covered with sauce when slow cooking.

Derby Party Bourbon-Glazed Short Ribs

Every year I host a Kentucky Derby party, and these ribs are always a hands-down favorite. They are rich and tender, and feature many Kentucky staples, including ribs, bourbon and brown sugar.

INSTANT POT FUNCTIONS		
• Sauté •		
• Slow Cook •		

3 lbs	boneless beef short ribs, in 2- by 2- by 8-inch (5 by 5 by 20 cm) pieces	1.5 kg
	Kosher salt and freshly ground black pepper	
	Virgin olive oil	
4	stalks celery, diced	4
3	carrots, diced	3
2	cloves garlic, minced	2
1	onion, finely chopped	1
¼ cup	tomato paste	60 mL
2	bay leaves	2
2 tbsp	chopped fresh rosemary	30 mL
2 tbsp	chopped fresh thyme	30 mL
2 tbsp	whole black peppercorns	30 mL
1	bottle (12 oz/341 mL) stout or dark beer	1
2 cups	bourbon, divided	500 mL
2 cups	apple cider, divided	500 mL
4 cups	ready-to-use beef broth	1 L
5	large shallots, thinly sliced	5
2 tbsp	packed brown sugar	30 mL
3 tbsp	prepared horseradish	45 mL
2 tbsp	butter, softened	30 mL

1. Season ribs with salt and pepper. Press Sauté; the indicator will read "Normal." When the display says "Hot," add 2 tbsp (30 mL) oil and heat until shimmering. Working in batches, add ribs and cook, turning often, for 5 to 7 minutes or until browned all over, adding more oil as needed. Transfer ribs to a plate.

2. Add 1 tbsp (15 mL) oil to the pot. Add celery, carrots, garlic and onion; cook, stirring, for 5 to 7 minutes or until browned. Add tomato paste and cook, stirring, for 7 to 10 minutes or until vegetables are caramelized.

3. Stir in bay leaves, rosemary, thyme, peppercorns, beer, 1 cup (250 mL) bourbon and 1 cup (250 mL) apple cider; boil, stirring occasionally, for 15 to 20 minutes or until sauce is reduced by half. Add broth, stirring well. Press Cancel. Add ribs.

4. Close and lock the lid and turn the steam release handle to Venting. Press Slow Cook; the indicator will read "Normal." Press Adjust twice to change the heat level to "Less." Use the ➕ button to increase the time on the display to 6:00.

5. When the timer beeps, remove the lid and check to make sure ribs are fork-tender. (If more cooking is needed, reset the slow cooker to "Less" for 30 minutes.) Discard bay leaves. Transfer ribs to a serving plate and cover loosely with foil.

6. Strain the pot juices, discarding solids, skim off fat and return juices to the pot. Press Sauté. Add shallots, brown sugar and the remaining bourbon and apple cider; cook, stirring occasionally, for about 10 minutes or until sauce starts to thicken. Add horseradish and butter, stirring until butter is melted. Season to taste with salt and pepper.

7. Pour enough sauce over the ribs to coat them. Serve with any remaining sauce on the side.

Tips

If you really want to take this dish up a notch, substitute apple-flavored brandy for the apple cider.

For a truly festive Derby party, serve with mint juleps and wear a fabulous hat.

Lamb Shanks with Red Wine and Mushrooms

Lamb is one of my favorite meats, and these slow-cooked shanks with a slightly sweet and tangy mushroom sauce are near the top of my favorites list. They are perfect for a special-occasion dinner.

MAKES 4 SERVINGS

INSTANT POT FUNCTIONS

• Sauté •

• Slow Cook •

1 cup	all-purpose flour	250 mL
2 tsp	kosher salt	10 mL
½ tsp	freshly ground black pepper	2 mL
4	lamb shanks, frenched (see tip, opposite)	4
4 tbsp	virgin olive oil, divided	60 mL
2	onions, sliced	2
4	cloves garlic, chopped	4
2 cups	ready-to-use beef broth	500 mL
1 cup	dry red wine	250 mL
⅓ cup	pure maple syrup	75 mL
2 cups	sliced mushrooms	500 mL
1 tbsp	butter	15 mL
3 tbsp	cornstarch	45 mL
3 tbsp	cold water	45 mL

1. In a medium bowl, combine flour, salt and pepper. Add lamb and toss to coat, shaking off excess flour. Discard any leftover flour mixture.

2. Press Sauté; the indicator will read "Normal." When the display says "Hot," add 2 tbsp (30 mL) oil and heat until shimmering. Working in batches, add lamb and cook, turning often, for 5 to 7 minutes or until browned all over. Transfer lamb to a plate.

3. Add onions and the remaining oil to the pot and cook, stirring, for 5 to 7 minutes or until onions are translucent. Add garlic and cook, stirring, for 30 seconds or until fragrant. Add broth, wine and maple syrup, stirring well. Return lamb to the pot, along with any accumulated juices. Press Cancel.

4. Close and lock the lid and turn the steam release handle to Venting. Press Slow Cook; the indicator will read "Normal." Press Adjust twice to change the heat level to "Less." Use the ✚ button to increase the time on the display to 7:00.

5. When the timer beeps, remove the lid and check to make sure the shanks are fall-off-the-bone tender. (If more cooking is needed, reset the slow cooker to "Less" for 30 minutes.) Transfer the shanks to a serving platter, cover with foil and let rest for 10 minutes.

6. Meanwhile, strain the pot juices, discarding solids, and return juices to the pot. In a small bowl, whisk together cornstarch and cold water. Press Sauté. Add the cornstarch mixture to the pot and cook, whisking, for 3 to 5 minutes or until sauce is the consistency of gravy. Serve gravy with lamb shanks.

Tips

To french lamb shanks, use a paring knife to trim off any excess fat and silverskin. Insert the knife near the narrow end of the shank, underneath a tendon, and cut toward the thicker part, severing the tendon from the bone. Rotate shanks and repeat until all tendons are severed. This step enables the meat to pull back from the bone during cooking.

These lamb shanks are fantastic with mashed potatoes and a side of steamed vegetables.

Depending on what type of shanks you purchase, you may want to ask your butcher how many you need per serving. Fore and hind shanks differ in size. In addition, American lamb and New Zealand lamb can be very different sizes.

White Bean and Garlic Dip

This dip is very similar to hummus but has more texture and a hint of Italian seasonings. Served with toasted pita chips, it's a great party starter. For best results, the beans should be soaked overnight, so start preparing this dip a day ahead of your event.

MAKES 8 SERVINGS

INSTANT POT FUNCTION
• Bean/Chili •

- **Preheat oven to 400°F (200°C)**
- **2 rimmed baking sheets, lined with heavy-duty foil**
- **Food processor**

6	8-inch (20 cm) pitas, each cut into 16 wedges	6
¾ cup	virgin olive oil, divided	175 mL
1 tsp	dried oregano	5 mL
	Kosher salt and freshly ground black pepper	
1½ cups	dried cannellini (white kidney) beans, rinsed	375 mL
	Water	
2	cloves garlic	2
¼ cup	loosely packed fresh parsley leaves	60 mL
	Juice of 1 lemon	

Tip

It is not strictly necessary to soak the beans overnight; however, doing so reduces the amount of gas they cause. If you decide not to soak, start with step 3 and increase the cooking time in step 4 to 35 minutes.

1. In a large bowl, toss together pita wedges, 3 tbsp (45 mL) oil, oregano, and salt and pepper to taste. Spread in a single layer on prepared baking sheets. Bake in preheated oven for 7 to 10 minutes or until lightly toasted and golden. Let cool completely, then store in an airtight container at room temperature for up to 1 day.

2. Place beans in a large bowl and add enough water to cover beans by 2 inches (5 cm). Let stand for 8 to 12 hours. Drain and rinse beans.

3. In the inner pot, combine beans, 2 tbsp (30 mL) oil and enough water to cover beans by 2 inches (5 cm).

4. Place the pot inside the cooker housing, close and lock the lid and turn the steam release handle to Sealing. Press Bean/Chili; the indicator will read "High Pressure." Use the ⊖ button to decrease the time on the display to 8 minutes.

5. When the timer beeps, press Cancel and let the pot stand, covered, for 15 minutes. After 15 minutes, turn the steam release handle to Venting and remove the lid. The beans should be very soft. (If more cooking is needed, reset to "High Pressure" for 5 minutes.) Drain and rinse beans. Let stand until cool.

6. In food processor, combine beans, garlic, parsley, ¼ cup (60 mL) oil and lemon juice; pulse until coarsely chopped.

7. Transfer bean dip to a serving bowl and season to taste with salt and pepper. Using the back of a spoon, make a depression in the dip and drizzle with the remaining oil. Serve with pita chips.

Tex-Mex Black Bean Dip

Serve up a zesty black bean dip from the Southwest to set the theme for your next hoedown. Your party guests will enjoy the deep and spicy flavors.

MAKES 12 SERVINGS

INSTANT POT FUNCTIONS
- Bean/Chili •
- Slow Cook •

1½ cups	dried black beans	375 mL
1½ cups	dried pinto beans	375 mL
	Water	
2 tbsp	virgin olive oil	30 mL
2	bay leaves	2
1	package (1.25 oz/37 g) taco seasoning	1
1 tsp	onion powder	5 mL
1 cup	frozen corn kernels	250 mL
1 cup	shredded Cheddar cheese, divided	250 mL
3 cups	ready-to-use vegetable broth	750 mL
2 cups	salsa	500 mL
3	green onions, thinly sliced	3
	Tortilla chips	

Tips

You can use the 10-minute quick soak method described on page 10 if you did not soak your beans overnight.

Instead of dried beans, you can use 1 can (14 to 19 oz/398 to 540 mL) each of black beans and pinto beans and start with step 5.

1. Place black beans and pinto beans in a large bowl and add enough water to cover beans by 2 inches (5 cm). Let stand for 8 to 12 hours. Drain and rinse beans.

2. In the inner pot, combine beans, oil and enough water to cover beans by 2 inches (5 cm).

3. Place the pot inside the cooker housing, close and lock the lid and turn the steam release handle to Sealing. Press Bean/Chili; the indicator will read "High Pressure." Use the ⊖ button to decrease the time on the display to 7 minutes.

4. When the timer beeps, press Cancel and let the pot stand, covered, for 15 minutes. After 15 minutes, turn the steam release handle to Venting and remove the lid. The beans should be very soft. (If more cooking is needed, reset to "High Pressure" for 5 minutes.) Drain and rinse beans. Rinse out pot.

5. In the pot, combine beans, bay leaves, taco seasoning, onion powder, corn, ⅔ cup (150 mL) cheese, broth, 2 cups (500 mL) water and salsa, stirring well.

6. Place the pot inside the cooker housing, close and lock the lid and turn the steam release handle to Venting. Press Slow Cook; the indicator will read "Normal." Press Adjust twice to change the heat level to "Less." Use the ⊖ button to decrease the time on the display to 3:00. Stir halfway through cooking time.

7. When the timer beeps, remove the lid and check to make sure the dip is heated through. (If more cooking is needed, reset the slow cooker to "Less" for 30 minutes.) Discard bay leaves.

8. Transfer dip to a serving bowl and garnish with the remaining cheese and green onions. Serve with tortilla chips.

Warm Chili Cheese Dip

This warm, hearty cheese dip is wonderful for game day parties — it's so filling it's almost a meal in itself. You can easily double the recipe to serve a larger group.

INSTANT POT FUNCTION

• Bean/Chili •

	Nonstick cooking spray	
1	onion, finely chopped	1
1	clove garlic, minced	1
1	can (15 oz/425 mL) chili without beans	1
8 oz	brick-style cream cheese, softened	250 g
1¼ cups	shredded Cheddar cheese	300 mL
1 cup	salsa	250 mL
3	green onions, thinly sliced	3
	Tortilla chips	

Tip

For the salsa, you can choose versions from mild to extra-spicy, depending on your preferences.

1. Spray the inner pot with cooking spray. Add onion, garlic, chili, cream cheese, Cheddar and salsa, stirring well.

2. Place the pot inside the cooker housing, close and lock the lid and turn the steam release handle to Sealing. Press Bean/Chili; the indicator will read "High Pressure." Use the ⊖ button to decrease the time on the display to 7 minutes.

3. When the timer beeps, remove the lid, stir dip thoroughly and check to make sure the dip is creamy and heated through. (If more cooking is needed, reset to "Less" for 2 minutes.)

4. Transfer dip to a serving bowl and garnish with green onions. Serve with tortilla chips.

Variation

Serve the dip in a hollowed-out sourdough loaf. Cut off the top and break it into bite-size pieces. Carefully pull out bite-size pieces from the core of the loaf. Pour the dip inside the bread bowl and serve with the bread pieces for dipping.

Pork and Shrimp Wontons

These little dumplings of joy are one of my most requested appetizers. They also make a wonderful light lunch, snack or dinner. While these are made with pork and shrimp, they can easily be varied to just pork or shrimp, or to use ground chicken.

MAKES 12 SERVINGS

INSTANT POT FUNCTIONS

• Sauté •

• Steam •

• **Instant Pot steam rack**

1 tbsp	sesame oil	15 mL
8 oz	ground pork	250 g
4 oz	shrimp, peeled, deveined and chopped	125 g
2	cloves garlic, minced	2
1 tbsp	minced gingerroot	15 mL
¼ cup	teriyaki sauce	60 mL
Dash	fish sauce (optional)	Dash
36	3-inch (7.5 cm) square wonton wrappers	36
	Water	
4	green onions, sliced	4

Tips

Wonton wrappers can be found in the frozen or produce section of well-stocked grocery stores or at Asian markets. If frozen, let thaw in the refrigerator overnight before using.

Serve with additional teriyaki sauce, soy sauce or your favorite sauce for dipping.

1. Press Sauté; the indicator will read "Normal." When the display says "Hot," add oil to the pot and heat until shimmering. Add pork and cook, breaking it up with a spoon, for 3 minutes. Add shrimp and cook, stirring, for 2 to 3 minutes or until pork is no longer pink and shrimp are transparent. Add garlic and ginger; cook, stirring, for 1 minute or until fragrant. Press Cancel.

2. Transfer filling to a bowl and add teriyaki sauce and fish sauce (if using), mixing well. Wash and dry the inner pot.

3. Working in batches, place wonton wrappers on a plate and add about 1 tbsp (15 mL) filling to the center of each. Using your fingers, brush the edges of the wrappers with water and fold into a triangle, squeezing out air and pressing down edges to seal. Repeat until all wrappers are filled.

4. Add 1 cup (250 mL) water to the inner pot and place the steam rack in the pot. Place about 12 filled wontons on the rack, overlapping slightly. Close and lock the lid and turn the steam release handle to Sealing. Press Steam; the indicator will read "High Pressure." Use the ➖ button to decrease the time on the display to 5 minutes.

5. When the timer beeps, press Cancel and turn the steam release handle to Venting. When the float valve drops down, remove the lid. The wontons should be hot and steaming. (If more cooking is needed, reset the steamer to "High Pressure" for 1 minute.) Transfer wontons to a serving platter, cover with foil and keep warm. Add water as necessary to maintain 1 cup (250 mL) water in the bottom of the pot. Repeat with the remaining wontons. Serve sprinkled with green onions.

Steamed Artichokes with Garlic Aïoli

There is something incredibly fun about pulling the leaves off steamed artichokes, dipping them in rich sauce and then scraping the delicate, meaty core. In my opinion, this is the ultimate conversation-food appetizer.

MAKES 2 SERVINGS

INSTANT POT FUNCTION

• Steam •

• **Instant Pot steam rack**

½ tsp	minced garlic	2 mL
½ tsp	paprika	2 mL
1 tsp	kosher salt, divided	5 mL
½ tsp	chili powder (optional)	2 mL
½ cup	mayonnaise	125 mL
2	lemons, divided	2
2	cloves garlic, peeled	2
2	sprigs fresh parsley	2
1	bay leaf	1
Pinch	freshly ground black pepper	Pinch
1 cup	water	250 mL
¼ cup	white wine vinegar	60 mL
2	medium artichokes, trimmed (see tip, at right)	2

1. In a small bowl, whisk together minced garlic, paprika, a pinch of salt, chili powder (if using), mayonnaise and the juice of 1 lemon. Set aside.

2. Cut the remaining lemon in half. Squeeze the juice into the pot and add the squeezed halves. Add garlic, parsley sprigs, bay leaf, the remaining salt, pepper, water and vinegar. Place the steam rack in the pot. Place artichokes, bottom side up, on the rack.

3. Place the pot inside the cooker housing, close and lock the lid and turn the steam release handle to Sealing. Press Steam; the indicator will read "High Pressure." Use the ⊖ button to decrease the time on the display to 6 minutes.

4. When the timer beeps, press Cancel and turn the steam release handle to Venting. When the float valve drops down, remove the lid. Check to make sure a knife inserted in the base of the artichokes encounters no resistance and the leaves pull easily from the base. (If more cooking is needed, reset the steamer to "High Pressure" for 1 minute.)

5. Transfer artichokes to a serving platter, stem side down. Serve with aïoli for dipping the leaves as you pull them off the artichoke. When you reach the center of the artichoke, scrape away and discard the prickly fuzz covering the heart. Cut the heart into sections for dipping.

Tips

To prepare the artichokes for steaming, cut off the stem and 1½ inches (4 cm) of the top. Using scissors, cut the sharp tips from the tops of the leaves. Remove any small, tough outer leaves near the base. You may want to rub the cut surfaces with lemon as you are cutting to prevent browning. Rinse artichokes well.

The aïoli can be made ahead, covered and refrigerated for up to 3 days. Bring to room temperature (about 30 minutes) before serving.

Desserts and Snacks

Pressure Cooker

Slow Cooker

continued on next page . . .

Desserts and Snacks
(continued)

Quick and Easy Cook Functions

Cherries Jubilee

This dessert was extremely popular during the first half of the 20th century and is still considered an elegant dessert for any occasion. Who knew it could be so simple? This version doesn't have the burst of flames, but the taste is just as stunning.

INSTANT POT FUNCTIONS

• Manual Pressure •
• Sauté •

1	lemon	1
1 lb	frozen sweet cherries (such as Bing)	500 g
½ cup	granulated sugar	125 mL
⅓ cup	white grape juice	75 mL
¼ cup	water, divided	60 mL
2 tsp	cherry extract	10 mL
¼ tsp	almond extract	1 mL
1 tbsp	cornstarch	15 mL
2 tbsp	cold water	30 mL
1 pint	vanilla ice cream	500 mL

Tip

You can use fresh sweet cherries instead of frozen. Wash and dry the cherries, then remove the pits. You will want to use kitchen gloves so the cherries do not stain your hands. It is best to pit cherries in a bowl in the bottom of your sink, as they will squirt staining juices when they are pitted.

1. Peel 2 wide strips of zest from the lemon and squeeze juice from ½ lemon.

2. In the inner pot, combine lemon zest, lemon juice, cherries, sugar, grape juice, ¼ cup (60 mL) water, cherry extract and almond extract, stirring well.

3. Place the pot inside the cooker housing, close and lock the lid and turn the steam release handle to Sealing. Press Manual; the indicator will read "High Pressure." Press Pressure once to adjust the pressure to "Low Pressure." Use the ⊖ button to decrease the time on the display to 7 minutes.

4. When the timer beeps, press Cancel and turn the steam release handle to Venting. When the float valve drops down, remove the lid. The cherries should give easily when pressed with a wooden spoon. (If more cooking is needed, reset the manual pressure to "Low Pressure" for 2 minutes.)

5. In a small bowl, whisk together cornstarch and cold water. Press Sauté. Add the cornstarch mixture to the pot and cook, stirring often, for 3 to 4 minutes or until sauce is thickened.

6. Scoop ice cream into serving bowls and drizzle with cherry sauce.

Red Wine and Citrus Poached Pears

Here, delicate pears are infused with red wine, citrus and spices until they are bursting with flavor and have a beautiful deep red color that makes for a striking dessert presentation.

MAKES 4 SERVINGS

INSTANT POT FUNCTIONS

• Manual Pressure •
• Sauté •

1	orange	1
1	lemon	1
4	large firm pears (such as Bosc), peeled, cut in half lengthwise, then cored	4
5	whole cloves	5
1	4-inch (10 cm) cinnamon stick	1
1 cup	granulated sugar, divided	250 mL
1½ cups	dry red wine	375 mL
¼ tsp	vanilla extract	1 mL
½ cup	crème fraîche or mascarpone	125 mL

Tip

Pears are frequently sold not quite ripe so they don't become damaged before you get them home. You will want to plan ahead to ripen them at home for a few days before cooking them. You can put them in a paper bag to speed up the ripening process.

1. Cut orange into quarters and squeeze juice from all quarters into the inner pot. Add one of the quarters to the pot. Cut lemon in half and squeeze juice from both halves into the pot. Add pears, cloves, cinnamon stick, ¾ cup (175 mL) sugar, wine and vanilla, stirring well.

2. Place the pot inside the cooker housing, close and lock the lid and turn the steam release handle to Sealing. Press Manual; the indicator will read "High Pressure." Use the ⊖ button to decrease the time on the display to 3 minutes.

3. When the timer beeps, press Cancel. Let stand, covered, until the float valve drops down. Turn the steam release handle to Venting and remove the lid. Check to make sure the pears are fork-tender. (If more cooking is needed, reset the manual pressure to "High Pressure" for 1 minute.) Using a slotted spoon, gently transfer pears to serving plates. Discard orange quarter, cloves and cinnamon stick.

4. Press Sauté and cook until wine is reduced by half. Drizzle sauce over pears.

5. In a small bowl, gently stir together crème fraîche and the remaining sugar. Serve a dollop next to each pear.

Peanut Butter Pecan Brownies

Chocolate, peanut butter and pecans are the magic trio in these gooey, moist brownies. Serve them warm or at room temperature; either way, they are sure to be a hit.

INSTANT POT FUNCTION

• Manual Pressure •

- **6-inch (15 cm) springform pan, sprayed with nonstick cooking spray**
- **Instant Pot steam rack**

⅔ cup	unsweetened cocoa powder	150 mL
¼ cup	all-purpose flour	60 mL
¾ cup	granulated sugar	175 mL
2	large eggs	2
½ cup	unsalted butter, melted	125 mL
½ tsp	vanilla extract	2 mL
½ cup	chopped pecans	125 mL
3 tbsp	peanut butter chips	45 mL
	Confectioners' (icing) sugar (optional)	

Tips

You can also use a 6-inch (15 cm) round metal cake pan in this recipe. Line the bottom of the cake pan with waxed paper or parchment paper lightly coated with nonstick cooking spray to make it easier to release your brownies from the pan.

You can use any variety of nuts and chips in this recipe; just keep the measurements the same.

1. In a large bowl, whisk together cocoa and flour.
2. In a medium bowl, whisk together sugar, eggs, butter and vanilla. Add to the cocoa mixture, whisking well. Fold in pecans and peanut butter chips. Pour batter into prepared pan.
3. Add 2 cups (500 mL) water to the inner pot and place the steam rack in the pot. Place pan on the rack. Close and lock the lid and turn the steam release handle to Sealing. Press Manual; the indicator will read "High Pressure." Use the ⊖ button to decrease the time on the display to 25 minutes.
4. When the timer beeps, press Cancel and let the pot stand, covered, for 10 minutes. After 10 minutes, turn the steam release handle to Venting and remove the lid. Check to make sure a tester inserted in the center of the brownie comes out clean. (If more cooking is needed, reset the manual pressure to "High Pressure" for 3 minutes.) Remove the steamer rack and the pan from the pot and let stand on the rack for 10 minutes, then remove the edges of the pan. Cut into 6 wedges. Sprinkle with confectioners' sugar, if desired.

French Yogurt Cake with Lemon Glaze

This classic French cake is light and moist and has a hint of tanginess. Because it is relatively plain, it lends itself to a variety of toppings. It can also be made ahead of time, so it is a perfect dish for entertaining.

MAKES 6 SERVINGS

INSTANT POT FUNCTION

• Manual Pressure •

- 6-inch (15 cm) springform pan, sprayed with nonstick cooking spray and dusted with flour
- Instant Pot steam rack

Cake

1 cup	all-purpose flour	250 mL
1½ tsp	baking powder	7 mL
½ tsp	kosher salt	2 mL
½ cup	granulated sugar	125 mL
1½ tsp	grated lemon zest	7 mL
2	large eggs, lightly beaten	2
½ cup	plain Greek yogurt (store-bought or see variation, page 213)	125 mL
¼ cup	vegetable oil	60 mL
½ tsp	vanilla extract	2 mL

Lemon Glaze

½ cup	lemon marmalade	125 mL
1 tsp	water	5 mL

Tips

The cake can be prepared through step 4 up to 3 days ahead of time. Keep it covered at room temperature. Prepare the glaze and glaze the cake just before serving.

Do not double this recipe. If you need twice the amount, make 2 batches.

1. *Cake:* In a medium bowl, whisk together flour, baking powder and salt.

2. In a large bowl, using your fingers, rub sugar and lemon zest together until sugar is moist. Whisk in eggs, yogurt, oil and vanilla. Fold in flour mixture until just combined. Pour batter into prepared pan, smoothing top with a spatula or the back of a spoon.

3. Add 1 cup (250 mL) water to the inner pot and place the steam rack in the pot. Place the pan on the rack. Close and lock the lid and turn the steam release handle to Sealing. Press Manual; the indicator will read "High Pressure." Use the ⊖ button to decrease the time on the display to 18 minutes.

4. When the timer beeps, press Cancel and let the pot stand, covered, for 10 minutes. After 10 minutes, turn the steam release handle to Venting and remove the lid. Check to make sure a tester inserted in the center of the cake comes out clean. (If more cooking is needed, reset the manual pressure to "High Pressure" for 2 minutes.) Using the handles of the rack, carefully remove the rack and the pan and let the pan stand on the rack until cool. Remove the edges of the pan and transfer cake to a serving plate.

5. *Glaze.* In a small saucepan over medium heat, combine marmalade and water; cook, stirring, for 3 to 4 minutes or until marmalade is liquefied. Strain glaze. Using a pastry brush, brush cake with glaze.

Classic Petite Cheesecake

Every time I tell someone I am making cheesecake in my pressure cooker, they look surprised. I, too, was skeptical at first, but this cheesecake is so easy and delicious, I make it every chance I get — and it consistently turns out firm and flavorful.

MAKES 8 SERVINGS

INSTANT POT FUNCTION

• Manual Pressure •

- **6-inch (15 cm) springform pan, buttered**
- **Food processor**
- **Instant Pot steam rack**

1¼ cups	graham cracker crumbs	300 mL
¼ cup	unsalted butter, melted	60 mL
1 lb	brick-style cream cheese, softened	500 g
½ cup	granulated sugar	125 mL
2	large eggs, at room temperature	2
1½ tbsp	all-purpose flour	22 mL
¼ cup	cottage cheese (preferably small-curd)	60 mL
	Grated zest and juice of ½ lemon	
½ tsp	vanilla extract	2 mL

1. In a small bowl, combine graham cracker crumbs and butter until evenly moist. Press into the bottom and halfway up the sides of the prepared pan.

2. In food processor, process cream cheese and sugar until smooth, scraping down the sides of the bowl as needed. With the motor running, add eggs through the feed tube and process until smooth. Add flour, cottage cheese, lemon zest, lemon juice and vanilla; process for 2 minutes or until smooth and creamy. Pour batter into the pan.

3. Add 2 cups (500 mL) water to the inner pot and place the steam rack in the pot. Place the pan on the rack. Close and lock the lid and turn the steam release handle to Sealing. Press Manual; the indicator will read "High Pressure." Use the ⊖ button to decrease the time on the display to 25 minutes.

4. When the timer beeps, press Cancel. Let stand, covered, until the float valve drops down. Turn the steam release handle to Venting and remove the lid. Check to make sure a tester inserted in the center of the cheesecake comes out clean. (If more cooking is needed, reset the manual pressure to "High Pressure" for 5 minutes.) Using the handles of the rack, carefully remove the rack and the pan and let the pan stand on the rack for 1 hour. Remove the edges of the pan and refrigerate for at least 6 hours or up to 2 days before cutting.

Variation

Instead of the graham cracker crumbs, use crushed vanilla or chocolate wafers, shortbread cookies or gingersnaps.

Dreamy Apricot, White Chocolate and Almond Cheesecake

Apricots, oranges and almonds make this cheesecake one of those desserts you dream about. You get sweetness, citrus flavor and creaminess all in one bundle.

MAKES 8 SERVINGS

INSTANT POT FUNCTION

• Manual Pressure •

- **6-inch (15 cm) springform pan, buttered**
- **Food processor**
- **Instant Pot steam rack**

4 oz	dried apricots, cut in half	125 g
	Grated zest and juice of 1 lemon, divided	
½ cup	orange juice	125 mL
½ cup	water	125 mL
1 tsp	almond or grapeseed oil	5 mL
1 cup	shortbread cookie crumbs	250 mL
¼ cup	finely chopped almonds	60 mL
¼ cup	unsalted butter, melted	60 mL
1 lb	brick-style cream cheese, softened	500 g
½ cup	granulated sugar	125 mL
2	large eggs, at room temperature	2
1½ tbsp	all-purpose flour	22 mL
½ tsp	almond extract	2 mL
2 tbsp	melted white chocolate	30 mL

1. In the inner pot, combine apricots, half the lemon zest and juice, orange juice, water and oil.

2. Place the pot inside the cooker housing, close and lock the lid and turn the steam release handle to Sealing. Press Manual; the indicator will read "High Pressure." Use the ⊖ button to decrease the time on the display to 5 minutes.

3. Meanwhile, in a small bowl, combine cookie crumbs, almonds and butter until evenly moist. Press into the bottom and halfway up the sides of the prepared pan.

4. When the timer beeps, press Cancel and let the pot stand, covered, for 10 minutes. After 10 minutes, turn the steam release handle to Venting and remove the lid. The apricots should be very soft. (If more cooking is needed, reset the manual pressure to "High Pressure" for 1 minute.) Mash apricots until mid-sized chunks remain. Transfer apricot compote to a small bowl and clean the pot.

5. In food processor, combine cream cheese and sugar; process until smooth, scraping down the sides of the bowl as needed. With the motor running, through the feed tube, add eggs and process until smooth. Add flour, almond extract and the remaining lemon zest and juice; process for 2 minutes or until smooth and creamy.

6. Spread half the cream cheese mixture evenly over the cookie crust. Add apricot compote and white chocolate to the remaining cream cheese mixture, stirring well. Spread evenly over the first layer.

7. Add 2 cups (500 mL) water to the inner pot and place the steam rack in the pot. Place the pan on the rack. Close and lock the lid and turn the steam release handle to Sealing. Press Manual; the indicator will read "High Pressure." Use the ⊖ button to decrease the time on the display to 25 minutes.

8. When the timer beeps, press Cancel. Let stand, covered, until the float valve drops down. Turn the steam release handle to Venting and remove the lid. Check to make sure a tester inserted in the center of the cheesecake comes out clean. (If more cooking is needed, reset the manual pressure to "High Pressure" for 5 minutes.) Using the handles of the rack, carefully remove the rack and the pan and let the pan stand on the rack for 1 hour. Remove the edges of the pan and refrigerate for at least 6 hours or up to 2 days before cutting.

Tip

The apricot compote recipe can be doubled and used as a topping for waffles, ice cream or oatmeal. Make sure to fill the pot no more than halfway full when increasing the compote ingredients. The compote can be stored in an airtight container in the refrigerator for up to 2 weeks. Small canning jars with lids work great for storing compote.

Bananas Foster Flan

This version of rich custard flan has the traditional creamy caramel sauce, but adds a touch of banana that is reminiscent of bananas Foster.

MAKES 6 SERVINGS

INSTANT POT FUNCTION

• Manual Pressure •

- **4-cup (1 L) round soufflé dish, bottom and sides buttered**
- **Fine-mesh sieve**
- **Instant Pot steam rack**

Sauce

¾ cup	granulated sugar	175 mL
½ cup	water, divided	125 mL
½ tsp	banana or vanilla extract	2 mL

Flan

3	large eggs	3
2	large egg yolks	2
⅓ cup	granulated sugar	75 mL
2 tbsp	banana-flavored syrup	30 mL
½ tsp	vanilla extract	2 mL
2 cups	milk	500 mL
½ cup	half-and-half (10%) cream	125 mL

1. *Sauce:* In a small saucepan, combine sugar and ¼ cup (60 mL) water. Bring to a boil over medium-high heat, stirring to dissolve the sugar. Boil, moving pan frequently but without stirring, for 5 to 7 minutes or until mixture becomes a light brown caramel color. Pour ¼ cup (60 mL) of the caramel into the prepared soufflé dish, tilting the pan so the caramel coats the bottom.

2. Add the remaining water to the caramel remaining in the pan and boil, stirring, for 2 minutes or until mixture is smooth. Transfer caramel sauce to a heatproof bowl and let stand until it becomes a heavy syrup. When caramel is cool, add banana extract, stirring well. Set aside.

3. *Flan:* In a medium bowl, whisk together eggs and egg yolks. Whisk in sugar, banana syrup and vanilla. Whisk in milk and cream. Strain through sieve into the soufflé dish.

4. Add 1½ cups (375 mL) water to the inner pot and place the steam rack in the pot. Place the soufflé dish on the rack. Close and lock the lid and turn the steam release handle to Sealing. Press Manual; the indicator will read "High Pressure." Use the ⊖ button to decrease the time on the display to 15 minutes.

5. When the timer beeps, press Cancel and let the pot stand, covered, for 10 minutes. After 10 minutes, turn the steam release handle to Venting and remove the lid. Check to make sure a tester inserted in the center of the flan comes out clean. (If more cooking is needed, reset the manual pressure to "High Pressure" for 2 minutes.) Using the handles of the rack, carefully remove the rack and the dish and let the dish stand on the rack until cool. Refrigerate for at least 6 hours or up to 3 days.

6. Run a knife around the edges of the flan. Place a serving platter on top of the dish and invert both platter and dish, transferring the flan to the platter. Drizzle some of the caramel sauce over top. Serve any remaining sauce on the side.

Tips

Leftover egg whites can be stored in an airtight container in the freezer for up to 3 months. Use them to make meringues and other desserts.

Banana-flavored syrup can be found in well-stocked grocery stores, online and in specialty coffee shops. It is a great addition to smoothies and is wonderful for flavoring coffee, too. If you cannot find it, use $1\frac{1}{2}$ tsp (7 mL) banana extract and 5 tsp (25 mL) liquid honey.

Salt Caramel Pots de Crème

These delicate pots de crème are soft little custards made of cream, milk and eggs. They can be flavored with a variety of ingredients, but for this version I've chosen salted caramel because it is one of my favorites.

INSTANT POT FUNCTION

• Manual Pressure •

- **Fine-mesh sieve**
- **Container with a spout**
- **Four 4-oz (125 mL) ramekins**
- **Instant Pot steam rack**

¾ cup	granulated sugar, divided	175 mL
1 tsp	sea salt, divided	5 mL
3 tbsp	water	45 mL
⅔ cup	heavy or whipping (35%) cream	150 mL
⅔ cup	milk	150 mL
4	large egg yolks	4

1. In a small saucepan, combine ½ cup (125 mL) sugar, a pinch of salt and water. Bring to a boil over medium-high heat, stirring to dissolve the sugar. Boil; moving pan frequently but without stirring, for 3 to 5 minutes or until mixture becomes a light brown caramel color. Carefully pour in cream and milk; cook, stirring, for 2 minutes or until bubbling. Let cool completely.

2. Meanwhile, in a medium bowl, whisk together the remaining sugar and egg yolks. Slowly whisk in cooled cream mixture until just combined. Strain through sieve into a container with a spout. Divide mixture evenly among ramekins. Cover each ramekin with foil, pinching tightly around sides.

3. Add 1 cup (250 mL) water to the inner pot and place the steam rack in the pot. Place ramekins on the rack. Close and lock the lid and turn the steam release handle to Sealing. Press Manual; the indicator will read "High Pressure." Use the ⊖ button to decrease the time on the display to 5 minutes.

4. When the timer beeps, press Cancel. Let stand, covered, until the float valve drops down. Turn the steam release handle to Venting and remove the lid. Check to make sure a tester inserted in the center of the custard comes out clean. (If more cooking is needed, reset the manual pressure to "High Pressure" for 2 minutes.)

5. Remove custards from pot, remove foil and let stand for 30 minutes or until cool. Sprinkle with the remaining sea salt.

Variations

Berry Pots de Crème: Omit step 1 and the sea salt and water. Reduce the granulated sugar to 6 tbsp (90 mL). In step 2, add the milk and cream, along with 1 tsp (5 mL) vanilla extract, to the sugar and egg yolk mixture, whisking until just combined. In step 5, serve with ½ cup (125 mL) berries, divided evenly among the pots, and drizzle with berry-flavored syrup.

Chocolate Pots de Crème: Omit step 1 and the sea salt and water. Reduce the granulated sugar to 3 tbsp (45 mL). In step 2, add the milk and cream, along with 6 tbsp (90 mL) unsweetened cocoa powder and 1 tsp (5 mL) vanilla extract, to the sugar and egg yolk mixture, whisking until just combined. In step 5, serve with dollops of whipped cream.

Tip

You can serve the pots de crème warm instead of cooled, if you prefer. They can also be covered and refrigerated for up to 2 days before serving.

Easy Crème Brûlée

This is hands-down one of my favorite desserts. First, your spoon hits the sugary glass topping, then you break through to the rich, heavenly, creamy custard. I am in pure ecstasy while I eat it, yet I never feel like I've overindulged.

MAKES 6 SERVINGS

INSTANT POT FUNCTION
• Manual Pressure •

- **Fine-mesh sieve**
- **Container with a spout**
- **Six 4-oz (125 mL) ramekins**
- **Instant Pot steam rack**

⅓ cup	granulated sugar	75 mL
6	large egg yolks (see tip, page 191)	6
1 cup	heavy or whipping (35%) cream	250 mL
1 cup	half-and-half (10%) cream	250 mL
2 tsp	vanilla extract	10 mL
⅓ cup	superfine sugar (see tip, below)	75 mL

Tips

Superfine sugar is often called baker's sugar. If you cannot find it, you can use turbinado sugar or pulse granulated sugar in a blender or grinder until fine.

You can prepare these through step 4 ahead of time (omit step 3). Let cool, then cover and refrigerate for up to 3 days. Bring flan to room temperature before adding sugar and broiling.

1. In a large bowl, whisk together sugar and egg yolks. Whisk in heavy cream, half-and-half and vanilla until just combined. Strain through sieve into container with a spout. Pour into ramekins, dividing evenly. Cover each ramekin with foil, pinching tightly around sides.

2. Add 1½ cups (375 mL) water to the inner pot and place the steam rack in the pot. Stack the ramekins on the rack, making sure they are level. Close and lock the lid and turn the steam release handle to Sealing. Press Manual; the indicator will read "High Pressure." Use the ⊖ button to decrease the time on the display to 6 minutes.

3. Meanwhile, preheat the broiler with the rack 4 inches (10 cm) from the heat source.

4. When the timer beeps, press Cancel and let the pot stand, covered, for 10 minutes. After 10 minutes, turn the steam release handle to Venting and remove the lid. Check to make sure a tester inserted in the center of the flan comes out clean. (If more cooking is needed, reset the manual pressure to "High Pressure" for 2 minutes.) Transfer ramekins to a baking sheet and remove the foil.

5. Sprinkle sugar evenly over each custard. Broil for 2 to 3 minutes, watching carefully and rotating as needed, until sugar has evenly melted and caramelized. Serve warm.

Variation

Omit the superfine sugar and steps 3 and 5. Top the custards with your favorite berries.

Lemon Mousse with Mixed Berries

This creamy mousse is made with a delightful pairing of lemon curd and yogurt and then topped with fresh berries and a hint of chocolate for a sweet and tart dessert. You will need to plan ahead, because the lemon curd needs to chill for 8 hours, but it can be made ahead and kept in the fridge for up to 7 days or in the freezer for up to 2 months.

MAKES 8 SERVINGS

INSTANT POT FUNCTION
• Manual Pressure •

- Food processor
- Two 8-oz (250 mL) canning jars with two-piece lids
- Instant Pot steam rack
- Eight 6-oz (175 mL) stemmed glasses or ramekins

Lemon Curd

½ cup	sugar	125 mL
3 tbsp	unsalted butter	45 mL
1	large egg	1
1	large egg yolk	1
	Grated zest of 1 lemon	
	Juice of 2 lemons (about ¼ cup/60 mL)	

Mousse

¾ cup	plain Greek yogurt (store-bought or see variation, page 213)	175 mL
1½ cups	heavy or whipping (35%) cream	375 mL
	Grated zest of 1 lemon	
2 tsp	freshly squeezed lemon juice (optional)	10 mL
	Fresh mixed berries	
	Cacao nibs	

1. *Lemon Curd:* In food processor, process sugar and butter for 2 minutes or until combined. With the motor running, add egg and egg yolk through the feed tube and process for 1 minute. Add lemon juice and pulse to combine. (The mixture will look slightly curdled.)

2. Divide the curd mixture evenly between the jars, cover with the flat lids and twist on the screwbands until they just catch.

3. Add 1 cup (250 mL) water to the inner pot and place the steam rack in the pot. Place the jars on the rack. Close and lock the lid and turn the steam release handle to Sealing. Press Manual; the indicator will read "High Pressure." Use the ⊖ button to decrease the time on the display to 10 minutes.

4. When the timer beeps, press Cancel and let the pot stand, covered, for 10 minutes. After 10 minutes, turn the steam release handle to Venting and remove the lid. Remove the jars from the pot and open carefully. Divide lemon zest evenly between the jars, stirring well. Replace lids and let stand for 20 minutes or until cool. Refrigerate for 8 hours.

5. *Mousse:* In a medium bowl, whisk together lemon curd and yogurt.

6. In another bowl, using an electric mixer on high speed, beat cream until stiff peaks form.

7. Fold whipped cream into curd mixture. Fold in lemon zest and lemon juice (if using). Divide mousse evenly among stemmed glasses, cover and freeze for at least 1 hour, until set, or for up to 2 days (if freezing for more than 1 hour, let thaw slightly in the refrigerator before serving).

8. When ready to serve, let mousse stand at room temperature for 10 minutes. Garnish with berries and cacao nibs.

Chocolate Chip Bread Pudding

What could be better than hassle-free bread pudding? Hassle-free bread pudding with lots of chocolate, of course. This rich dessert is always inviting, but the simplicity of this recipe makes it even better.

MAKES 8 SERVINGS

INSTANT POT FUNCTION

• Manual Pressure •

- **4-cup (1 L) round soufflé dish, bottom and sides buttered**
- **Instant Pot steam rack**

3 tbsp	unsalted butter, softened	45 mL
6	slices French or Italian bread	6
3	large eggs	3
⅓ cup	granulated sugar	75 mL
1½ cups	half-and-half (10%) cream	375 mL
2 tsp	vanilla extract	10 mL
2 tsp	grated orange zest	10 mL
⅔ cup	semisweet chocolate chips	150 mL
½ cup	chopped walnuts	125 mL
	Whipped cream	
½ tsp	ground nutmeg	2 mL

1. Butter both sides of bread and cut into 2-inch (5 cm) square pieces. You should have about 6 cups (1.5 L).
2. In a large bowl, whisk eggs. Whisk in sugar, cream, vanilla and orange zest.
3. Add half the bread pieces to the prepared soufflé dish. Pour half the egg mixture on top. Sprinkle with half the chocolate chips and half the walnuts. Repeat layers. Press bread down into liquid to make sure it gets soaked. Let stand for 10 minutes. Cover with foil, pinching tightly around sides of dish.
4. Add 2 cups (500 mL) water to the inner pot and place the steam rack in the pot. Place the soufflé dish on the rack. Close and lock the lid and turn the steam release handle to Sealing. Press Manual; the indicator will read "High Pressure." Use the ⊖ button to decrease the time on the display to 20 minutes.
5. When the timer beeps, press Cancel and let the pot stand, covered, for 10 minutes. After 10 minutes, turn the steam release handle to Venting and remove the lid. Check to make sure a tester inserted in the center of the pudding comes out clean. (If more cooking is needed, reset the manual pressure to "High Pressure" for 5 minutes.) Remove the dish from the pot, remove the foil and let stand for at least 10 minutes or until ready to serve.
6. Top pudding with dollops of whipped cream and sprinkle with nutmeg.

Variation

Cranberry Almond Bread Pudding: Substitute dried cranberries for the chocolate chips and slivered almonds for the walnuts.

Maple and Raisin Rice Pudding

Rice pudding is one of the classic comfort foods. Add some maple syrup, raisins and just a hint of cinnamon, and you will swoon over the results.

MAKES 6 SERVINGS

INSTANT POT FUNCTIONS

- Sauté •
- Manual Pressure •

2 tbsp	unsalted butter, divided	30 mL
1 cup	Arborio or other short-grain white rice	250 mL
2 cups	water	500 mL
½ tsp	vanilla extract	2 mL
⅓ cup	raisins	75 mL
1½ cups	milk	375 mL
⅓ cup	pure maple syrup	75 mL
	Ground cinnamon (optional)	

Tip

When using the Quick Release method to release pressure, keep your hands and face away from the hole on the top of the steam release handle so you don't get scalded by the escaping steam.

1. Press Sauté; the indicator will read "Normal." When the display says "Hot," add 1 tbsp (15 mL) butter to the pot and heat until melted. Add rice and cook, stirring, for 1 to 2 minutes or until rice is coated and starting to crackle. Press Cancel. Add water, the remaining butter and vanilla extract.

2. Close and lock the lid and turn the steam release handle to Sealing. Press Manual; the indicator will read "High Pressure." Use the ⊖ button to decrease the time on the display to 7 minutes.

3. When the timer beeps, press Cancel and turn the steam release handle to Venting. When the float valve drops down, remove the lid. Check to make sure the rice is tender. (If more cooking is needed, reset the manual pressure to "High Pressure" for 2 minutes.)

4. Stir in raisins, milk and maple syrup. Press Sauté and cook, stirring often, for 4 to 6 minutes or until pudding is your desired consistency. (Note: it will continue to thicken after it is removed from the heat.) If desired, sprinkle with cinnamon.

Variation

Cranberry Rice Pudding: In place of the raisins, use dried cranberries. Substitute ½ cup (125 mL) granulated sugar for the maple syrup. Garnish with cardamom instead of cinnamon, if desired.

No-Bake Baked Apples

The smell of baking apples and cinnamon wafting through the house takes me back to childhood. When I walked into Grandma's house and sniffed the air, I knew I was about to get the best treat ever.

MAKES 4 SERVINGS

INSTANT POT FUNCTION

• Slow Cook •

4	apples (see tip, below)	4
2 tbsp	packed dark brown sugar	30 mL
1 tbsp	dried cranberries	15 mL
½ tsp	ground cinnamon	2 mL
¼ tsp	ground allspice	1 mL
1 tbsp	unsalted butter	15 mL
½ cup	apple juice	125 mL

Tips

Apples that are good for baking, such as Cortland, Empire or Braeburn, will work best in this recipe. Select apples that are uniform in size and are nicely proportioned.

This recipe can also be made in 3 to 4 hours. In step 3, press Adjust once to change the heat level to "More." Use the ➖ button to decrease the time on the display to 3:00. Continue with step 4.

1. Using a paring knife or an apple corer, core each apple, leaving ½ inch (1 cm) at the bottom intact. Peel a 1-inch (2.5 cm) section around the top of the apple.

2. In a small bowl, combine sugar, cranberries, cinnamon and allspice. Press mixture into apple cores, dividing evenly. Top each with one-quarter of the butter.

3. Add apple juice to the inner pot and place apples in the pot. Close and lock the lid and turn the steam release handle to Venting. Press Slow Cook; the indicator will read "Normal." Press Adjust twice to change the heat level to "Less." Use the ➕ button to increase the time on the display to 6:00.

4. When the timer beeps, remove the lid. The apples should be tender and slightly collapsed. (If more cooking is needed, reset the slow cooker to "Less" for 1 hour.)

South Pacific–Inspired Bananas Foster

Super-quick, super-easy and definitely decadent, this version of bananas Foster is screaming with flavor, has a unique tropical twist and is truly a crowd-pleaser.

MAKES 12 SERVINGS

INSTANT POT FUNCTION

• Slow Cook •

	Nonstick cooking spray	
1 cup	packed dark brown sugar	250 mL
½ cup	unsweetened coconut milk	125 mL
½ cup	dark rum	125 mL
⅓ cup	unsalted butter	75 mL
8	ripe bananas, cut into ½-inch (1 cm) slices	8
2 cups	pineapple chunks	500 mL
½ tsp	ground cinnamon	2 mL
2 pints	vanilla ice cream	1 L

Tips

For the sake of convenience, precut fresh pineapple is sometimes worth reaching for. If cutting your own, cut it into 1-inch (2.5 cm) chunks. Either way, you can't go wrong.

You can also use drained canned pineapple chunks in place of the fresh pineapple.

Leftover bananas Foster can be stored in an airtight container in the refrigerator for up to 3 days. Reheat in the microwave or in a small saucepan until heated through.

1. Spray the inner pot with cooking spray. In a medium bowl, combine sugar, coconut milk, rum and butter. Pour into the pot.

2. Place the pot inside the cooker housing, close and lock the lid and turn the steam release handle to Venting. Press Slow Cook; the indicator will read "Normal." Press Adjust twice to change the heat level to "Less." Use the ⊖ button to decrease the time on the display to 1:00.

3. When the timer beeps, press Cancel. Remove the lid and whisk mixture until smooth.

4. Add bananas, pineapple and cinnamon to the pot, stirring well. Close and lock the lid and turn the steam release handle to Venting. Press Slow Cook; the indicator will read "Normal." Press Adjust twice to change the heat level to "Less." Use the ⊖ button to decrease the time on the display to 0:30 and set a timer for 15 minutes.

5. After 15 minutes, remove the lid and check to make sure the sauce has a syrupy consistency. (If more cooking is needed, cover and continue cooking until the timer beeps.)

6. Divide ice cream among serving bowls and spoon bananas Foster around ice cream.

Cherry Dump Cake

It doesn't get much easier than this. Four ingredients, four minutes prep, four steps, four hours of hands-off slow cooking. I wish I could say it was four calories, but after your first taste, I am sure you won't mind.

MAKES 6 SERVINGS

INSTANT POT FUNCTION

• Slow Cook •

- 6-inch (15 cm) springform pan, sprayed with nonstick cooking spray
- Instant Pot steam rack

1	can (21 oz/595 g) cherry pie filling	1
1	box (18.25 oz/515 g) yellow cake mix	1
½ cup	unsalted butter, melted	125 mL
⅓ cup	chopped walnuts	75 mL

Tip

This cake can also be made in 2 to 2½ hours. In step 3, press Adjust once to change the heat level to "More." Use the ⊖ button to decrease the time on the display to 2:00. Continue with step 4.

1. Pour pie filling into prepared pan.

2. In a small bowl, combine cake mix and butter. Spread over pie filling. Sprinkle with walnuts.

3. Add 2 cups (500 mL) water to the inner pot and place the steam rack in the pot. Place the pan on the rack. Close and lock the lid and turn the steam release handle to Venting. Press Slow Cook; the indicator will read "Normal." Press Adjust twice to change the heat level to "Less." Leave the time at 4:00.

4. When the timer beeps, remove the lid and check to make sure a tester inserted in the center of the cake comes out with a few moist crumbs. (If more cooking is needed, reset the slow cooker to "Less" for 30 minutes.) Spoon into dessert bowls.

Lemon Spoon Cake

Frankly, I think all cakes should be eaten with a spoon, so you get every last yummy morsel. So take this opportunity to make a creamy, citrusy cake in your slow cooker and enjoy every mouthwatering bite.

MAKES 12 SERVINGS

INSTANT POT FUNCTION

• Slow Cook •

4 cups	all-purpose flour	1 L
2 cups	granulated sugar, divided	500 mL
1 tbsp	baking powder	15 mL
2	large eggs	2
1¼ cups	unsalted butter, melted, divided	300 mL
1 cup	half-and-half (10%) cream	250 mL
	Grated zest and juice of 4 lemons (about ⅔ cup/150 mL juice), divided	
1 cup	water	250 mL
	Whipped cream	
	Fresh raspberries	
	Fresh mint leaves (optional)	

Tips

The cake can be cooled and stored in an airtight container in the refrigerator for up to 5 days. Bring to room temperature before serving.

This recipe can be halved. In step 2, pour the batter into a 6-inch (15 cm) springform pan sprayed with nonstick cooking spray. Continue with step 3. In step 4, add 1 cup (250 mL) water to the inner pot and place the Instant Pot steam rack in the pot. Place the pan on the rack. Increase the cooking time to 2 hours.

1. In a large bowl, whisk together flour, 1 cup (250 mL) sugar and baking powder.

2. In another large bowl, whisk eggs. Whisk in 1 cup (250 mL) butter, cream and half the lemon zest and juice. Add flour mixture, mixing well. Pour batter into the inner pot.

3. In a small saucepan, bring 1 cup (250 mL) water to a boil. Stir in the remaining sugar, butter, lemon zest and lemon juice until combined. Pour over batter.

4. Place the pot inside the cooker housing, close and lock the lid and turn the steam release handle to Venting. Press Slow Cook; the indicator will read "Normal." Press Adjust once to change the heat level to "More." Use the ⊖ button to decrease the time on the display to 1:30.

5. When the timer beeps, remove the lid and check to make sure a tester inserted in the center of the cake comes out with a few moist crumbs. (If more cooking is needed, reset the slow cooker to "More" for 30 minutes.)

6. Spoon into dessert bowls, add a dollop of whipped cream to each serving and arrange raspberries around the cake. Garnish with mint leaves, if desired.

Glazed Lemon Poppy Seed Cake

This classic summertime cake is quick and easy to make. The zesty tang of the lemons and the bit of crunch from the poppy seeds make it a memorable dessert. And you don't even need to heat up the kitchen!

MAKES 8 SERVINGS

INSTANT POT FUNCTION

• Slow Cook •

- **4-cup (1 L) round soufflé dish, sprayed with nonstick cooking spray**
- **Instant Pot steam rack**

1½ cups	all-purpose baking mix (such as Bisquick)	375 mL
½ cup	granulated sugar	125 mL
2½ tbsp	poppy seeds, divided	37 mL
1	large egg	1
1½ tsp	grated lemon zest	7 mL
½ cup	sour cream	125 mL
2 tbsp	buttermilk	30 mL
1 tsp	vanilla extract	5 mL
2	lemons	2
2 cups	confectioners' (icing) sugar	500 mL

Tip

Instead of the lemons, you can use 2 tsp (10 mL) grated orange zest in step 2 and ¼ cup (60 mL) freshly squeezed orange juice in step 5. Garnish with orange peel strips.

1. In a medium bowl, whisk together baking mix, granulated sugar and 2 tbsp (30 mL) poppy seeds.

2. In a large bowl, whisk egg. Add lemon zest, sour cream, buttermilk and vanilla, stirring well. Whisk in dry ingredients until blended. Pour into prepared soufflé dish and use the back of a spoon or a spatula to smooth the top.

3. Add 2 cups (500 mL) water to the inner pot and place the steam rack in the pot. Place the soufflé dish on the rack. Close and lock the lid and turn the steam release handle to Venting. Press Slow Cook; the indicator will read "Normal." Press Adjust once to change the heat level to "More." Press ⊖ to decrease the time on the display to 2:30.

4. When the timer beeps, remove the lid and check to make sure a tester inserted in the center of the cake comes out clean. (If more cooking is needed, reset the slow cooker to "More" for 30 minutes.) Remove the rack and dish from the pot, run a knife around the edges of the dish, invert the cake onto the rack and let stand until cool. Transfer wire rack, with cake, to a plate.

5. Using a peeler, cut long, curling strips of peel from 1 lemon. Juice both lemons and measure ¼ cup (60 mL) juice (reserve any extra for another use).

6. In a small bowl, whisk together confectioners' sugar and lemon juice. Drizzle glaze over cake. Sprinkle with the remaining poppy seeds. Cut cake into wedges and serve garnished with lemon peel strips.

Butterscotch Pudding Cake

Rich and luscious butterscotch flavors lace this moist and unmistakably decadent dessert. Serve it warm, with butterscotch pecan or vanilla ice cream, and your guests will swoon.

MAKES 8 SERVINGS

INSTANT POT FUNCTION

• Slow Cook •

- **6-inch (15 cm) springform pan, sprayed with nonstick cooking spray**
- **Instant Pot steam rack**

1	box (18.25 oz/515 g) yellow cake mix	1
1	box (3.9 oz/110 g) instant butterscotch pudding and pie filling	1
4	large eggs	4
2 cups	sour cream	500 mL
1 cup	water	250 mL
½ cup	vegetable oil	125 mL
1 cup	butterscotch chips, chopped	250 mL
1 cup	chopped pecans	250 mL

Tip

The Slow Cook function performs best when you keep the lid closed throughout the cooking time and resist the urge to peek. Every time you remove the lid, the heat escapes from the pot and alters the cooking process.

---

1. In a large bowl, combine cake mix, pudding and pie filling, eggs, sour cream, water and oil. Using an electric mixer on medium speed, mix batter for 2 minutes, scraping down sides as needed. Pour batter into prepared pan.

2. Add 2 cups (500 mL) water to the inner pot and place the steam rack in the pot. Place the pan on the rack. Close and lock the lid and turn the steam release handle to Venting. Press Slow Cook; the indicator will read "Normal." Press Adjust twice to change the heat level to "Less." Leave the time at 4:00.

3. When the timer beeps, remove the lid and check to make sure the cake is set around the edges and soft in the center. (If more cooking is needed, reset the slow cooker to "Less" for 30 minutes.) Press Cancel. Cover the pot and let stand for 25 to 30 minutes or until cake is set.

Chocolate Turtle Pudding Cake

You know those oh-so-tempting little chocolate turtles that scream to you in the checkout lane? Well, you don't have to worry about whether to give in to their temptation anymore, because you can make an even better version at home in your slow cooker.

MAKES 8 SERVINGS

INSTANT POT FUNCTION
• Slow Cook •

1½ cups	all-purpose baking mix (such as Bisquick)	375 mL
1¼ cups	packed brown sugar, divided	300 mL
½ cup	unsweetened cocoa powder	125 mL
½ cup	milk	125 mL
½ cup	caramel sauce, divided	125 mL
	Nonstick cooking spray	
1⅔ cups	hot water	400 mL
½ cup	chopped pecans	125 mL
	Sea salt (optional)	

1. In a medium bowl, combine baking mix, 1 cup (250 mL) brown sugar, cocoa, milk and ¼ cup (60 mL) caramel sauce, stirring well.

2. Spray the inner pot with cooking spray. Spread caramel mixture over the bottom of the pot. Sprinkle with the remaining brown sugar. Pour hot water on top; do not stir.

3. Place the pot inside the cooker housing, close and lock the lid and turn the steam release handle to Venting. Press Slow Cook; the indicator will read "Normal." Press Adjust twice to change the heat level to "Less." Use the ⊖ button to decrease the time on the display to 2:00.

4. When the timer beeps, remove the lid and check to make sure a tester inserted in the center of the cake comes out clean. (If more cooking is needed, reset the slow cooker to "Less" for 30 minutes.) Press Cancel. Let stand, uncovered, for 15 minutes to cool.

5. Pour the remaining caramel sauce over top and sprinkle with pecans and sea salt, if using.

Chocolate Lava Cake

This showstopping rich and creamy dessert combines fudge cake, chocolate pudding and chocolate chips for the trifecta of decadent chocolate desserts. Serve with vanilla ice cream.

INSTANT POT FUNCTION

• Slow Cook •

• **Parchment paper**

	Nonstick cooking spray	
1	box (18.25 oz/515 g) moist chocolate fudge cake mix	1
3	large eggs, beaten	3
3¼ cups	milk, divided	800 mL
⅓ cup	vegetable oil	75 mL
1	box (3.9 oz/110 g) instant chocolate pudding and pie filling	1
2 cups	milk chocolate chips	500 mL

Tips

All the ingredients you need are included here. Do not add any additional ingredients mentioned on the cake box.

Any moist chocolate cake works well in the recipe. Some of my other favorites are a triple-fudge cake mix, dark chocolate cake mix and devil's food cake mix.

1. Line the inner pot with parchment paper and spray with cooking spray.

2. In a large bowl, combine cake mix, eggs, 1¼ cups (300 mL) milk and oil. Pour into prepared pot.

3. In a medium bowl, whisk together pudding and pie filling and the remaining milk. Pour over batter; do not mix. Sprinkle chocolate chips over top.

4. Place the pot inside the cooker housing, close and lock the lid and turn the steam release handle to Venting. Press Slow Cook; the indicator will read "Normal." Press Adjust twice to change the heat level to "Less." Use the ⊖ button to decrease the time on the display to 2:30.

5. When the timer beeps, remove the lid and check to make sure the cake is set and the pudding is starting to bubble. (If more cooking is needed, reset the slow cooker to "Less" for 30 minutes.) Serve immediately.

Rocky Road Chocolate Cake

This cake is a chocolate lover's dream. It begins with chocolate cake, loads of chocolate pudding and chocolate chips, and then gets crowned with slightly melted marshmallows and toasted pecans. Serve with vanilla ice cream.

MAKES 10 SERVINGS

INSTANT POT FUNCTION

• Slow Cook •

- **4-cup (1 L) round soufflé dish, sprayed with nonstick cooking spray**
- **Instant Pot steam rack**

1	box (18.25 oz/515 g) German chocolate or other chocolate cake mix	1
1	box (3.9 oz/110 g) instant chocolate pudding and pie filling	1
3	large eggs	3
3¼ cups	milk, divided	800 mL
1 cup	sour cream	250 mL
⅓ cup	unsalted butter, melted	75 mL
1 tsp	vanilla extract	5 mL
1	box (3.4 oz/96 g) chocolate cook-and-serve pudding and pie filling	1
1½ cups	miniature marshmallows	375 mL
1 cup	semisweet chocolate chips	250 mL
½ cup	toasted chopped pecans (see tip, below)	125 mL

Tips

Toast pecans in a small skillet over medium-high heat for 3 to 4 minutes or until lightly browned.

Any moist chocolate cake works well in the recipe. Some of my other favorites are triple-fudge cake mix, dark chocolate cake mix and devil's food cake mix.

1. In a large bowl, using an electric mixer on medium speed, beat cake mix, instant pudding and pie filling, eggs, 1¼ cups (300 mL) milk, sour cream, butter and vanilla for 2 minutes, scraping down the sides of the bowl as needed. Pour batter into prepared soufflé dish. Sprinkle cook-and-serve pudding and pie filling over top.

2. In a small saucepan, heat the remaining milk over medium heat, stirring occasionally, for 3 to 5 minutes or until bubbles start to appear. Slowly pour milk over pudding.

3. Add 2 cups (500 mL) water to the inner pot and place the steam rack in the pot. Place the soufflé dish on the rack. Close and lock the lid and turn the steam release handle to Venting. Press Slow Cook; the indicator will read "Normal." Press Adjust twice to change the heat level to "Less." Leave the time at 4:00.

4. When the timer beeps, remove the lid and check to make sure a tester inserted in the center of the cake comes out with a few moist crumbs attached (the cake will set more in step 5). (If more cooking is needed, reset the slow cooker to "Less" for 15 minutes.) Press Cancel.

5. Sprinkle cake with marshmallows, chocolate chips and pecans. Let stand, uncovered, for 15 minutes or until marshmallows are slightly melted.

Moist and Luscious Carrot Cake

My mother made one of the best carrot cakes. It was always moist, was filled with carrots and had the right balance of spices. The slow cooker makes this no-fail combination easy to achieve.

INSTANT POT FUNCTION

• Slow Cook •

- **6-inch (15 cm) springform pan, sprayed with nonstick cooking spray**
- **Instant Pot steam rack**

¾ cup	all-purpose flour	175 mL
½ tsp	baking powder	2 mL
½ tsp	baking soda	2 mL
½ tsp	ground cinnamon	2 mL
Pinch	ground cloves	Pinch
Pinch	kosher salt	Pinch
½ cup	packed brown sugar	125 mL
1	large egg, at room temperature	1
⅓ cup	vegetable oil	75 mL
¾ cup	shredded carrots	175 mL
	Confectioners' (icing) sugar	

Tip

There are so many fun stencils you can buy — or you can make your own with whatever forms and shapes you like. Place a stencil on top of the cake and then sprinkle the cake with confectioners' sugar. Remove the stencil to reveal your decoration.

1. In a small bowl, combine flour, baking powder, baking soda, cinnamon, cloves and salt.

2. In a large bowl, whisk together brown sugar and egg. Gradually whisk in oil. Stir in flour mixture until just combined. Fold in carrots. Pour batter into prepared pan. Gently tap pan on countertop to release any bubbles.

3. Add 2 cups (500 mL) water to the inner pot and place the steam rack in the pot. Place the pan on the rack. Close and lock the lid and turn the steam release handle to Venting. Press Slow Cook; the indicator will read "Normal." Press Adjust once to change the heat level to "More." Use the ⊟ button to decrease the time on the display to 3:00.

4. When the timer beeps, remove the lid and check to make sure a tester inserted in the center of the cake comes out clean. (If more cooking is needed, reset the slow cooker to "More" for 30 minutes.) Using the handles of the rack, carefully remove the rack and the pan and let stand on the rack for 1 to 2 hours or until cool.

5. Run a knife around the inside of the pan and remove the edges. Run the knife along the bottom of the cake and transfer cake to a serving plate. Sprinkle with confectioners' sugar.

Pumpkin Pie Custard

I remember the first year my grandmother made a crustless pumpkin pie for Thanksgiving. It was all the rage at that time. The crust lovers at the table were disappointed, but the flavor of the pie was outstanding. For this recipe, I'll call it custard, so as not to mislead the crust fans.

MAKES 6 SERVINGS

INSTANT POT FUNCTION
• Slow Cook •

- **4-cup (1 L) round soufflé dish, sprayed with nonstick cooking spray**
- **Instant Pot steam rack**

2 cups	pumpkin purée (see tip, below)	500 mL
¾ cup	packed brown sugar	175 mL
½ cup	all-purpose flour	125 mL
1 tsp	ground cinnamon	5 mL
½ tsp	ground nutmeg	2 mL
½ tsp	baking powder	2 mL
¼ tsp	ground cloves	1 mL
¼ tsp	kosher salt	1 mL
Pinch	ground ginger	Pinch
2	large eggs, beaten	2
1	can (12 oz or 370 mL) evaporated milk	1
2 tbsp	unsalted butter, melted	30 mL
2 tsp	vanilla extract	10 mL

Tip
You can use a 15-oz (425 g) can of pumpkin pie filling for this recipe, but I prefer to use pie (sugar) pumpkins. Cut the pumpkin in half and remove the seeds, then bake it upside down on a foil-lined baking sheet at 350°F (180°C) for 45 minutes or until caramelized juices appear around the edges of the pumpkin. Scoop out the pumpkin and pulse to your desired consistency in a food processor.

1. In a large bowl, combine pumpkin, brown sugar, flour, cinnamon, nutmeg, baking powder, cloves, salt, ginger, eggs, evaporated milk, butter and vanilla, mixing well. Pour batter into prepared soufflé dish.

2. Add 2 cups (500 mL) water to the inner pot and place the steam rack in the pot. Place the soufflé dish on the rack. Close and lock the lid and turn the steam release handle to Venting. Press Slow Cook; the indicator will read "Normal." Press Adjust once to change the heat level to "More." Use the ⊖ button to decrease the time on the display to 1:30.

3. When the timer beeps, press Cancel. Press Slow Cook. Press Adjust twice to change the heat level to "Less." Use the ⊕ button to increase the time on the display to 4:30.

4. When the timer beeps, remove the lid and check to make sure a tester inserted in the center of the custard comes out clean. (If more cooking is needed, reset the slow cooker to "Less" for 30 minutes.) Using the handles of the rack, carefully remove the rack and the dish and let stand on the rack for 1 to 2 hours or until cool.

5. Remove the edges of the pan. Cut custard into slices or spoon into dessert cups.

Tiramisu Bread Pudding

Combine espresso, Kahlua, light cheese and cocoa with cubes of bread, and what do you have? The most downright luscious dessert you can imagine in a slow cooker.

MAKES 10 SERVINGS

INSTANT POT FUNCTION

• Slow Cook •

- **6-cup (1.5 L) casserole dish, sprayed with nonstick cooking spray**

$\frac{1}{3}$ cup	granulated sugar	75 mL
$1\frac{1}{2}$ tbsp	instant espresso granules	22 mL
$\frac{1}{2}$ cup	water	125 mL
2 tbsp	Kahlua	30 mL
2	large eggs, lightly beaten	2
2 cups	milk, divided	500 mL
8 cups	cubed French bread	2 L
$\frac{1}{3}$ cup	mascarpone cheese	75 mL
1 tsp	vanilla extract	5 mL
2 tsp	unsweetened cocoa powder	10 mL

1. In a small saucepan, combine sugar, espresso and water. Bring to a boil over medium heat. Boil, stirring, for 1 minute. Remove from heat and stir in Kahlua. Let cool.

2. In a large bowl, whisk together eggs and $1\frac{3}{4}$ cups (425 mL) milk. Gradually whisk in espresso mixture. Stir in bread until well coated. Pour mixture into prepared casserole dish and let stand until bread is well soaked.

3. Place the dish in the inner pot. Close and lock the lid and turn the steam release handle to Venting. Press Slow Cook; the indicator will read "Normal." Press Adjust twice to change the heat level to "Less." Use the ⊖ button to decrease the time on the display to 2:00.

4. When the timer beeps, remove the lid and check to make sure a tester inserted into the center of the pudding comes out clean. (If more cooking is needed, reset the slow cooker to "Less" for 30 minutes.)

5. In a small bowl, whisk together mascarpone, the remaining milk and vanilla until smooth.

6. Spoon pudding into dessert bowls, top with sauce and sprinkle with cocoa.

Festive Peppermint Bark Pretzels

Everyone delights in a homemade gift, and these festive pretzels are colorful and easy to make in your slow cooker.

INSTANT POT FUNCTION

• Slow Cook •

- **Waxed paper**
- **Gift boxes**

3 cups	pretzel nuggets	750 mL
3 cups	white or vanilla candy coating, coarsely chopped	750 mL
3 cups	white chocolate chips	750 mL
8 oz	white chocolate baking bars, broken into pieces	250 g
4 cups	hard peppermint candies, finely crushed, divided	1 L
½ tsp	peppermint extract	2 mL

Tip

Wrap the hard peppermint candies in waxed paper and use a rolling pin or meat mallet to crush them. Make sure to crush them evenly into small pieces so that all pieces will work well as coating.

1. In the inner pot, combine pretzels, candy coating, chocolate chips and baking bars.

2. Place the pot inside the cooker housing, close and lock the lid and turn the steam release handle to Venting. Press Slow Cook; the indicator will read "Normal." Press Adjust twice to change the heat level to "Less." Use the ⊖ button to decrease the time on the display to 2:00.

3. When the timer beeps, remove the lid and check to make sure the chocolate is melted and combined. (If more cooking is needed, reset the slow cooker to "Less" for 30 minutes.) Press Cancel.

4. Add 2½ cups (625 mL) peppermint candies and peppermint extract, stirring well to coat. Drop by heaping spoonfuls onto waxed paper, leaving space in between. Sprinkle the remaining peppermint candies over top. Let stand until firm, then divide evenly among gift boxes.

Oktoberfest Candied Almonds

My first experience with these little gems was at Oktoberfest in Munich, decades ago. They were warm, fragrant and entirely scrumptious. Since then, I have seen them at festivals and fairs, but nothing compares to that first experience, other than making them at home.

MAKES ABOUT 3 CUPS (750 ML)

INSTANT POT FUNCTION

• Slow Cook •

• **Rimmed baking sheet, lined with parchment paper**

1 cup	granulated sugar	250 mL
1 cup	packed brown sugar	250 mL
2½ tbsp	ground cinnamon	37 mL
Pinch	kosher salt	Pinch
1	large egg white	1
2 tsp	vanilla extract	10 mL
3 cups	raw almonds	750 mL
	Nonstick cooking spray	
2 tbsp	water	30 mL

Tips

Candied almonds are best when served warm.

You can purchase cone-shaped treat bags online and add your almonds to them for the traditional eating experience.

1. In a large bowl, combine granulated sugar, brown sugar, cinnamon and salt.

2. In medium bowl, whisk together egg white and vanilla until frothy. Add almonds, tossing to coat. Add to the sugar mixture and toss to coat.

3. Spray the inner pot with cooking spray. Pour the almond mixture into the pot.

4. Place the pot inside the cooker housing, close and lock the lid and turn the steam release handle to Venting. Press Slow Cook; the indicator will read "Normal." Press Adjust once to change the heat level to "More." Leave the time at 4:00. Stir every 20 minutes during the cooking time.

5. When the timer beeps, press Cancel. Pour water over almonds, mixing well and separating almonds as necessary. Close and lock the lid. Press Slow Cook. Press Adjust twice to change the heat level to "Less." Use the ⊖ button to decrease the time on the display to 1:00. Stir every 20 minutes during the cooking time.

6. When the timer beeps, remove the lid and check to make sure almonds are well coated. (If more cooking is needed, reset the slow cooker to "Less" for 20 minutes.) Pour almonds onto prepared baking sheet and separate any that are stuck together. Let cool slightly.

Homemade Yogurt

Yogurt is so easy to make in your Instant Pot, you may never buy commercial yogurt again. Keep it on hand, as it is wonderful for breakfast, as a snack, as an alternative to sour cream or as an ingredient or topping in many dishes.

INSTANT POT FUNCTIONS

- Steam -
- Yogurt -

- **Four canning jars (preferably 8 oz/250 mL), with two-piece lids**
- **Instant Pot steam rack**
- **Instant-read thermometer**

| 4 cups | milk | 1 L |
| | Yogurt starter with live active cultures (see tips, opposite) | |

• Jar Method •

1. Divide milk evenly among jars, leaving room at the top for the starter and leaving jars uncovered.

2. Add 1 cup (250 mL) water to the inner pot and place the steam rack in the pot. Place the jars on the rack. Close and lock the lid and turn the steam release handle to Sealing. Press Steam; the indicator will read "Normal." Use the ⊖ button to decrease the time on the display to 1 minute.

2. When the timer beeps, press Cancel. Let stand, covered, until the float valve drops down. Turn the steam release handle to Venting and remove the lid. Carefully transfer the jars to the countertop and let stand until an instant-read thermometer inserted into the center of a jar registers between 105°F and 115°F (41°C and 46°C).

3. If you are using a purchased yogurt starter, follow the directions on the package for the amount of starter to add to each jar. If you are using a previous batch of homemade yogurt as a starter, add 1 tbsp (15 mL) yogurt to each jar, stirring well.

4. Return the uncovered jars to the rack. Close and lock the lid and turn the steam release handle to Sealing. Press Yogurt; the time on the display will initially read 8:00 and then start counting up.

5. After 8 hours, the timer will beep and the indicator will read "Yogt"; press Cancel twice. Turn the steam release handle to Venting and remove the lid. Remove the jars from the pot. The yogurt should be firm when the jar is tilted. (If more cooking is needed, return the jars to the pot and reset the cooker to Yogurt for 30 minutes, repeating as needed.)

6. Cover jars with the flat lids and twist on the screwbands until there is a little resistance. Let stand for 2 hours or until cool. Refrigerate for at least 6 hours, until chilled, or for up to 10 days.

• Pot Method •

1. Add milk to the inner pot. Close and lock the lid and turn the steam release handle to Sealing. Press Yogurt. Press Adjust once to change the heat level to "More." The indicator will read "Boil."

2. When the timer beeps, press Cancel twice. Turn the steam release handle to Venting and remove the lid. Let stand, uncovered, until an instant-read thermometer registers between 105°F and 115°F (41°C and 46°C).

3. If you are using a purchased yogurt starter, follow the directions on the package for the amount of starter to add. If you are using a previous batch of homemade yogurt as a starter, add ¼ cup (60 mL) yogurt to the milk, stirring well.

4. Close and lock the lid and turn the steam release handle to Sealing. Press Yogurt; the time on the display will initially read 8:00 and then start counting up.

5. After 8 hours, the timer will beep and the indicator will read "Yogt"; press Cancel twice. Turn the steam release handle to Venting and remove the lid. The yogurt should be firm when the pot is lifted and tilted. (If more cooking is needed, reset the cooker to Yogurt for 30 minutes, repeating as needed.)

6. Spoon yogurt into jars, cover with the flat lids and twist on the screwbands until there is a little resistance. Let stand for 2 hours or until cool. Refrigerate for at least 6 hours, until chilled, or for up to 10 days.

Variations

Homemade Greek Yogurt: After step 5, pour the yogurt into a nut milk bag or fine-mesh kitchen towel set inside a strainer and over a bowl. Let drain in the refrigerator for 4 to 6 hours or until desired consistency. (The liquid left in the bowl is whey. Whey can be refrigerated for up to 7 days for use in smoothies and juices, to add protein, vitamins and minerals. Whey can also be used as a cooking liquid for rice, grains and pasta.) Spoon yogurt into jars, cover with the flat lids and twist on the screwbands until there is a little resistance.

Thicker Greek-Style Yogurt: If using the jar method, stir $1/2$ tsp (2 mL) dried milk powder into each jar in step 1. If using the pot method, stir 2 tsp (10 mL) dried milk powder into the milk in step 1. Drain as in the Homemade Greek Yogurt variation.

Flavored Yogurt: Add 1 tbsp (15 mL) flavored syrup, such as strawberry, raspberry or pomegranate, per 1 cup (250 mL) milk to your yogurt after it has chilled or when adding the culture in step 3; stir well.

Jam or Jelly Yogurt: Add 1 tbsp (15 mL) jam or jelly per 1 cup (250 mL) milk to your yogurt after it has chilled or when adding the culture in step 3; stir well.

Berry Yogurt: Add 2 tbsp (30 mL) fresh or thawed frozen berries per 1 cup (250 mL) milk to your yogurt after it has chilled or when adding the culture in step 3; stir well. If adding fruit to jars in step 3, you may need to divide the milk, starter and fruit among 5 jars instead of 4 to allow for the added volume of ingredients.

Tips

Use only jars and lids that are specifically made for canning; they will reduce the potential for breakage and will properly store your yogurt.

Before starting, make sure all of your containers and tools are clean.

Purchase high-quality yogurt with live active cultures to use as your starter.

You can also purchase packaged yogurt starters for yogurt-making. You will need to adjust the amount of starter to the volume of milk based on the package instructions.

Save some of your homemade yogurt, in a separate jar, to use as the starter for your next batch. Homemade yogurt can be refrigerated for up to 7 days for use as an active starter.

You can adjust the yogurt incubation time in step 4 by using the ➖ or ➕ button to decrease or increase the time. Packaged yogurt starters may direct you to cook the yogurt for more or less time than the preset 8 hours on the cooker. You can also adjust the time if you are using a homemade starter. Decreasing the time will result in a less tangy yogurt.

Pacific Island Rice Pudding

This creamy rice pudding is layered with mangos and pineapple, then topped with kiwis, nuts and coconut for a sweet and tangy dessert with a bit of crunch. The presentation is so beautiful, it will impress everyone.

MAKES 6 SERVINGS

INSTANT POT FUNCTIONS
• Rice •
• Keep Warm •

1½ cups	Arborio or other short-grain white rice	375 mL
1	cardamom pod	1
2 cups	water	500 mL
2 tbsp	granulated sugar	30 mL
1 tsp	salt	5 mL
1¾ cups	coconut milk	425 mL
½ cup	half-and-half (10%) cream	125 mL
2 cups	pineapple chunks	500 mL
2 cups	cubed mango	500 mL
2	kiwifruits, sliced and quartered	2
3 tbsp	chopped macadamia nuts	45 mL
2 tbsp	shredded sweetened coconut	30 mL

Tip
Any combination of your favorite fruits will work well in this recipe. You can also use raisins or dried cranberries, and other types of chopped nuts.

1. In the inner pot, combine rice, cardamom pod and water.

2. Place the pot inside the cooker housing, close and lock the lid and turn the steam release handle to Sealing. Press Rice; the indicator will read "Low Pressure." Leave the time at 12 minutes.

3. When the timer beeps, press Cancel and turn the steam release handle to Venting. When the float valve drops down, remove the lid. Check to make sure the rice is done to your liking. (If more cooking is needed, cover the pot and let stand for 2 minutes.) Discard cardamom pod. Let stand, uncovered, for 15 to 20 minutes or until cool.

4. Gently stir in sugar, salt, coconut milk and cream. Close and lock the lid and turn the steam release handle to Venting. Press Keep Warm and heat for 20 to 30 minutes or until the flavors have melded and rice is heated through.

5. In parfait glasses or bowls, layer ⅓ cup (75 mL) each of the pineapple, rice pudding and mango. Add another layer of pudding. Distribute kiwis, macadamia nuts and coconut evenly over top.

Quick Classic Tapioca Pudding

I've always found tapioca pudding tantalizing, but hesitated to make it often because it required soaking the tapioca overnight. Now, with the multicooker, this pudding can finally be made quickly.

MAKES 8 SERVINGS

INSTANT POT FUNCTION

• Porridge •

- **4-cup (1 L) round soufflé dish, sprayed with nonstick cooking spray**
- **Instant Pot steam rack**

1	large egg yolk	1
2 cups	milk	500 mL
½ cup	small pearl tapioca, rinsed	125 mL
⅓ cup	granulated sugar	75 mL
1½ tsp	grated lemon zest	7 mL
Pinch	kosher salt	Pinch
¼ cup	water	60 mL
	Ground nutmeg	

Tips

When preparing porridge using the Manual Pressure or Porridge functions, make sure to fill the pot no more than halfway full. Do not attempt to double or triple the recipe; otherwise, the exhaust valve may become clogged as the porridge froths up under pressure.

In step 3, make sure to wait the additional 5 minutes after the float valve drops down before venting and removing the lid; otherwise, the milk may foam up too quickly.

Do not use quick-cooking tapioca. If the package says to soak the tapioca overnight, you have the right type; however, you do not need to soak it before making this recipe.

1. In a medium bowl, whisk together egg yolk and milk. Add tapioca, sugar, lemon zest, salt and water, stirring well. Pour into prepared soufflé dish.

2. Add 1 cup (250 mL) water to the inner pot and place the steam rack in the pot. Place the soufflé dish on the rack. Close and lock the lid and turn the steam release handle to Sealing. Press Porridge; the indicators will read "High Pressure" and "Normal." Press Adjust twice to change the cooking duration to "Less" (the time on the display will read "15").

3. When the timer beeps, press Cancel. Let stand, covered, until 5 minutes after the float valve drops. Turn the steam release handle to Venting and remove the lid.

4. Serve warm or let cool, then cover and refrigerate for at least 1 hour (or up to 2 days) and serve cold. Sprinkle with nutmeg before serving.

Index

Library and Archives Canada Cataloguing in Publication

Haugen, Marilyn, author
175 best Instant Pot recipes : for your programmable electric pressure cooker / Marilyn Haugen.

Includes index.
ISBN 978-0-7788-0542-7 (paperback)

1. Pressure cooking. 2. Cookbooks. I. Title. II. Title: One hundred seventy-five best Instant Pot recipes.

TX840.P7H39 2016   641.5'87   C2016-903861-0

175 Best Instant Pot® Recipes

The Instant Pot will help you make healthier and more delicious foods that are easy and fast to prepare, *and* it uses less energy and requires less cleanup than conventional cooking methods. Now that's a seriously appealing combination! Marilyn has created inviting, mouth-watering Instant Pot recipes for every meal of the day. In a hurry? Done. Low and slow? Got it. The perfect rice or risotto? No problem. Entertaining? Marilyn has got you covered.

Impress your family and friends with the wide variety of satisfying dishes you can quickly and easily create in your multicooker!

These recipes are sure to become family favorites that will be requested again and again.

MARILYN HAUGEN is passionate about cooking and entertaining and has turned this passion into a successful cookbook career. Visit her blog, FoodThymes.com.

For more small appliance books and recipes, visit: http://smallappliance.robertrose.ca

ALSO AVAILABLE

$19.95 USA
$19.95 CAN

Robert ROSE

ISBN 978-0-7788-0542-7

9 780778 805427

PRINTED IN CANADA

Visit us at www.robertrose.ca